Bataan and Beyond

*Number Six: The Centennial Series of
the Association of Former Students
Texas A&M University*

Bataan and Beyond

Memories of an American POW

By JOHN S. COLEMAN, JR.

Foreword by THOMAS DOOLEY

 Texas A&M University Press COLLEGE STATION

Library of Congress Cataloging in Publication Data

Coleman, John S   1902–
    Bataan and beyond.

    (The Centennial series of the Association of Former
Students; no. 6)
    Includes index.
    1. World War, 1939–1945—Prisoners and Prisons,
Japanese. 2. World War, 1939–1945—Personal
narratives, American. 3. Coleman, John S., 1902–
4. World War, 1939–1945—Philippine Island.
5. Philippine Islands—History—Japanese occupation,
1942–1945. 6. Prisoners of War—Philippine Islands—
Biography. I. Title. II. Series: Texas. A & M
University, College Station. Association of Former
Students. The Centennial series of the Association of
Former Students, Texas A & M University; no. 6.
D805.P6C64   940.54'83'73   78-6365
ISBN 0-89096-055-0

Manufactured in the United States of America
THIRD PRINTING

Contents

List of Illustrations

Foreword

At the end of 1940 Douglas MacArthur, USA Retired, with the appointed rank of Field Marshal of the Philippine Army, was slowly putting together the defense forces that were to take over upon the withdrawal of American Forces scheduled for 1946.

Although the question of war did not arise in the winter of 1940–1941, the thinking changed in that spring of 1941. In July, 1941, General MacArthur was recalled to active duty by President Roosevelt and placed in command of all U.S. forces in the Far East.

Training programs were accelerated, American dependents were returned to the States on ships that brought officers and noncommissioned personnel to cadre and train with new Philippine units. This program would have provided a respectable defense by late spring of 1942. But the Japanese strike on Pearl Harbor occurred December 7, 1941 (December 8 in Philippines), and at 12:30 on that date heavy bomber and fighter attacks on Clark Field and other airfields throughout the islands sent untrained, inadequately equipped units to combat positions. Although most U.S. and Philippine fighter aircraft had been alerted and were in the air earlier that day, they had landed to refuel and to lunch and were destroyed on the ground. With this severe loss of aircraft and the imminent landings of Japanese amphibious forces, the Provisional Air Corps Regiment was formed to add to the ground defenses. This unit brought about the ground combat experiences of John Coleman.

War Plan Orange No. 3 was a variation of a plan developed about twenty years earlier. In the event of successful enemy landings on the main island of Luzon, the American and Philippine units were to fight delaying actions and withdraw into Bataan Peninsula. The plan envisioned a six-month stand on Bataan and Corregidor, by which time aid from the United States would arrive.

Since the strike on Hawaii precluded a supply line to the Far East, the Philippine effort was doomed. Half rations went into effect in early January and careful allotment of ammunition enabled the continuation of a defense until April 9, when Bataan fell. With no buffer left, the Japanese moved heavy artillery to the depth of Bataan and brought concentrated fire and aerial bombardment on Corregidor, which culminated in surrender on May 6, 1942.

A relatively small force of underfed, inadequately trained, poorly equipped soldiers had delayed several months the Japanese timetable for their conquest of the Far East. This, perhaps, saved Australia and provided the base from which the Pacific campaign was initiated.

Major Coleman, fortunately, was able to compile and bring home a diary of his experiences. He has described in some detail the battle for Bataan, its closing days and the almost intolerable Death March to the first of several prisoner-of-war camps. His account of the odious state of POW life is presented in straightforward, unemotional narrative.

Bataan and Beyond serves well to remind us of the dark days of the beginning of World War II. Let us hope that the book will remind us that our defenses must be maintained at a standard that will preclude future U.S. military forces from experiencing the humiliations and deprivations of surrender and imprisonment.

Thomas Dooley
Col. USA Retired
Aide-de-camp to
General Jonathan M. Wainwright
August, 1941–September, 1947

Bataan and Beyond

1. *On My Way*

San Francisco, August 28, 1941. War clouds were rolling and tossing in the Pacific. It had become no secret that in Europe we had taken sides; there was no further choosing. I knew at this time that my assignment to foreign duty in the Philippine Islands was going to be a lot of war for my side. The Japanese were favoring Germany.

My family had gone with me as far as they could, to the port of embarkation. My daughter, Lennie Lou, ten years old, and my son, Spencer, six years old, had not the least idea of danger. My wife, Ethel, fearing that I might never return, was practically sick with the responsibility I had left her.

This was my first sea voyage. I was assigned to a cabin with two other officers aboard the *President Pierce*. This ship had been a luxury liner but had been converted to an army troop transport. I met a friend of mine from Texas Agricultural and Mechanical College, class of 1929, Captain Harry O. Fisher with the Army Engineer Corps. After going aboard I met Colonel Emeral Cane, who had one battalion of the 200th Anti-Aircraft National Guard Regiment on this ship to the Philippine Islands. This battalion was from New Mexico. I had no troops assigned to me but would get my assignment after I arrived at Manila, P.I.

The day before we arrived in Hawaii, the sea became very rough and there were many seasick soldiers. I was assigned the officer-of-the-day duty. This was my first time to inspect a troop ship. When I went into the troop quarters there was a rancid, sour smell of seasick soldiers. The quarters were in order and clean. When we went through the refrigerated food storage room, we found they had been having some refrigeration trouble, and some beef had to be disposed of because of spoilage. I can remember the things I did wrong more easily than those that I did right.

The night before going into port we were told that we would have a practice "blackout." The whole ship was to be in complete darkness as far as observation from the outside was concerned. After giving the guards their information, and posting guards in special areas, and ordering all lights out above deck, I reported to the ship's captain that the blackout was secure.

The captain took a hasty glance out over the ship. He called me into his cabin and said, "Captain Coleman, you have not closed the hatches and there is a reflection of light from the hatch doors."

I did not know what a hatch was but soon learned. I said, "Very well, Sir. They will be closed." I went down to the corporal of the guard and told him that the hatch doors would have to be closed.

He said, "Very well," and closed all of the hatch doors. This may have been a practice blackout, but they never allowed the lights on anymore until we arrived in Manila, P.I., two weeks later.

When we went into port at Honolulu, I did not know, nor did the army troops know, that they must be in number-one uniforms to appear on the upper deck when going into port. The ship's captain called me into his cabin and said, "Captain Coleman, look down there on the top deck; very few of these men are in number-one uniform. Get the guards word to send all men below deck who are not dressed properly."

I believe 90 percent of all personnel were on the upper deck looking over the port area and the scenery as we were docking. When we docked we were told that we would be there one day and to report back to the ship at 6:00 P.M.

I told the captain that I was ready to turn over my duty to the next officer of the day. He said, "You will have to wait until he comes on board the ship, so I can sign the ten or twelve prisoners over to him." These prisoners were some soldiers who had missed the last ship out of San Francisco to Hawaii or the Philippine Islands. These men had been kept in the brig of the ship since sailing from San Francisco. After all personnel, except the men on duty, had left the ship, the prison officer came aboard and signed for the prisoners.

The officer to whom I had assigned the prisoners asked me if I would like to make a tour of the island. I told him I sure would like to and he said he could get as many trucks as we needed for our personnel. I asked him to get four trucks. Each truck would carry from twenty-five to twenty-eight men. Everyone had a head start on me and I had to hurry to get enough men to fill the trucks. I had some competition with the women taxi drivers as everyone wanted to ride in a taxi driven by a woman. Most all of the taxis were driven by women and most of the men had already taken taxis for downtown Honolulu. I was able to get only three truckloads of men. Everyone was eager to take the scenic trip, if he knew about it. It was an interisland excursion and free to all army personnel. On this all-day tour we went completely around the island of Oahu, visiting some of the places that were destined to make history in about three months, such as Schofield Barracks and Pearl Harbor.

At 6:00 P.M. everyone was aboard the *President Pierce* and ready to go to Manila. The Hawaiian Chamber of Commerce put on a special show for us on the pier after we were all aboard the ship. There was hula dancing and Hawaiian songs. Their last song was "Aloha." This was very beautiful and quite appropriate. We left with 90 percent of them never to return.

The next morning as the sun came up on the beautiful blue Pacific, on one side of our transport was a camouflaged man-of-war, a destroyer. I felt that we were nearer to being in war than I had thought with a continuous blackout of our ship and now a destroyer escort. After we had sailed around the south end of Mindanao and across the deepest water in the world, the first typhoon hit our ship. It rained in sheets and the wind blew so hard that our ship lay almost on its side continuously. The waves were going over our top deck. Our destroyer escort was under the waves most of the time. Visibility was from zero to fifty yards for two days. We were traveling at about five knots, and every ten minutes the ship's horn was sounded to prevent our colliding with the escort vessel.

Just before we entered Manila Bay, fighter planes (P-40's) began flying over us; then submarines came up out of the water on both sides of us. We were given a royal welcome. When we started to enter Manila Bay, a new ship's pilot took over the ship to guide her through the mine fields. There was a concentration of war preparations. When we floated up to Pier Five in the Manila harbor, there was a U.S. transport leaving the pier. The American soldiers and sailors who lined the rail yelled, "Suckers! Suckers!" at us. We decided that they had been in the Philippines a long time or else did not like their assignments or were just razzing us.

As we were disembarking, the army band was playing "God Bless America." This gave us a thrill and made us proud of our assignment:

to protect our country. The officers who did not have troop assignments were taken to the army and navy club by taxi. No one had ever told me that they drove on the left side of the road instead of the right side as we do in the United States. When the taxi driver started to the officers' club, I thought he was drunk or crazy, he was driving so fast and on the left side of the street all of the time. It looked as if we were going to have a wreck at any moment. After I realized it was the law here to drive on the left side, I felt much better. We were welcomed by the officers who had been in the Philippine Islands a long time and the drinks were on the house.

My orders were to report to the commanding officer of Nichols Field. This field was a fighter base for the defense of the Philippine Islands. We were taken by taxi from the army and navy club to Nichols Field. I was assigned an apartment in the bachelor officers' quarters. It took about two days to get my permanent assignment. I was assigned as adjutant to the 27th Materiel Squadron. I was to start immediately to train them for infantry combat. This training was extra. They had their regular airplane service and maintenance work at the air field. They also furnished work details at different air fields in the Philippines for repair parts to all airplanes.

I did regular adjutant work with the 27th Materiel Squadron for about one month; then I was transferred to the Headquarters & Headquarters Squadron. At the same time, I was asked by the commander, Colonel Churchill, to be adjutant to Nichols Field, but I did not think I was ready for such a big job. Anyway, having been trained as an infantryman and just transferred to the Air Corps was a big change of duties and I needed more training for this kind of job. I was given the job of auditing all of the squadron's books at Nichols Field, besides my regular adjutant's job.

About December 1, 1941, the squadron commander of the 27th Materiel Squadron, Major Griffin, was leaving to go back to the States. His five-year reserve commission was up. He had been in the Philippines three years and wanted to go home. He told me that he thought we were going to have war very soon and they had sent his family back to the States. General Douglas MacArthur would not give him permission to leave the Islands because of the threat of war. Major Griffin did not accept his next five-year commission and went home, paying his own way back to the States on the last ship out of the Philippine Islands before the start of the war. He gave a master sergeant fifty dollars for his place on the ship. This sergeant was taken prisoner and later died in prison. I was assigned to take command of this 27th Materiel Squadron. This position was supposed to be commanded by a major, and Colonel Bill Maverick, the commanding officer at Nichols Field at this time, recommended me to General MacArthur for a commission as major, but this position recommendation was turned down.

About December 1, we had orders for all personnel to wear steel helmets, side arms, and gas masks at all times. A close security was also ordered for Nichols Field. This was to be defended from parachute troops, sabotage, or agitated mobs that might attack the field. I was put in charge of the ground defense of Nichols Field. We immediately built seven machine gun emplacements and put First Lieutenant Shelton H. Mendelson in charge of this platoon.

Those responsible for assembling and repairing airplanes were working twenty-four hours a day. The P-40's that were shipped to us in crates were being assembled as fast as possible. A long heavy runway was being built to accommodate our large B-17's. There were several hundred civilians working at Nichols Field on these jobs. Preparation for war was fast and furious now.

When I was officer of the day, an order came by telephone from General MacArthur's headquarters, telling me to have all of our planes near the runways dispersed. At that time they were lined up in order in a straight line near the runways. I told this officer that we had many training planes out and to disperse all the planes on the ground without warning all of the pilots in the air, could cause many collisions as they returned to the runways. He said, "Have those planes dispersed immediately."

I called the control tower and told them to notify all pilots in range before they landed that the planes had been dispersed. We scattered these planes out so they would not be easily hit by attacking planes. Revetments were being constructed by our engineers to protect the planes on the ground.

2. *Disaster Strikes*

Then came that horrible, eventful Sunday morning, about seven o'clock December 8, 1941. My house boy came into my room with a newspaper. The headlines were, "PEARL HARBOR BOMBED BY JAPANESE." We went to breakfast; then I went to my office, the headquarters of the 27th Materiel Squadron. Everything was in an uproar and, of course, everyone was sad. We had twenty shoeshine boys on duty that morning and I put them all to digging slit trenches near the banks of the Parañaque River, which was near our squadron headquarters. I knew trenches would be of more help than shined shoes. Here and in future months I was reminded of these words of Ralph Waldo Emerson:

> Not gold, but only men can make
> A nation great and strong;
> Men who for truth and honor's sake,
> Stand fast and SUFFER LONG.
>
> Brave men who work while others sleep,
> Who dare while others shy,
> They build a nation's pillars deep,
> And lift them to the sky.

At this time the 27th Materiel Squadron was scattered in small details all over the Philippine Islands. First Lieutenant Wayne Van Voorhis had a detail at Clark Field; Lieutenant Morton Deeter was to take a platoon to Lipa to build an auxiliary air field. We also had a detail at Del Monte Air Field in Mindanao. All of these were to keep repairs for all kinds of planes.

We expected to be bombed Monday night and needed to lessen the danger of being caught in a large concentration of troops. I made reconnaissance of an area three miles northwest of Nichols Field to move my unit to, where they could rest at night and the cooks could go on with their business without being on edge all the time for fear of being bombed.

My roommate at the bachelor officers' quarters was Captain McCorkle. He was in command of the 2nd Observation Squadron. He had come with me to the Philippine Islands from Camp Bowie, Texas. We met back at our room about eight o'clock that evening and we predicted that we would be bombed before daylight the next day. We agreed that, if the air-raid siren sounded, we would go to our head-quarters and have all of our men who were not on machine guns or other detail assignments do the same so that they could be used for emergency duty.

About 1:30 A.M., Monday morning, December 9, the air-raid siren sounded. We went to our post. About two o'clock the all clear sounded. We went back to bed. Then at four o'clock the air-raid siren sounded again. Captain McCorkle and I again went to our head-quarters. I checked two defense machine gun emplacements on my way. In about thirty minutes the warning sounded again. We could hear heavy motors coming from the west. Everything was blacked out.

Bombs began to fall in my officers' quarters and in the hangar areas. Our fifty-caliber defense machine guns were firing wide open. The all clear sounded soon. Wounded men began coming into our first-aid station and I began checking on all of my men in the area. Our P-40 airplanes began coming back to refuel after attacking the Japanese bombers. One of my machine gunners opened up again. I ran over to this emplacement and stopped the operator from firing at our planes. There was a lot of confusion and noise with many motors in the air and fire truck sirens blaring. I came back to the slit trench near my headquarters and sat down for a short rest. Many of my en-listed men were crowded around to find out what had happened. One of my men came up and sat down near me. The moon was shining brightly and I could see a dark creeping thing on his left arm and hand. I looked closer and it was blood. I said, "You need to go to the first-aid station."

He said, "I was over there a minute ago and they were so crowd-ed I could not get in."

I could see he was losing lots of blood, so I had him come with me. We went over to the first-aid station and had his arm dressed. His arm was broken and part of the bone was protruding. He was one of my fifty-caliber machine gunners. When I asked him how it hap-pened, he said, "I hate to tell you because I did what you had in-structed us not to do. When those planes came over I loosened the clamp that holds the barrels on the tripod so I could maneuver the gun easier. When a bomb hit close by, the concussion of the bomb blast caused the gun to spin around and I reached in to stop it so I could continue to fire and it hit my arm." I had two men wounded and one killed by a hangar door falling on him that night. No runway was hit and only one plane wheel was damaged.

I went back to my room and found that the second bomb that was dropped at Nichols Field had hit on my front porch, completely riddling everything with shrapnel. It blew everything in my room into the adjoining room and destroyed about ten rooms in like manner. I went into the room just south of mine, to see if I could find some of my clothes, and found a headless lieutenant in a sitting position in a chair. Evidently he had started to put on his shoes to go to his foxhole, because he had one shoe on. The concussion from the bomb apparently snapped off his head.

The day before it had been rumored that the war might still be averted. This came from the higher echelon of those in command of the Philippine Islands. We did not know how badly we were hurt at Pearl Harbor or how fierce this attack was. I had no doubt that we were at war for sure. We moved the 27th headquarters out three miles northwest of Nichols Field to the site I had reconnoitered a few days earlier so the men could get some rest and not be subjected to bombings. This move was made the morning of December 9.

We had two more machine gun emplacements constructed for the defense of the field. Telephone lines were strung to each of the emplacements from the command post. These men were furnished food from our field kitchen. It was everyone's duty to help fight the fires after every bombing. At this time I sent Lieutenant Deeter to Lipa to build an auxiliary air field with one platoon of men and equipment. It was reported that on the morning of the ninth, when we got our first bombing, flares had been shot up along the water's edge on Dewey Boulevard in Manila. These bombers left the edge of the water and flew directly over Nichols Field. There were also some lights on near this spot. The Japanese navigators were flying along the edge of the water until this signal went up which directed them to Nichols Field. We sent one squad of our men to patrol this area for saboteurs. This report had been discounted as false by headquarters for the U.S. Army Forces in the Far East (USAFFE), but it was true. Later our squad shot a man who lit a skyrocket nearby when they could hear Japanese motors approaching. They also captured a Japanese woman who raised all of her window shades and turned on a light. This patrol continued to operate until we evacuated Nichols Field.

I had deployed one platoon of the 27th Materiel Squadron on a ridge overlooking Nichols Field. They were digging foxholes and machine gun emplacements. The air corps personnel had not been issued a full complement of infantry equipment. They only had a few infantry picks and shovels with which to dig the foxholes. I had just warned them to hurry and get dug in because we could get a heavy bombing any minute. Each man who was not busy digging would say, "I'm waiting for Joe to get his foxhole dug so I can use his pick and shovel." They had it organized so they could wait their turn to use the equipment we had. I went into the air base headquarters which was in a bomb shelter, the only one at Nichols Field. It was about fifty yards from where the platoon was digging in. I had been talking to our base commander, Colonel Maverick, and just as I stepped out the door to go back where my men were I heard a terrible roar. I looked up and counted ninety-six heavy bombers flying at about twenty-one thousand feet. Our anti-aircraft shells were exploding just below them. We just did not have anti-aircraft weapons that were capable of firing to that altitude. I ran back into the bomb shelter just as a five-hundred-pound bomb hit near the southwest corner of the shelter. One hit the center of the north side, just off the shelter. There was a pen made of railroad irons in the center of the shelter and everyone was in this pen on hands and knees. The shelter rocked like a kite in the wind. Concrete dust fell on us, but there were no chunks of concrete. The railroad irons, stacked in there to protect the personnel in case the top fell in, had served their purpose. A chaplain said, "Let's repeat the Lord's Prayer." Everyone joined in until we got about half through and the bombs quit falling.

Our communications operator was near the southwest corner of the shelter when the first bomb hit. He was not under the railroad irons' protection. He began to yell and have fits. We all realized he was shell shocked. A doctor gave him something to quiet him. I started out the door again and a Zero fighter plane sprayed the door with bullets. It was gone before I realized what had happened. I ran out to the platoon on the ridge. One of our P-40's flew low in front of my troops where they were dug in. It was on fire and two Jap Zeros were in pursuit and firing at it. All of my men opened fire with rifles and machine guns. Our P-40 went into Manila Bay about one-half mile from us. One of the Zeros went into the water too.

When I got back to the platoon, one would have thought it was a prairie dog town. Everyone was digging a foxhole. They were using large bolts, bayonets, tire tools, or just anything they could dig with. They were not waiting for the next man to get through with his pick and shovel. One sergeant who was digging a hole for a machine gun dug so deep he had to throw some dirt back in the hole so he could man the machine gun. I had noticed that same sergeant when the Jap Zeros were pursuing our P-40; he did not have the barrel mounted on a tripod. He put it in the fork of a mesquite tree and was firing from that position. It would slip almost out of the fork of the tree and he would stop firing long enough to put it back.

In the meantime our coast guard went out to rescue the P-40 pilot. He was not hurt but did lose his plane. The Zero that my unit had shot down sank into the water with the pilot in the cockpit. When the Zero was pulled from the water, it had several hundred bullet holes through the fuselage but was not disabled, due to heavy armament. The pilot had a bullet hole through his temple. One lucky shot had killed him.

This flight of bombers had dropped many five-hundred-pound bombs over Nichols Field, but most of the ninety-six bombers unloaded on Cavite, our naval base. They did not hit our runways or damage any of our fighter planes. They set fire to our post exchange and the 27th Materiel barracks. They cracked our large cement water storage tank about in the middle. One bomb went through the center of my office and turned over the heavy steel safe. A large part of their bombs landed on the edge of Manila and along the slough. They killed a large number of civilians. I went down to help fight the fire in the post exchange and in my old barracks. I went into my office that the bomb had wrecked, and the large safe was turned over on its side. I tried to work the combination, but during the confusion it did not work. The next morning I worked the combination on the first try and took out our squadron cash.

On the way back to our camp we had three trucks in a group, and we were attacked by a squadron of Jap planes. We scattered in every direction, leaving the trucks on the side of the road. There were no trees large enough to stop a bullet, but there was some brush and a buffalo wallow. The buffalo wallow was dry and in most places had a bank around it about two feet high. It was thirty feet across. We got into the buffalo wallow and when the planes made a dive to strafe us, we would lie against the bank on the side of the approach for protection. One of the planes made three passes, strafing us each time and kicking the dirt over us when the bullets hit the bank just above us. The third time, I ran across the wallow to the opposite side and I stepped in a buffalo track that had been made in the mud, turning my ankle while I was looking up at the plane. I had to crawl the rest of the way. The Jap pilot probably thought he had hit me. He did not come over again.

I was taken to the Fort McKinley hospital where they X-rayed my leg. The doctor showed me a clear streak above my left ankle on the X-ray; he said my leg was fractured. He taped my leg and ankle, then picked me up in his arms and put me in a hospital bed. I told the corpsman who brought me to the hospital that, if they would find me a pair of crutches, I would go back to my headquarters. They soon found me a pair of crutches. They carried me to the ambulance. All of my officers were out on assigned details, so I had to operate the squadron from the bed for about two weeks. I received a call from General MacArthur's headquarters telling me to take the three cargo planes that I had left to Australia. Under the conditions we were in, I could not leave my squadron. I sent three pilots, one very sick man, and one who had his leg broken to Australia. I never heard whether they arrived in Australia or not. Two of our large cargo planes had just landed at Clark Field when they received their first heavy bombing. Both of them were demolished on the ground.

That first night, after fracturing my leg, I was miserable. It rained most of the night and the tarpaulin that I was sleeping under leaked. It was cold and the water would run into my blanket. I would try to turn over, but my leg ached and was very painful every time I moved. The water kept trickling through on me all night. The next day my men set up a pup tent under some bushes to conceal me from planes. They also had a good mattress on level ground for me to lie on in the pup tent. I had telephone communications with each of my platoons.

3. *New Defense Plans*

I was still using one crutch when I received a call from General Mac-Arthur's headquarters, December 23, about 1:00 P.M. The caller asked me how long it would take me to get my squadron down to Pier Five, at Manila. I told him that I did not have a single truck in camp, but that I could get to Pier Five by five o'clock. He said, "Five o'clock, hell! Make it four o'clock."

I said, "Very well, Sir." Lieutenant Deeter had one platoon and two trucks at Lipa, which was thirty miles away. One group was at the Philippine Air Depot. There were two security patrols down in Manila and those manning machine gun emplacements at Nichols Field. I had my clerk contact them by telephone. I went out on the highway near by and in a few minutes a large moving van came along. I stopped it and commandeered it. The driver said he was sent by his company to move someone from town to the country. I told him that the army had priority now and that I would give him a receipt for the use of the van. He and our cooks loaded up our squadron's cooking equipment and what canned goods we could carry. We hid the rest under straw and bushes. I called Lieutenant Deeter at Lipa and told him to come to Pier Five immediately. We were leaving Manila.

We did not know where we were going and did not have room for any excess baggage. Most of my men had already lost everything they had in the barracks fire. December 23, I was at Pier Five by four o'clock, but the rest did not arrive until almost five o'clock. The men at the Philippine Air Depot did not join our unit until we were on Bataan. The men at Lipa did not take time to unload a tractor from one truck and a grader from another. They arrived at Pier Five at five o'clock. There was a large interisland ship that they began loading us onto. I was helping unload and dropped a typewriter on my right big toe just as I was putting it into the loading net. My toenail soon turned black and a corpsman bored a hole in it to let the blood out. It looked as if I were going to be accident prone.

While we were loading this interisland ship, two of our submarines surfaced near the pier and began taking on battery water. They had been there about fifteen minutes, when the air-raid sirens sounded. The submarines closed their hatches and left the dock immediately. They were about half-submerged when the fighter planes came over. They flew close to the water but did not strafe or bomb the submarines. Those of us on the pier lay down as close to the pier warehouse as we could get. Nothing happened. Large clouds of black smoke were boiling up from the navy storage area between Cavite and Nichols Field. There were one million gallons of oil being destroyed. We were trying to use the scorched-earth policy, leaving nothing of value for the enemy to use.

By dark we had loaded about fifteen hundred men and the essential belongings on the ship. There were so many soldiers on the ship that we could only sit down on the deck; no one could lie down. We still had not been told where we were going. We hoped we were going to run the blockade on our way to Australia. This being a very dark night, we thought we had a very good chance to get through the blockade. We moved out from the pier swiftly, then slowed down when we reached the mine field. Suddenly we stopped. Someone said, "Do you suppose we are having engine trouble?" We continued to sit there in the water for an hour, then two, then it extended until daylight. Our hopes of going to Australia vanished. There were just too many men on this small ship to undertake such a long voyage. Our hopes of running the blockade had vanished by 3:00 A.M. It was dawn, Christmas Eve morning. We moved a short distance to a small village on the south end of the Bataan Peninsula. We soon found out that we were getting into position to defend the Bataan Peninsula. Evidently we had abandoned the Rainbow Plan to defend the Philippine Islands on the beach landings. We were taking up the Operation Orange 3 Plan to defend Bataan and Corregidor. Holding these locations would be a thorn in the side of the Japanese when it came to occupying other areas farther south. This did not look good to us. The Air Corps Regiment had not been briefed or given any details of this new plan. We still had not been issued a full complement of infantry equipment. We would certainly need some trench mortars and more entrenchment equipment. None of my men had raincoats and just about one-fourth of them had shelter halves.

Mariveles was a shallow-water port and the ship could not get closer than a quarter of a mile to the pier. The captain of the ship blew his horn to signal for a barge to come out and take us to shore. The barge came up on one side of the ship and dropped a large rope net along the side of the ship from the upper deck so the men could get on the barge. The barge could only carry fifty men at a time. I noticed that it would take a long time to unload the ship, so I went to the captain of the ship and asked him to order another barge to unload from the other side of the ship. I knew as soon as the sun came up we could expect the Japs to attack us with bombs and strafing. He said he did not have the authority to use more than the one barge. I tried to persuade him to get another barge so we could unload faster. I knew if we were bombed or strafed, some of the men would abandon ship and attempt to swim to shore. There could be several drowned. The ship's captain refused to expedite the unloading. I went back to the main deck and got four more captains and a major to insist that the ship's captain order another barge. After a rather heated argument, he secured another barge to come along the other side of the ship to double our capacity to unload.

Just as we had unloaded all of the men and had made one trip unloading equipment, a flight of Jap dive bombers came over strafing and bombing. All of the soldiers had time to take cover in the brush along the beach. The first flight over set fire to our ship and it sank in thirty minutes. Had we not secured the second barge, about half of the men would have still been on the ship waiting to be unloaded.

Most of our equipment was still on the pier when the bombing took place. We had to flee for protection, leaving it there. When the bombing was over, each unit sent a detail to get what equipment was left. Lieutenant Deeter saw some of the finance department detail get our typewriter that I had earlier dropped on my toe. He argued with the finance officer, but he being a captain, Lieutenant Deeter lost the argument. Later we did get our typewriter.

We were unloaded at Mariveles without any transportation, but with orders to move about eight miles north and secure a camp site where we could continue training this squadron for combat duty. I decided to try my luck on the main road near Mariveles. I had not waited long when a Filipino came along in an old Ford truck. I stopped him and told him we needed to use his truck to transport men and equipment about eight miles north. I explained to him that I had the authority to commandeer his truck and would give him a signed receipt for the use of it so he could get his pay. He was very courteous and said we could use it as long as we needed it. I started the men marching north. We loaded the equipment on the truck and, with

Lieutenant Deeter in charge, I started it north also. I marched with the men. As soon as Lieutenant Deeter had unloaded the equipment, he was to set the kitchen up and send the truck back for a load of men. We continued this shuttle process until all the men had been picked up and moved to the new camp site. The last load was picked up within four miles of the camp.

Lieutenant Deeter had selected a dandy camp site near a heavily wooded area. There was a clear creek nearby for plenty of fresh water and we were out of the mosquito area. Our next problem was a supply of food. This exact area was where I had read about Frank Buck capturing the world's largest python snake in 1928. Later I shot one about twelve feet long, for food. This was the first time that I had helped anyone eat snake. It tasted like the white meat of a chicken.

The road to Manila had not been closed by the enemy at this time. General Jonathan M. Wainwright was fighting a delaying action against those that had landed at Lingayen Gulf, while General Albert M. Jones was fighting a delaying action against those that had landed south of Manila. I sent the commandeered truck to Manila with five men. They were to pick up four army trucks and bring back five truckloads of Type C rations and staple food. They were to get the food at the army depot or warehouse at the port area. In the meantime, I set up an infantry combat training program for this air corps squadron.

I noticed that, all along the road from Mariveles to our camp, there were fifty-five–gallon drums of gas on the side of the road about every quarter of a mile. Our supply or quartermaster department was doing a good job. I understood this gas supply was distributed in this manner all the way from the top of the Bataan Peninsula to Mariveles on the main road. Any truck with a gas pump could fill up out of these barrels.

Christmas Day 1941, after a long, hot day of training, we went down to Manila Bay for a swim and bath. Along the edge of the water it was shallow, so we had to get out from shore some fifty yards before we could get in water deep enough to swim. There was high brush along the edge of the beach. It was about four o'clock in the afternoon, and we had just gotten out in water three or four feet deep when we heard a flight of Japanese fighter planes. There were about one hundred of us in the water and some started to run through the

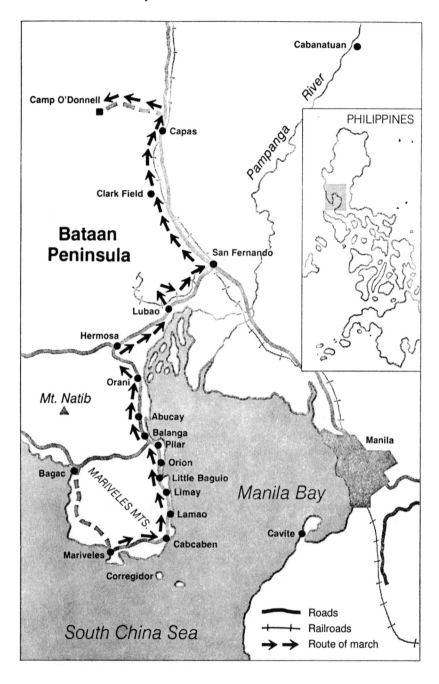

water to shore. I shouted for them to dive under the water. These planes came over the mountains and swooped down on us like hawks. It is hard to stay under salty water, so we learned fast to hold on to the bottom, using rocks and seaweed. We were strafed and could hear the bullets pop on top of the water, but not a single man was hit. This stopped our bathing during the daylight hours.

In our infantry training we went through the extended order drill, with some bayonet training, some scouting, and patrol work as well. It was an unusual sight for me to see my airplane mechanics, thirty to thirty-five years old, doing this kind of training. Usually men eighteen to twenty-five years old were given training such as this. I explained to them that there was no alternative, that each man must accept infantry training for his own protection and for the efficiency of our fighting force. We had few airplanes and everyone would have to do what he could to defend the Bataan Peninsula. This was our only hope to delay the enemy until we could be supplied with materiel and recruits from the United States.

That night our supplies came from Manila. Our plan had worked out perfectly so far. The five men sent in for supplies had come back with four good trucks and five loads of food. We took the commandeered truck back to the owner at Mariveles. I signed a receipt for the use of it as I had agreed to do and thanked him for his cooperation. We had to let two of our neighboring units have two of our trucks. Every other day we would send the two trucks back to Manila to get what food they could find. Finally our trucks could not get food. They said the warehouse was empty. They brought back a truckload of Canadian motorcycles. They had gotten them off a Canadian ship that was anchored in Manila Bay. The next day I went back to Manila to see if I could get something more profitable or useful to us than motorcyles. Master Sergeant Brennison, our supply sergeant, went with us. His wife was in the hospital in Manila and had given birth to a boy that the sergeant had not seen until that night. It was also the last time he was to see his son. He left his wife five hundred dollars in cash. That night we loaded up wheat flour, cooking starch, and small items, all that we could find. While we were doing this, the Japs were bombing part of the city of Manila, though it had been declared an open city by General MacArthur. A church was bombed and set afire one block from where we were.

We found out that the invading army from the north was about to cut the road between Manila and Bataan. We hurried back toward Bataan. After we turned southwest from San Fernando, we could see the flashes and hear the rumble of artillery from the north. Some bombs had hit the road in a few places that we had to drive around. By this time most of the gasoline drums that had been plentiful a few days ago were gone or empty. The large gasoline dump where we had stored thousands of gallons of gasoline and oil near Nichols Field had been burning for days. The burning oil and gas caused a great cloud of smoke in the Manila area. This was our last trip to Manila until we surrendered several months later.

The Jap planes became more numerous from day to day, bombing our motor pools, Cabcaben Air Field, and Corregidor. Many bombers were shot down by our anti-aircraft units. One day while our anti-aircraft guns on Bataan were firing at planes over the area, we were sitting under some trees to hide us from observation. I had taken my gas mask off my shoulder and laid it against a tree trunk where I had been sitting. I moved around on the other side of the tree to get in the shade. Just as I sat down, a copper head to an anti-aircraft shell came down and hit my gas mask, cutting it in half. I had moved just in time to prevent getting hit.

All of the Air Corps Regiment continued to train and drill in infantry tactics, such as setting up outposts, counterattacks, and bayonet drills. Certain ones were selected to train for scout and patrol duty. Having been an infantry officer, I was used to help train several squadrons. We had classes in the care and maintenance of our rifles and machine guns. We went down on the beach for some target practice. This was done while the armies of Generals Wainwright and Jones were delaying the invading armies. The delay was to keep them scattered and give us time on Bataan to stop them as they entered the Bataan Peninsula.

On January 1, we received orders to cut our rations in half. This meant two light meals a day. One about daylight; the other after dark. This cut us down to about two thousand calories per day. We began getting some supplies from the army supply dump, such as bread enough for one slice per man, a small piece of boiled beef and gravy once a day, with coffee twice a day. The Air Corps Regiment became known as the Provisional Air Corps Regiment in the office of the

USAFFE. We in the regiment only knew it as the Air Corps Regiment.

4. *Near the Front*

On January 10 our regiment received orders to move up to a position one-half mile west of Orion. We moved that night when it was dark and foggy. We dug foxholes and established a defensive position. We also cleared some brush for lines of communication. In my battalion were the Headquarters & Headquarters Squadron, the 19th Bomb Group, the 7th Materiel Squadron, and the 27th Materiel Squadron. To our right flank was the American 31st Infantry and to our left flank was the 2nd Observation Squadron and the rest of the Air Corps Regiment. Beyond this was the Philippine Army. One night soon after the 31st Infantry Regiment was ordered to go north, my squadron was ordered to take up the position the 31st Infantry Regiment had occupied. This meant that the 27th Materiel Squadron had to be scattered pretty thin. I had the irrigation ditches opened up to our immediate front. This flooded the rice paddies with about six inches of water all over the field. This protected us from infantry and tank attacks. After we had been in this position about two days, I was told to stop anyone on the coastal or main road to Mariveles. The coastal road ran through the right side of our sector. I was to keep all soldiers with me until further notice. We were to be furnished food for the number that we took coming back from the north. Most of these men were the retreating American and Philippine armies from General Jones' command.

I took one squad with me to a deep cut in the highway where we dug foxholes, so we could use Molotov cocktails on the Japanese tanks if it became necessary to stop them. The first truck that I stopped was full of dead bodies. There were some Filipino soldiers hitchhiking on this truck. They were riding on the fenders and bumpers of the truck. After questioning the driver about his cargo, I flashed a light into the rear of the truck that had a tarpaulin over it. It had what looked like twenty-five or thirty bodies stacked in it. We let the driver proceed but kept the other soldiers. I asked them where they were going and they said they were going to Mariveles to meet their comrades. I asked them where their lieutenant was and they said he had been killed in action, as were most of the other soldiers in their unit.

We stopped 127 Filipino soldiers that night. We took them to our kitchen area where they were fed. All of these soldiers were hungry and thirsty and had had very little sleep or rest. A Filipino officer came for them and reorganized their unit.

About two nights later, I received an order by walkie-talkie to prepare my unit to move up. After seeing the casualties coming from the north, I knew this move meant the front lines of battle. I went back to my headquarters and told all of my men to pack up and prepare to move. I told them we would get transportation as near to the front as was possible, as we had to protect the safety of the buses. It was January 19 when we moved near the Abucay line.

Everything became very quiet; no one spoke out loud. It was nearing sunset. They rolled their packs and were in line in a few minutes. No one asked any questions. They had been expecting this move. Those long, large school buses, without tops, came into the area. The kitchen equipment was loaded into the only truck we had. The men were loaded into the buses by nine o'clock that night. It was a very dark night and everything was blacked out. The buses began to move north. I did not have to warn the men about lighting cigarettes because they had none to light. We could see, far in the north, flashes of heavy artillery like an advancing thunderstorm. No one talked or joked as the men usually did. We followed the coastal road for about seven or eight miles, then turned west on a dirt road that was very rough. We passed a first-aid station that had a dim light inside. We could see shadows of men working around a table, probably giving first aid to several soldiers. Soon we came into a heavily wooded area. The trees here were very tall and slim and thick on the ground. We had to cross some narrow bridges. One man walked along in front of the bus holding a flashlight pointed to the ground or bridge. All lights had to be concealed to keep the enemy from reacting with artillery. This was as far as it was safe for the buses to go. It was now 1:30 A.M. I told my men to get some sleep but not to put up any pup tents; in fact very few of them were ever issued pup tents.

I was called to regimental headquarters and given my orders. The 1st Battalion under Major O'Brian was to be the advance unit, and I was to have charge of the advance point. This meant that my men would be the first to come in contact with the advancing Japanese Imperial Army in this sector. We were to contact them on our left flank in the rough mountain area. This would keep our main force, in the level land, from being out-flanked. We were to start moving out at 4:30 A.M. I had almost one hour and fifteen minutes of sleep that night. We ate a light breakfast and then organized the advance unit. It was the 27th Materiel Squadron. We marched in columns of four for a short time until it began to get light; then the advance point, our unit, went into diamond formation. I was in the center of the diamond. I had two scouts out in front to check out every possible ambush location.

About eleven o'clock that morning we came upon a large sugar cane field. This was a perfect set up for an enemy ambush. I had the column halt and sent scouts around the edge of the cane field looking for signs of Japanese. They did not find any tracks of Japs going into the field, but they did report that there were some tracks just to the south of the field. I went over to look at the tracks and they were prints of the split-toed rubber shoes that most of the Japs wore. We tracked them to the northwest and found where they had probably eaten breakfast. There were paper wrappers and crumbs of their emergency rations that we called "dog biscuits." There were probably eight of them from the number of tracks. This alerted us; there must be Japs in this immediate area.

Due to the visibility of our area to the front, I had two rifle squads take up a skirmish formation. This way we could move faster without danger of ambush. We had tracked them about one mile farther northwest when we heard rifle fire. It sounded like our .30/.30 rifle fire. We saw two Filipino soldiers running toward us. They did not have their guns and were terribly frightened. They said their squad had been ambushed and they were the only ones not killed. We insisted on one of them going back with us to where the ambush took place and sent the other one on west to the headquarters of his unit, which was the 31st Filipino Regiment. One of my soldiers saw a Jap run across an opening, fired; he went down. Then some others shot Japs as they were running north. There were nine dead Filipino soldiers and one Jap where the ambush had taken place.

The Japs were numerous and were running northwest out of our designated area. I thought it best to contact the Filipino unit that was responsible for that area or we might be fired upon from one of our neighboring units by mistake. In fact the Filipino unit was in our sector when they were ambushed. When I talked to the Filipino commander, Colonel Erwin, he said the Japanese were coming by one trail over the mountains to within about two miles of our front. We decided to observe the trail with field glasses and soon saw some start over the trail. We called in our artillery to stop them from retreating over this trail. Colonel Erwin then sent a company up in this canyon to mop up the area about two hours after the artillery attack. This stopped them from coming over the mountain trail and attacking our main forces on the left flank.

We received orders to move about four miles back and make camp for the night. We had started to camp in a beautiful valley with some trees and lots of good water, but after we had halted and assigned areas for each unit, we were told that a platoon of twenty-five Japs had been killed in this area the day before. We decided we would need a better defensive position. We moved to a higher area, making it easier to defend against snipers. That night we could see flashes of artillery in the northeast along the Abucay line. The battle for Bataan had begun in earnest. The next morning there were lots of dive bombers in the air. We kept under cover and were not bombed or strafed.

Our whole army did not have a good defensive position across Bataan at this time, but we were putting forth a slowing process so they could be more easily stopped at our main line of defense, which we had previously prepared near Orion, west across the peninsula. The next night we had moved about four miles farther south of this flank position. I probably committed an error here. When First Sergeant Boston and I were setting up our perimeter guard positions, we were making reconnaissance of the area and walked right up on a man hiding in the brush along a single trail. We both held our guns on him for a minute and looked to see if there were any other men in the area. He did not look like a Jap, but looked like a tall, slender Filipino farmer. He had a bamboo cane pole about six feet long, with a bandana handkerchief tied around a small bundle on the end of the pole. He was on his knees, sitting back on his heels, and was hunched over as if he were hiding. Many of the Filipinos in this area could not speak English. He did not say a word but acted very scared. We walked up to within ten feet of him. He did not have a gun or knife that we could see, so we left him and went on about our business. When we returned to camp we reported this to Colonel Laughing-house, the battalion commander. He criticized me for not bringing him in for questioning. He said the man might have been a sniper, with his gun hidden, or a spy, reporting the movement of the military units in this area.

We posted our guards and twice in the night I was awakened by rifle fire. When I would investigate, there would be no movement or sound in the area. The guard would say, "I heard something in that area, but did not see anything." Each time it was in a canyon or a low place. The next morning, in each place where the guards had fired we found a large, grey, dead monkey.

5. *Front-Line Troops*

The next day we received orders to move back to a line west of Orion, which we had prepared before coming to Abucay. This was January 24. This area near Orion also had the world's heaviest malaria mosquito infestation. We were ordered to keep a rear guard out to cover our retreat, in case the Japanese were following us very closely. We loaded the kitchen equipment into the only truck we had. I sent Lieutenant Deeter and Mess Sergeants Yount and Smith along to locate a camp site for the kitchen. As soon as the truck was unloaded it was sent back for a load of men. It continued this shuttle until all of the men were picked up. In the meantime we would be marching toward Orion. We completed our move about sundown. After each unit of the 1st Battalion of the Air Corps Regiment had gotten its assignment on the front line, we had to establish our outpost to protect our units from sudden attacks.

When we were about three hundred yards out in front of our new line, I saw some Japanese soldiers run into a bamboo thicket. Most of the area in no man's land was rice paddies, but there was a line of small trees and brush where the creek bed had been. This was the best location for our outpost. The bamboo thicket was just beyond where we established our outpost. I thought this area needed to be cleaned out to protect us that night. I realized that this was just a Jap patrol, but they had followed us pretty closely. The artillery did a good job of saturating the bamboo thicket. When I came back to our lines, the engineers were putting up the barbed-wire entanglements in front of our lines.

Lieutenant Deeter reported that he had found an excellent place for our kitchen. It was seven kilometers to the rear of our lines, with lots of good water and a bluff to the north which would protect the kitchen from artillery fire. The only drawback was that we had to cross an exposed ridge to get the food from the kitchen to our unit. That meant that we could only be supplied with food during the dark hours: early morning and late at night. We were on short rations and only fed twice a day anyway.

The 27th Materiel Squadron was used as a battalion reserve. In case of an attack on any unit, we were to go to their aid or make a counterattack on the heaviest concentration of enemy fire. We cleared the trails out, where there was brush, so we could be of help immediately to any unit. About eleven o'clock that night a runner came to me from the 2nd Observation Squadron with the message that Captain McCorkle had been shot four times while trying to establish his outpost. Captain McCorkle had been my roommate and best friend. I had trained with him at Camp Bowie, Texas, and we were sent to the Philippine Islands at the same time.

I went over to his headquarters. They were waiting for an ambulance. He had received three machine gun bullets near the center of his stomach and one through his left shoulder. He complained about a rock being under his left shoulder, but the corpsman said he thought a bullet had lodged under his left shoulder blade. His first sergeant told me what had happened. He said they had started to establish their outpost about sundown, when they received some gun fire from a small barrio to their immediate front. They were pinned down for a few minutes. Captain McCorkle called for heavy rifle fire to be laid down in the area where the fire was coming from. He then raised up to rush the area and a machine gun opened up, stopping their attack. The captain's runner crawled up behind a small rice paddy terrace and rolled the captain onto his shelter half. He then crawled backward, dragging the captain by holding the shelter half in his teeth. The captain was pulled to a safe place where he could be put on a stretcher. Captain McCorkle died about one o'clock the next morning.

About half-past two that morning, the regimental commander told me to report to his headquarters immediately. When I arrived the colonel told me that Captain McCorkle had died. Then he said, "You will be in charge of the counterattack to retake this outpost." He said, "There is between a company or a platoon of Japanese troops in the area that had repulsed Captain McCorkle's attack. We will furnish you a company of men selected from each unit of the Air Force regiment. They will be ready and assembled at a certain point by 3:30 A.M., and you will be ready to jump off at 4:30 A.M., and we will give you artillery support when you are ready."

I asked the colonel to notify my battalion commander that I would be on this mission and he said he would do so. About 3:30 A.M. I had a meeting of the company officers who were assigned to this mission and we went over the plan of attack. We moved to the jumping-off area. My runner, Donald Stover, and I made a reconnaissance of the area to our immediate front.

It was a bright, moonlit night just before the moon was going down. There were tall coconut trees in all of this area. They waved in the breeze this warm summer morning. Normally it would have a romantic effect, but it was very different in this instance. We jumped from one tree to another as we approached the barrio's buildings, from which the firing came that had killed Captain McCorkle. We were within seventy-five yards of the first building. We were convinced that the terrain was smooth enough that we would not be surprised by an ambush up to a certain point to where the artillery could take care of anything that could happen from there on.

My runner and I went over to our right where we had been told that, at this outpost, there was a telephone with connections to our regimental headquarters. By this time the moon had gone down and it was very dark in the wooded area. We came up to the outpost and I could hear a voice but could not understand what was being said. It sounded like a challenge but not in English or Spanish.

I said, "American." They continued to challenge. I felt a .45 pistol in my left side. I said, "Americano." By this time there were two rifles aimed at us. The officer with the pistol pushed it hard against my left side, and I told him I wanted to talk to the regimental colonel.

He said, "What do you want to tell the colonel?" I told him that I had orders to call the regimental headquarters and tell them that we would be ready to jump off at 4:30 A.M. and to start the artillery at that time.

This Filipino would not let me talk, but he took the receiver and said, "White is to black as black is to white." This was code, of course, but I could hear the colonel's voice over the receiver. He said the artillery would start at 4:30 A.M. We went back to where our men were waiting. The officers had each unit in place and ready when we got the orders. Daylight had begun to break in the east. The beginning of a clear, hot day.

At 4:30 A.M. the artillery barrage started. We followed it as closely as was safe. Dust and leaves were thick in the air. The Japanese artillery counteracted by firing on our artillery emplacements, which they spotted by the flash of our batteries. They could not fire on us for fear of killing their own men. We did get some trench mortar burst. When we got to the group of buildings, where the machine gun fire came from, we could see a few Japs running out the back of these buildings and into the brush. Our men would shoot them as we would shoot jackrabbits. It did not take us long to retake our outpost. These buildings had not been occupied since the war started, and brush and weeds had taken over. The 2nd Observation Squadron reestablished their outpost. When we withdrew to our area, there was one trench mortar that kept firing from the cliff north of the area, but it was not doing any damage that I could see. The day had become hot again and our men were glad to get back to the shade and eat breakfast.

When I returned to my headquarters, I received a call from my battalion commander, Colonel Bill Maverick, wanting to know where I had been and why I had not told him I was going to be gone. I told him I had asked the regimental commander to call him and let him know that I was on this mission and he had agreed to do so. Colonel Maverick was very unhappy and told the regimental commander so. The next time I called Colonel Maverick personally and let him know that I was going to make a counterattack, and who would be in charge of my unit while I was away.

The Japs kept a tight pressure by heavy patrols on the entire front line for several days. We heard by our intelligence lines that the hospitals in Manila were full of Japanese soldiers with malaria. The

Americans and Filipinos were not doing much better. We had no quinine. When our men had a malarial chill, they would just lie around for a few days until the fever left, and then they would go back on duty. They were not sent to the hospital. Our rations were cut in half again in February. This made us get two very light meals a day. Never did we have more than one slice of bread at each meal. If we could find a mule, horse, or carabao (water buffalo), we would have some meat. We had no refrigeration facilities, so fresh meat would not keep very long.

One night while it was quiet in our sector, I thought I would get a good night's sleep. I took off my trousers and shoes so I could relax. About 4:00 A.M., the Jap artillery opened up on our sector. I put on my shoes and grabbed my trousers and jumped into my foxhole just about the time a shell hit near by. I had one leg in my trousers and the dirt from the shell burst filled my foxhole and my trousers before I could put them on.

The Jap patrol finally found what they thought was a weak point in the Filipino army unit to the left of the "flying infantry" regiment. Twice in a two-month period, I went over there with our unit to replace a hole in their lines.

Every few days each unit sent out a fifteen-man intelligence patrol. They were not to enter into a fire fight if they could prevent it but were to get certain information. Most of these patrols would slip behind the Jap lines and stay all day. They would go under darkness and return under darkness. To get behind the lines, we found a place where we could wade across the river near Manila Bay that the Japs used as a buffer zone in that area. The patrols would get in the rice paddies along the main road, where the rice straw was high, and lie there all day in the hot sun and count the vehicles, the artillery pieces and such, the number of Jap troops coming and going back from the front. This way we could tell when to expect a push from the build-up.

The following is an example of how our intelligence patrols worked, showing the high morale of our troops:

January 29, 1942, I was asked to furnish an intelligence patrol to get certain pertinent information from the enemy lines. Volunteers were requested. Due to the high morale of the squadron and the extreme confidence in Lieutenant Deeter as a patrol leader, all who were able volunteered. Only fourteen were needed, so the first fourteen to volunteer were accepted. They received their orders from the battalion intelligence officer. They were to proceed to Balanga and ascertain whether or not there were Japanese troops in that town. Orders were to fight if necessary to accomplish the mission. The patrol passed the outpost line of resistance at twelve midnight. At 4:00 A.M. the morning of the thirtieth, the patrol arrived at a point one kilometer from the town of Balanga. Here they were met by a patrol from the 31st Filipino Army Regiment. A few hours prior to this meeting, the 31st patrol had attempted to cross the bridge into Balanga and were attacked by Japanese forces. Three of their men were killed and two were wounded. The remainder were forced to withdraw. After receiving this information, our patrol proceeded under cover. They used the cover of the bar ditch and scattered trees along the road toward the Balanga bridge. Rice paddies were solid on each side of the road and could give little cover protection. It was good daylight when they moved up to within 150 yards of the bridge. Lieutenant Deeter used his field glasses to examine the bridgehead carefully. What appeared to be a machine gun emplacement at the farther abutment of the bridge was faintly outlined through the field glasses. No personnel could be seen. The patrol proceeded down the river to where a better view could be had by climbing a tree. Here with the use of the glasses the position of the Japs could be seen. Two Jap soldiers and the machine gun emplacements were visible. The positions were observed for about one hour. No other soldiers appeared during this time. Lieutenant Deeter assured himself that there were Japanese troops in Balanga, in as much as the bridgehead was in Balanga. This was his mission, but he felt that more information would be helpful. He wanted to find out, if possible, the strength the enemy had at Balanga. They waded the Talisay River, which was about three and one-half feet deep at the shallowest place they could find and about fifty yards across. Three men were sent across first to cover the others while they crossed. As they were entering the outskirts of the city, they stopped several Filipino civilians who were running away. Some of the Filipinos were being put to hard labor digging ditches for the Japs. After several had been questioned, it was pretty certain that there were forty or fifty Japanese soldiers stationed in Balanga. The patrol decided to withdraw. It was sunup and a clear, hot day. The Japanese tactics had been to let a patrol by and then ambush them as they started to withdraw. Lieutenant Deeter knew that to take the same route out would mean suicide, so they withdrew through the rice paddies, on their knees, slipping from one terrace to another until they were out of rifle range. They were sure they had been observed by the Japs before crossing the river, because there had been no cover to conceal their movements in broad daylight. They had gone behind the enemy lines and outmaneuvered them by not returning the same way they came in, which looked like the only possible way to withdraw. This patrol was out eighteen hours and returned with much more information than had been asked for, without getting into a fire fight.

Every man in my unit went on one of these patrols at one time or another. The morale continued to be high even though they were continuing to lose weight. At first we had some type of emergency rations to send on these patrols until we received orders from the corps headquarters to turn in our Type C rations to be redistributed. We had been using these rations only on the thirty-six–hour patrols because rice balls would spoil in twelve hours. The other units had eaten up their Type C rations, while we had saved ours for this special purpose. I did not know how the units in the rear could use these rations to a better advantage than we were doing. We held out sending them to the rear and kept using them until a detail was sent to pick them up. We also had five twelve-gauge shotguns we were using on these patrols and we received orders to turn them in, because it was against the international law to use shotguns in combat. I did comply with this request.

One time an intelligence patrol from another unit came back from patrol duty and reported that a boatload of Jap soldiers went up a certain river in *boncas** in no man's land about twelve midnight every night. When it came our time to go out on this patrol, we were ordered to bring back a live Japanese soldier for interrogation. We decided this could be done by setting up an ambush at the point where the lieutenant had seen the *bonca* full of Japanese soldiers. Lieutenant Deeter was to take this fifteen-man patrol. My personal runner, Donald Stover, wanted to go. He said, "I want to get me a 'nippie.' " He borrowed my .45 Colt automatic, fastened four hand grenades on his

---

* Where possible, the spelling of Filipino and Japanese words has been verified, but in some cases the author has spelled terms phonetically, as he heard them at the time.

belt, and took a Browning automatic rifle with him. The others in the patrol were almost as well prepared for combat. This time they were to enter into fire fighting if necessary to achieve their objective: to get a live Jap soldier.

They decided first to throw a hand grenade into the boat, then completely cover from the bank anything that moved. If the boat sank, certain ones were designated to concentrate on one Jap soldier by using man power or force. The others that tried to escape would be shot. Lieutenant Deeter borrowed my field glasses so he could watch for a Jap patrol. The lieutenant briefed his patrol and told them of his plan to take as many alive as would surrender. If none offered to surrender, then they would take them by force. They crossed our front lines a little after dark. Since the river was narrow at the point set for the ambush, a hand grenade could easily be thrown into the boat from the bushy bank. They approached this area and waited for the boat.

All of the 27th Materiel Squadron, and others in the battalion that knew of this patrol and its mission, were anxious to find out what success they had. About 3:00 A.M., Lieutenant Deeter's patrol returned. The lieutenant came up to my bunk, threw his helmet down in disgust, and said, "That lying lieutenant who made that report to the intelligence battalion ought to be court-martialed. He didn't even look into the river as he reported." He said, "We got into position as planned and just at twelve o'clock, when the Japanese boat was supposed to come along according to the report, we heard a noise that sounded like oars paddling a boat in the river. We rushed up to surprise them and blast part of them out of the water. It was light enough that we could see some large fish breaking the water, splashing around. We checked closer and found that this was a shallow place in the river that the large fish were trying to cross to go upstream." This was a very disappointed patrol. But morale remained high and they always seemed eager to go on these patrols.

6. *Desperate for Food*

I could tell that the Filipino army units were getting weaker and it was much easier for the Japs to break through their front lines. Our own men were growing weaker and getting poorer every day from the lack of food. We had to forage on the land for most of the food we received. We were getting from 1,000 to 1,400 calories a day. Our men would go out into no man's land at night and get rice from what straw stacks they could find, bringing it back and threshing it out in the daytime. For a while we could find some of our army mules or horses that had been turned loose. Due to our lack of refrigeration, we only killed what we could eat in a day. In fact, I appointed one man to bring us one mule or horse a day until he could no longer find one. We tried the large red monkey meat, but this did not work too well. The meat was tough and stringy. We dynamited some fish in Manila Bay. We tried to use some abalone (shell fish) but because our meals were always cold when we were served, this was too tough. For example, one morning we were being served (always in line) and I was at the end of the line and last to be served. I noticed several of the men sitting cross-legged on the ground, with their mess kits in their laps, chewing what looked like meat, but they never swallowed any of it. (We had a rule that no one would gripe about the food or how it was served.) When I received my portion of meat and gravy—no bread—I started to eat this meat. It tasted like fish, but I could not bite through it. It was just like trying to bite through rubber. I would get a good bite on the meat then take my whole hand and try to pull off a bite. It would stretch like rubber and slap me in the face. I went over to Mess Sergeant Van Hook and asked him if someone had lost a rubber shoe heel. The sergeant said, "No, that is abalone, and when it's eaten hot it is tender, but when it gets cold, it's hard to eat." The abalone was shaped like a shoe heel and about the same size.

The sergeant said, "On our way from the kitchen to the front lines, we were attacked twice by low-flying planes." Each time they left the truck to find a place to hide. One time bullets pierced the gravy and abalone containers as well as the cab of the truck. He showed me where there were three bullet holes in the containers that had our food in them. A lot of the gravy had leaked out. The truck was not disabled though. I told him they would have to leave the kitchen area about fifteen minutes earlier while it was still dark enough that the planes could not see them. All of this interruption caused the food to be cold and the mess sergeants could not help it. Not one of my men complained. They were grateful to get anything to eat.

After we had established the line west of Orion, General Mac-

Arthur would not let our artillery shell churches in no man's land or in the enemy territory. We had suspected that the Japs were using the church steeples as observation stations. Several times our patrols had gotten into fire fights or ambushes near the community of Pilar. At Pilar there had been a sugar mill and a rice grinding station; that is, they had some mill stones there used for grinding rice or corn. Some of our patrols had reported this. A platoon of men were sent to Pilar to get these mill stones to be used for our purpose, but the Japs had beaten us to them. Our men, when on patrol, would go by the sugar mill and eat some of the black strap molasses that was in the tanks. They would bring back full five-gallon containers by putting each one on a stick so two could carry it between them. We would eat this straight like candy. The containers were five-gallon gasoline cans.

One night while one of our patrols was in that area, they had a fire fight with a platoon of Japanese. They were chased out. The next time one of our patrols started to get some molasses, they noticed it smelled like kerosene. They checked further and found that the Japs had poured kerosene in every vat. This ruined the taste of the syrup and made our men very angry.

We could tell by the way our patrols were followed, and from the artillery strikes, that certain church steeples were being used as observation posts. In order to be sure of this, before reporting it to the higher ups, we sent a patrol to a church in Pilar in the early morning after good daylight. When two men entered the church, they saw closets on each side. Just after entering the church, one man opened a closet door and saw a Jap pack lying on the floor. He told the soldier on the other side, "There are Japs in here." The other soldier was in the process of opening a closet door on the other side, when the first one spoke. He opened the door and there was a Jap sitting on the floor with an automatic rifle in his hand. The sergeant tried to shut the door, but before he could, he was shot three times in the stomach. He fell in the entrance of the church and the other soldiers pulled him from the building. The patrol surrounded the church so no one could escape. Four entered the church, opened the closet where the Jap was, and threw in a hand grenade; at the same time the others were firing into the pulpit area. They heard a sound from that area and threw two grenades behind the pulpit. They killed five Japanese in this church. They were equipped with walkie-talkie communications. They had been climbing up into the steeple, as there were cigarette stubs that had been thrown down several days before.

After this incident and others were reported to General MacArthur, the artillery orders were changed. They were told not to spare the churches, if it was suspected they were harboring enemy personnel.

There were several hundred Filipino men working on building roads from our front lines to the rear. When they got near the front lines, they continued to build small fires to cook their rice for the noon meal. Twice I had asked them not to build fires in our area for fear of drawing artillery fire or getting bombs dropped on us. One day at noon a flight of dive bombers came over us as usual. Our air-raid guards reported the sound of motors in the east and overhead. All at once one of these planes peeled out of formation and dropped bombs within fifty yards of my headquarters. The leaves and dust were still falling when I ran over to where the bomb had hit. A fragment bomb had been dropped in the fire where the five Filipinos had just started a fire to cook their rice. Three of the five were killed. One was crawling toward an old fence where there was a piece of baling wire. He took this wire off the fence, wound it around his leg above the knee, and twisted it tight with a bayonet. The bone was protruding on both sides of his leg below the knee. One of the dead, I noticed, had a piece of shrapnel about the size of an axe protruding from the center of his backbone just above his hips. The carabao that was tied to a tree within ten feet of the fire was switching his tail because of the leaves and dust falling on his back. Our corpsman gave the wounded men shots to ease them; then they were moved by ambulance. I heard later that the man who tied the wire around his leg to stop the blood had to have his leg amputated but was doing all right. The other man died due to the loss of blood.

Someone in our battalion mounted a battery of two fifty-caliber machine guns on two bicycle wheels so it could be moved more easily to counterattack the dive bombers. We soon learned that a fifty-caliber weapon could not bring down a heavily armored Jap plane unless it was hit in the belly. These planes became very numerous. They would dive like they were going to unleash their bombs, and if the angle was not right, they would pull up and make another run, releasing the bombs when everything was just right. They had no opposition. Everywhere this mounted machine gun would fire on them, they would come back and saturate the area with bombs. We had them firing this mobile machine gun out away from everyone. It did knock down one dive bomber that I know about.

On March 12, each of the front line units received a radiogram from Corregidor telling them that General MacArthur had been ordered to Australia. The general said, "I will return." That same evening the 19th Bomb Group was bombed again. I went over to see how much damage had been done. The bomb shelter they had under a tree had gotten a direct hit on the top. Four men were in the shelter, one in each corner. When I arrived, three were sitting limp in their corners and one other came out of the shelter, ran about fifty feet, and fell dead. The three in the shelter were unconscious. Their eyes were blood shot. They had blood coming out of their ears. These men were ready for duty the next day.

Each day a slow-flying observation plane would come over us in the morning and burst a bale of propaganda leaflets over our lines. These sheets of paper would trickle down over our area. They would have every kind of propaganda picture on them. Some had the picture of a Filipino who had been captured, sitting at a dinner table loaded with good things to eat, and his wife holding a child in her arms while she waited on him. It said, "You too can enjoy this if you will come to the coconut grove with your rifle over your left shoulder and the barrel pointing down. This leaflet will be accepted as your ticket and any number can enter. You will be treated well."

Another of the leaflets pictured a battle ground, after a battle, with dead men lying all around. A rifle with a bayonet was stuck in the ground with a helmet on top of the gun stock. It read, "This is what you will look like if you don't surrender by a certain time." One day we received a sex leaflet showing the privates of a beautiful, blond woman. This series was entitled, "You too can enjoy this if you will surrender." Having these leaflets dropped every morning was like getting the newspaper delivered to us, only we knew it was propaganda.

One morning about 4:30, there was an annoying sound. It was coming from the back of our lines and sounded like a fire fight. All the sound came from something about the size of a Japanese rifle. I think they were dropped from an airplane during the day and they had a time fuse on them. They could have been clusters of large firecrackers. They came at a time when we were having lots of sniping and the men would mention how this was getting on their nerves. We knew the line could break anywhere and the Japs could get behind us before we were aware of it. During the day or night we didn't call each other by our names, for fear of getting picked out at night. If a Jap heard your name was Joe, that night someone would yell, "Joe, come here and help me a minute." The next morning we would find "Joe" with his throat cut. We were harassed in another way. About daylight there was a large howitzer shell burst back of our lines. These shells would explode five or six times at one-minute intervals. This would wake everyone up; this harassment went on for quite some time. The shells never did hit anyone or any of our vehicles, but the loss of sleep hurt the men and was wearing on their nerves. We thought the shells were coming from a boat in Manila Bay.

Seeing the once-healthy soldiers tiring easily and most of them having malaria fever (each had lost twenty or thirty pounds of weight) was pathetic. I decided that I would go to the rear, where I had known there were some food dumps, and beg food for these men. This did not hurt my ego in the least, because I knew these soldiers were doing their best with what they had. I went like a hobo to two supply depots from Little Baguio to Cabcaben and begged for food. At each place they just did not have any food, but at the last place I went they gave me a gallon glass jug of vinegar. They were all very sympathetic. I stopped in at a motor pool where I knew several officers and had dinner. At noon just as we sat down to an improvised table, we heard the drone of heavy motors coming from the west. Everyone ran for his foxhole, but there was not an extra one for visitors, so this being a heavily wooded area, I ran to the trees. These trees were banyan trees and had very large roots extending out of the ground. Three bombers came over but only one dropped several bombs. I could hear the bomb-bay doors open and could see the bombs as they fell toward us. I jumped behind one of the large tree roots, the bombs exploded, and a large shrapnel hit the tree that I was behind. These were fragment and phosphorus bombs. The phosphorus bombs set fire to two truck tires and leaves and brush. Everyone put on his gas mask to help fight the fires, but I had left my gas mask at my kitchen when I started back to beg for food. The phosphorus was so strong that it burned my throat and nostrils. This was certainly not a good time to be without a gas mask. I thought for a while they had dropped poison gas.

I thought of my military training and what I had been taught to do if caught without a gas mask. This was to find a ledge or cliff where fresh air comes up, then hang your head over this and it would get you away from the gas. There was a cliff about fifteen feet away from me, so I ran over there. That was the best deep breath I ever took as I hung my head over the cliff. When the phosphorus gas was dispersed, I went back and helped put out the fire. Then I said, "Let's finish our dinner." There was not a single officer who came back to the table to finish his dessert, which was tomato bread pudding. I ate all five of the officers' desserts. The mess sergeant had one leg blown off and died a short time later.

I took a boat at Cabcaben soon after sundown to go to Corregidor. When I arrived there later that night, it looked as if the only place for me to sleep was on the cement floor in the Malinta tunnel. I saw Lieutenant Andy James, who was reared at Dalhart, Texas, near my home. He had been one of my lieutenants in the 27th Materiel Squadron. He was now decoding messages in the decoding room on Corregidor, except he had been assigned as a patient in the hospital with a case of malaria. He told me he had been pretty sick but was getting ready to check out of the hospital and return to the decoding room to sleep. He said, "You sleep in my hospital bed tonight and I will check out tomorrow instead of today. That way you will have a good bed to sleep in tonight." I went into the hospital and went to bed in Lieutenant James' bed. I slept like a baby all night. Everything was quiet and the bed was so soft. About 4:30 the next morning, a nurse woke me up and started to give me a shot. I didn't like the looks of the needle, so I quickly told her I was Captain Coleman from Bataan and that I was sleeping in Lieutenant James' bed. The light was very dim and she did not pay any attention to what I said. If she did, she did not believe me or else thought I was delirious. She was going to stick me anyway. I rolled over on the other side of the bed, she came around there and I rolled back over on the other side. Then she called a male nurse. He came running down to my bed. He was about six-feet-three and weighed at least two hundred pounds. When he came over to my side of the bed, I rolled over on the side where the nurse was and jumped out of bed, grabbed my trousers, and ran into the rest room. The corpsman followed me and when he came in where it was light enough to see me, he said, "You are not Lieutenant James. You must be from Bataan. You are too dark to be from Corregidor." He wanted to know why I was in the hospital in the lieutenant's bed. I explained to him that the lieutenant had just given me a good place to sleep that night since he could sleep in the decoding room.

For breakfast we had two slices of bacon and one slice of bread. That I remember; we might have had more. This was the first bacon that I had eaten in two months. I talked to General Wainwright that morning at his headquarters. He was worried about our not getting any supplies and the way the war was going in general. He had high praise for the defenders of Bataan and asked about the condition of my men. I told him that they were slowly starving to death. They were so weak it took an extra effort for them to get out of their foxholes. All of them had had malaria or were having it. We could not send the sick to the hospital or we would have no one on the main line of defense. I told him I feared that the next big push the Japs would make would be the end of the Bataan defense. Then I told him my mission; to beg food for my men.

He said he could not give me extra food, because they expected Corregidor to hold out after Bataan fell or was resupplied from the States. He said, "If we furnish supplies for you, we would have to let the Filipinos have food too, to keep them fighting. This would deplete our supplies here on Corregidor too much. We just do not have the food to spare. He finally wrote me out an order for one 120-pound box of shredded coconut and one number-two can of fruit cocktail. The fruit cocktail was for my dinner the next day on my way back to the front lines. About ten o'clock that morning Corregidor had a heavy bombing attack. Everyone in the area was in Malinta tunnel. All that we could hear was the sound of the motors and the thud of the bombs as they hit on top of the tunnel. Some rocks would roll down the hill toward the entrance of the tunnel.

That day at noon we had carabao meat for lunch served on a table. The officers sitting on each side of me pushed their meat away and said, "I can't eat that meat." I was quick to say, "Let me have it; I believe I can eat it." Those on Corregidor were skimping and conserving food too, because one never saw a fat soldier there.

After dark I boarded the boat that took me back across the three miles of water to Cabcaben on Bataan, with my 120-pound box of coconut and one gallon of vinegar. After I got to Cabcaben, I had to spend the night at an engineers' headquarters. For breakfast we had a glass of chocolate milk and Type C rations. Now my problem was to figure out how I was going to hitchhike my way back to my kitchen area, which was eight or ten miles. I rode north with a couple of military police to Limay; then I had them call my kitchen and asked them to send a truck for me. They could not because they were out of gas but said the Headquarters & Headquarters Squadron could send a truck for me if I would give them half of the coconut and vinegar. I had no alternative but to accept their offer.

While I was waiting for the truck to pick me up, the military police asked me if I had a first-aid kit, which I did. They asked me to go to a certain place and doctor a woman who had been hit with shrapnel. I went over to see if I could help the woman. It was a very pitiful sight. There was an old man holding a baby that looked to be about two weeks old. The baby was crying. A little girl about two years old had had part of her left cheek blown away. She had quit crying and the blood was almost dry. The mother had part of the muscles torn off her left arm and about half of her left breast. Milk was oozing out of the wound on her breast, and she was still bleeding. I bandaged her arm and breast and asked where her husband was. She said, "He is across the road in the shade of a tree, on a stretcher." I went across the road to see about the man. He had had his head blown off and it was lying under his arm on the stretcher. He looked to be fifty-five or sixty years old. She said about eleven o'clock that morning he had looked over a bank toward a battle area and an artillery shell exploded nearby, snapping off his head. I went back to the military police and asked them if I could use their walkie-talkie. I called the corps hospital and asked them to come and get the woman and the two children. They said they would.

About this time the truck came for me and I went back to my kitchen area. On the way we were bombed once and strafed once. I remembered something that I had read, that went something like this: "During war the defending front line troops will suffer more for the want of food than any of the other units," and this trip made me believe this statement. The men were fed much better behind the lines than on the front lines. There had been a bad breakdown in our food supply and its final distribution.

7. *The Handwriting on the Wall*

When I returned to my headquarters, I had orders to make out a plan of attack to dislodge the Japanese from our immediate front, also a plan to withdraw. I knew it was impossible for us to build up a strong attack unless we had the support of new troops. I believed this part of the order was to camouflage or soften the withdrawal orders. This was to keep from killing our morale before we had to retreat. I talked with several of my sergeants and set up a hypothetical plan like this: if we were supplied with troops, would we want them to relieve us from our front-line duty; or would we want to make a push first and then let them take over? Although we had been on the front lines for three months without any relief, they said, "We would want to run the Japs out of their first line of defense before we let anyone take our place." They said, "We can whip them anytime, but we do not have the supplies or personnel to hold what we would gain."

The plans to attack and to withdraw were made and sent to the corps headquarters. Then we got orders to build a regimental reserve line. That would be a defensive position with foxholes dug for each unit. We had no reserves to occupy this emplacement, so we knew it would be we that would occupy it. This was in a half-moon–shaped defense. The 27th Materiel Squadron was on the extreme left flank of the Provisional Air Corps Regiment. This would put my squadron in the 2nd Battalion area. I never knew why this was done just for the regimental reserve. This took us two days to complete.

The next day we received an extremely heavy bombing from five-hundred-pound bombs. It uprooted trees that were from forty to seventy feet high. I was very nearly covered up in my foxhole. Blood ran out of both my ears from the concussion. My unit did not suffer any casualties except shell shock. My youngest soldier came up and lay down at my feet, wheezing and groaning as if he were choking to death. I had a corpsman give him a shot to relax him and sent him back to the kitchen to help carry wood for the cooks for a couple of days. The next day he came back with the chow truck. He said, "Captain, I'm not yellow. I could not help doing what I did, but I want to be up here with my buddies."

I told him, "I know you could not help it. Excitement causes the throat muscles to tighten, causing you to choke." The next morning we had a heavy shelling and were afraid there would be an infantry attack with it. I checked all of my men in the foxholes. There was one in which I could not see any movement, so I ran over there and lay down near the hole. The shells were still falling close. This soldier was in the bottom of his foxhole chewing off his fingernails. I had him stand up and let me look at his nails. They were all bloody and eaten into the quick. I told him to pull himself together and get ready for an infantry attack. He said, "But Ca-Ca-Captain, I'm afraid."

I told him, "I'm afraid too, but each of us has a job to do and if we do not do it, the Japs will take our lives."

He acted sullen and stubborn. I took out my pistol and told him to stand up and get ready like the rest of the soldiers. He got his rifle above the foxhole and I went back to my foxhole. We did not get the expected infantry attack and the next day I sent this man back to the hospital as a shell shock victim. I was sorry I had been overpersuasive. He died a few days later.

By this time every soldier in my unit had malaria. Very few ever went to the hospital. The hospital did not have any medicine for them and the men wanted to stay on the line of duty. We were expecting more attacks on our front lines. Every night some of our tanks would come up to help us hold the line. They could not stay there during the daylight hours, for fear of being destroyed by Jap artillery. Each night as they came up, they would run over our telephone lines and cut them. We were supposed to call our headquarters every thirty minutes to let them know the situation. Our telephone-line repairmen would start at each side where the line was intact and slide their hands along the line until they found the cut. This was done on the darkest nights and the lines could be repaired in a short while. Even though the tanks caused us some trouble, we surely were glad to have their support. We felt more secure with them there to help us. Nearly all of our artillery batteries had been silenced by the five-hundred-pound bombs the Japs were using.

Our artillery had been doing an excellent job. They could silence a Japanese artillery piece five minutes after it started firing. Our military force had been using the Bataan Peninsula to have their maneuvers on for years. They had accurate maps and had drawn them off in grids. You could tell a liaison officer that you wanted fire on a certain numbered grid and he could put it on there immediately. This caused the artillery to fight a duel every night.

On April 6, when I awoke and looked toward the north through the haze and fog, I could see a sausage-shaped observation balloon high over the Japanese lines. This was out of range for any weapons we now had. Our artillery could range fourteen miles, but we did not have any near the front to use. We also did not have any airplanes. I just knew, "this is it," but what could we do about it? They could see every move we made and where we were.

Colonel Bill Maverick, the 1st Battalion commander, called me to his headquarters. He told me to put someone in charge of the 27th Materiel Squadron, that he was appointing me to be his executive officer. Colonel Maverick said, "I have been a flying officer for twenty years and know very little about maneuvering troops. You have proved to us that you know the infantry business. You will prepare to withdraw this battalion to the regimental reserve line."

This order had come from the regimental commander. The movement was to be made in the morning. I said, "Colonel, I believe the first thing to do will be to get those men with malaria, the sick and wounded that cannot march, sent back to the hospital. None of our men are able to carry those water-cooled machine guns or the fifty-caliber guns that we mounted on tripods. We will have to put these in a truck to destroy them or send them to the rear for someone in better shape than we are to use them."

We gave the problem of picking up the machine guns and the unnecessary baggage to the transportation officer. When our sick men were taken back, it took at least one-third of our battalion. My old standby, Lieutenant Deeter, adjutant to the 27th, had to go to the hospital. Lieutenant Wayne Van Voorhis was put in charge of the 27th Materiel Squadron.

We had taken the fifty-calibre machine guns off destroyed P-40 airplanes. Someone at the Philippine Air Depot had made tripods to fit them so they could be used as infantry weapons. This battalion had more machine guns than an ordinary infantry regiment.

Supper, April 6, was the last time I was to eat with my old 27th Materiel Squadron. I had never known a more obedient or harder working unit than they had been. That night the mess sergeant told me we had only enough food for one more meal and it would all be rice. We did not know where we could get any more food. This was also the situation with all the rest of the Air Corps Regiment.

Our intelligence reported that the heavy drive was on. Fresh troops from Singapore, called "the Shanghai Division," were attacking in our area. This was the division that had taken the British and the Australians at Singapore in February. Artillery had been concentrated on the Filipino troops to our left. They were being shelled day and night. We could look up the valley to the west and see artillery burst all day, sending dust and mud into the air. There seemed to be an abundance of artillery pieces all along the Japanese lines. The night of April 6, I stayed up all night, with one hundred other men posted on the left flank of the regiment, expecting to have to make a counter-attack. This didn't take place because of the size of the breakthrough on the Air Corps Regiment's left. By daylight the morning of April 7, the Japanese had cut through on our left as far as seven kilometers to the south. They had taken the kitchen area of the 27th Materiel Squadron.

We received orders from regimental headquarters to abandon the immediate front lines and take up the regimental reserve position to protect our flanks. We also found that the Filipino unit, the 31st Infantry on our right flank between the 1st Battalion and Manila Bay, had begun to withdraw. They were not even with our regimental reserve lines, but several miles to the south. This left our right flank open. After we were in position on the regimental reserve line, I went back to the regimental command post.

The regimental colonel said, "This is where our command post will be and if you have any information send it to us."

At this time there were no airplanes or artillery bothering us. All seemed to be quiet. I went back to the battalion command post. Colonel Maverick said, "The intelligence patrol that we sent out thirty-six hours ago should be back by now."

I did not know about this patrol. They had been sent out before I was appointed executive officer. The patrol came from the 7th Materiel Squadron, with a Lieutenant Rice in charge. Colonel Maverick and I went up on a knoll near our headquarters and took a look toward our immediate front, using my field glasses. There were hundreds of small boats along the bay up near Pilar. At the same time we could see thousands of Japanese in skirmish formation spread across our front for at least one-half mile. I gave the glasses to the colonel and when he looked, he said, "Oh, Captain, we will never overcome this."

We heard rifle and machine gun fire to our left and to the rear. I knew we did not have any machine guns. Colonel Maverick and I went back to the regimental command post, leaving four runners and our supply officer at the battalion headquarters. There were runners from all the units coming into the regimental command post wanting to know what to do. A runner from the 2nd Observation Squadron said tanks and infantry had cut off the 27th Materiel Squadron and half of the 2nd Observation Squadron. He said the tanks and infantry were coming in behind us. They could not find anyone at the regimental command post and neither did we.

There had been several hundred Filipino civilians working on the roads just to the rear of our lines for about five miles. These men and some Filipino soldiers, without their rifles, began to run into our lines by the hundreds, yelling, "Tanks! Tanks!" Many of them had been wounded, some had arms dangling, some were lame, with fresh blood on them.

Colonel Maverick said, "We've got to do something." He turned to me and said, "Captain Coleman, you take charge of this regiment. We are about to be surrounded." By now I could see dust and hear automatic gun fire as well as what I thought was twenty-millimeter gun fire every few seconds. This sound had to be coming from tanks. I could not see any tanks, but I could hear motors, see trees and brush shaking, and hear the machine gun fire. There was a ravine to our left that had large boulders in it that prevented the tanks from coming completely across the rear of our lines until they found a crossing about even with our front lines.

I squatted down in kneeling position and sent written messages by each runner, telling the squadron commanders of each unit to come out in order to our right flank, on double time. This would leave the tanks on the west side of the rough ravine. Our troops would be moving east. I could see, to the immediate front, waves of Jap soldiers coming across the rice paddies near our old front line. Our troops had begun to fire on them, making them run a little way and then hit the ground; then others would come up running, while we were getting lots of rifle fire from the front.

The entire regiment was soon on the move to the south. They had come out of this pocket on double time and in order. The civilians were choking up the road, so we traveled off the road. Soon flight after flight of strafing planes came from the north swooping down on the road full of civilians, leaving many wounded and dead after each pass. The civilians would scatter but would soon be back on the road.

A runner from the 1st Battalion Headquarters reported to me that Lieutenant Rice and his twelve-man patrol had returned to their unit. They had entered into a fire fight with the Japs at our old front lines. Lieutenant Rice did not know that we had moved back to the regimental reserve lines and he was lost for a while.

We did not have a single weapon that would knock out a tank and I was at a loss to know what to do since I had not heard from a higher echelon. I knew I could be court-martialed for ordering a retreat. To get surrounded would mean that we would be subjected to dive bombing and strafing, as well as being sitting ducks for artillery. If surrounded, we could not move and I knew we were outnumbered probably fifty to one.

The 2nd Battalion commander, Lieutenant Colonel J. W. Sewall, could not be found before I took over the regiment. He may have been cut off with the 27th Materiel Squadron or the 2nd Observation Squadron.

When we had traveled south to the first military crest that looked like a good defensive position, I ordered the regiment to deploy along this line. We could see a lot of scrub trees and brush, before getting into a clearing in front of us. I did not know whether these scrub trees would stop the tanks or not. Our visibility was good for 150 yards to our immediate front. I checked the line to the west to see that all of the regiment was in place for an infantry attack. As far as I could tell, everything seemed to be in order. Colonel Maverick stayed at the regimental command post. Just as I was returning from the west end of the line, I saw scrub trees and brush in front of us shaking, and the dust rising. I could hear the clank, clanking of the tanks following us.

I had hurried so much to see that everything was in place that I was just about exhausted.

A runner from the regimental colonel had just reported to Colonel Maverick that we were to set up a defensive position some ten miles farther south near a certain kilometer. I did not have a map, but it sounded like it was on the coastal road near the bay since it was marked off in kilometers. I knew the Japs were farther south than we were on the west, because I could hear Jap artillery fire to the southwest of us. We were fighting a running battle to keep from getting surrounded. I found out later that it had been reported that the Air Corps Regiment had been completely surrounded and lost.

The Jap tanks and infantry were about on us. We had to act fast. I ordered each unit to double-time and follow the unit to the east of them. This was done so that the last unit out would not have to take the brunt of the attack and be cut off. To our rear (south) were heavy brush and scrub trees, so it would be impossible to move through and keep a squad intact. The last unit was to fight a rear-guard action if the Japs closed in.

After we had marched about two miles, we found the regimental colonel and his staff in a jeep parked under a large tree that had been uprooted by a bomb. Colonel Maverick went up to the regimental colonel and asked him, "Where have you been?"

He said, "We have been back at corps headquarters trying to find out what to do."

Colonel Maverick had some bad words for him and told him, "If we ever get back to the States, you will be court-martialed for leaving your unit in such a critical situation, without leaving someone in charge. If we had waited fifteen minutes longer, we would have been completely surrounded and could not have fought our way out of the encirclement."

The regimental colonel gave me a map and showed me where we would form another defensive line. He wanted to know how long it would take me to get this unit down there. I told him, "If we have no further interference from the Japs, we will be there by 3:30 in the morning."

He didn't brief me on where any of our friendly troops were or where the enemy was. I asked him if he could find any food anywhere for these men; they had had nothing to eat since supper last night. He said he would try to arrange for something, but he never did.

They turned the jeep around and turned south ahead of our regiment. This was about five o'clock in the afternoon. We crossed the Mamala River without a bridge. Soon we were in a heavy forest. This would keep the dive bombers and strafing planes off our columns. We didn't see or hear the tanks again. I was worried about the fate of the 27th Materiel Squadron. They had been very faithful and hard-fighting men. I was hoping that they, along with those from the 2nd Observation Squadron, had been able to move south and would rejoin the regiment.

When we were well into the heavy forest, I gave the men a twenty-minute break. They were hot and tired, in fact, exhausted. This gave them a chance to pour the water out of their shoes and wring their socks out after wading the river. There was not much talk. I am sure they had a lot on their minds and were wondering just what might be our fate in the next two days. I told them to dispose of their gas masks and anything else they didn't have to have. We were never issued a full complement of infantry equipment. Most of them threw away their blankets, shaving equipment, and digging tools. About all they kept were their rifles, bayonets, and bandoleers of shells. Some had the machine gun bandoleers draped over their shoulders. They kept their water canteens, mess kits, and first-aid kits. Those who had chlorine flakes to sterilize their water kept them. No extra clothes were kept. I knew they realized that the way things were going, something different had to happen. Where we were located on Bataan now, the Japanese artillery could completely cover every foot of the area that the American and Filipino troops occupied.

We had been told several weeks before that the Japs would not take prisoners. It looked like it was going to be another Alamo, a fight to the finish. With no food, no artillery, no machine guns or planes, something had to happen fast if we were to hold out. I heard no complaint from the men. They were all trying to do what they had been trained to do. I told them where our next line would be.

We formed into columns of fours and moved out onto the main road. We moved slowly on this dusty, hot road, halting only for about ten minutes at intervals. After dark we had another twenty-minute break. I knew these men were all very tired after a whole day of marching, running, fighting, and dodging strafing planes. I could not visualize our ever moving again, after we took up our next defensive line, without some food and rest. We had not had sufficient food for the last three months.

Colonel Maverick marched by my side all night long. Sometime during the night, just after we got on a paved road, we saw Colonel Erwin and part of his 31st Filipino Regiment. They could not give us any information. They did not know the location of any of the units at this time. Colonel Erwin did not say where his next line of defense would be. His morale was very low. We came to the kilometer where we were supposed to meet the regimental commander. This was where the next defense line was to be set up according to his orders. It was now about three-thirty the morning of April 8. The regimental colonel and his staff were waiting in the jeep for us. The regiment was given a rest period while I talked to the colonel. He and his staff remained in the jeep. He looked at his map by flashlight; then he said, "No, this is not the place where you are to form the defensive line; it is back up the road about a mile." This stunned me—to think that all of these tired, hungry soldiers had to retrace their steps one mile. This was a useless and uncalled-for mistake. I hated to tell the officers and men that we had overrun the position by a mile.

We formed columns of fours again and marched back north one mile. We were to take up a position to hold the Japs a little longer. Just as we had retraced our steps that one mile, the regimental commander and his staff drove up in the jeep. He said, "No, this is not the right location. It is back where you were a while ago." Gee! I dreaded to tell these hungry, sleepy soldiers that we had to turn around and go back over this mile to the place where we had been before.

The day was just breaking when we finally got to the right position to establish our defensive line. The regimental colonel was there to show me on his map where we were to take up our position. It was on a slope of a brush-covered ridge about one-half mile west of where we were. I asked the colonel if he had made reconnaissance of the area.

He said, "No, you will make it for me."

Again Colonel Maverick came unbuckled and told him that it was his place to make the reconnaissance. Colonel Maverick told him,

"You are imposing on Captain Coleman to require him to make a reconnaissance that you were supposed to make. It could have been done while you were waiting for the regiment to arrive."

The regimental colonel said, "My headquarters will be here [pointing to the map] in a rock ranch house. Send runners to report to me every hour to keep me posted on how the battle is going." This rock house was about one mile from the defensive position and should not have been more than two or three hundred yards. Again we were not given any information as to where our friendly troops were or how near the enemy was. I was never to learn how the colonel received his communications telling him to form a defensive line at this place or whether it had just been his own idea. I did not know if we were to coordinate this position with some other units or not.

Colonel Maverick and I decided we would leave our troops there to rest while we made the reconnaissance of the position. We could not take a chance of putting troops in an area that had not been reconnoitered. We went west one-half mile to look our position over. To our immediate front was a steep hill with brush on top and a few scrub trees. The hill was some one hundred feet higher than our present position. To us it looked as if it would be suicide for us to take up the position that we were told to occupy. We would be sniped to death.

When we walked to the west end of our position, we met Colonel Jasper Brady, who was in charge of the 31st American Infantry. We told him of our mission and the problem of the steep hill in front of the position. He said, "You would be taking a big chance to take up a position here. If it were my decision, I would put the regiment on the hill to our front."

Colonel Maverick and I decided that we would take up our position on this hill within the next hour. Colonel Brady was making reconnaissance of his area. He said, "My regiment will be back here on your left at three o'clock this afternoon. They are still two miles north of here." The terrain was very rough with a stand of heavy brush some eight feet high.

Colonel Maverick and I rushed back to where our troops were resting. We had a surprise awaiting us. The supply officer of the regiment, Major O'Brian, came up and said, "We have a little bit of food for your men for breakfast." I went over to where they had started feeding them from a field kitchen. They were giving them three table-spoons full of watery rice and one tablespoon of condensed milk per man. This field kitchen was from my old 27th Materiel Squadron. They had reorganized this field kitchen and had come to feed the 27th Materiel Squadron with all they had left, which was not enough for one squadron, but was divided among a regiment.

I was feeling very bad. I was tired and my head was swimming as if I had fever. I asked a corpsman to take my temperature and it was 102 degrees. At first I thought it was fatigue and the adverse conditions we had been experiencing. Later I found out that I was taking malaria. I could not eat the thin rice, but I took the tablespoon of condensed milk as if it were medicine. It had been twenty-four hours since we had eaten anything.

It was now good daylight and we had to get into our defensive position before the dive bombers became active. We hoped to get in position without the Japanese knowing our location. We knew that as soon as the sun came up the observation planes would become numer-ous. The advance combat troops of the Japanese army could contact us at any time now. There was a light foggy overcast, but we knew it would clear up soon.

On our way to our position on top of the hill we came into an opening in the trees and brush. There were some fifty Filipino soldiers there changing from their khaki military clothes to civilian clothes. They had hidden their guns and ammunition in preparation to sur-render to the Japs as civilians. Colonel Maverick jerked his .45 pis-tol out of the holster and pointed it at them. He told them to get their uniforms back on, that the fighting was not over. They hesitated and I pulled my pistol out and about then our troops came into the clear-ing.

They started putting their uniforms back on. Since they were not in uniform, we could not tell who their officers were. Colonel Mav-erick asked them, "Where are your guns?" They told him and he said, "Get your guns and get in the battle." They started picking up their guns. We had to hurry to get to our position. It was sunup.

This hill was so steep that we had to cut places to put our feet, like a ladder or stair steps. The top of the hill was almost flat except for the outcropping of rocks. We could not have dug foxholes even if we had had the tools—the hill was too rocky. After each unit was in place, I sent two runners back to regimental headquarters at the rock ranch house. This was 9:00 A.M. The runners were back in about forty-five minutes and reported that they had found the ranch house, but there was no one there.

We had planned to have each squadron fire simultaneously if the enemy was in a concentrated formation. We did not believe that they knew our whereabouts at this time. There was a clearing in the brush and trees for three-quarters of a mile east of us and on the south slope of the ridge. By firing all at one time, we would not be giving our position away. By eleven o'clock that morning, I could see, with my field glasses, the enemy moving up artillery pieces in the hills about two miles to the northwest of our front. This was in the 31st Infantry's area. Soon Japanese infantry began showing up in the clearing on our right side about one-quarter mile away. They were marching south in columns of fours. They were going around this steep hill that we were on. They made excellent targets. Our squadrons began firing blasts, and a whole Japanese platoon or squad would be wiped out before they knew where the fire came from. The Japs would all hit the ground. If there were any left able to move, they would start rolling for cover. We would have to use a few snipers to stop anything that moved. Our men were never fired on or detected by the ground troops. For about four hours there would be platoons or squads show up in the clearing. This was so successful some of our officers asked enlisted men to let them use their rifles.

At about four o'clock in the afternoon everything became quiet and no Japanese were in sight. This was the "lull before the storm." About 4:30 everything began to happen to us. Three dive bombers flew from the west with the sun and dropped fragment and phosphorus bombs all over the hill. The Jap artillery fired point blank at us. The fragment pieces of the bombs would hit the rocks and splatter them like fragments of steel. Many were killed or wounded in a very short time. The hill shook from the explosions of the bombs and artillery shells. Fires were started by the phosphorus bombs. Since it was the dry season, the brush and grass burned as if kerosene had been thrown on it. A strong southwest wind fanned the flames.

When the dive bombers first came out of the sun, I was looking through my field glasses at the artillery being moved to emplacements northwest of us. When I saw the bombers, I looked for a low place to lie in. There was a place that looked like a low spot that was filled with leaves. I jumped into this place and shoved the leaves away, and could get my head, shoulders, and chest below ground level. I had the only map in the regiment in my hand. I had just checked all the roads and trails to and from this area. I was thinking that, from the way those artillery pieces were being positioned, we might have to move from this location pretty soon.

When the first three dive bombers dropped their load, a shrapnel hit me in the leg at shoe-top level and some phosphorus splattered on the top of my left hand. I turned around and grabbed my ankle. I could smell flesh and leather burning. I took hold of the bomb fragment that was embedded in my leg and pulled it out. It was lying flat against the bone in my leg. I burned my index finger and thumb pulling the shrapnel out. By this time the phosphorus had started to burn my hand, and I could smell burned flesh and phosphorus everywhere. I washed the phosphorus off my hand with water from my canteen.

Everyone was yelling for a corpsman. We had only two for the entire regiment and they had very little first-aid equipment left. I ran back to our headquarters where Colonel Maverick was and told him we would have to withdraw as soon as possible. He agreed. The artillery just would not let up, and the fire was getting worse and worse.

8. *Our Last Retreat*

I sent runners to each squadron commander, asking them to report to me. A corpsman took my temperature; it was 103 degrees. I had never felt worse in my whole life and this was not a good time to be in this physical condition. From where I stood waiting for the squadron commanders, I could see human flesh stuck in the scrub trees and bushes. The smell of burned human flesh and TNT that hovered in the heavy brush on this hill was terrible.

I knew that the rate of march to withdraw would have to be slow. Two days of fighting without food or sleep had exhausted everyone. There were many wounded who would have to be carried. Always before, they could be sent back to the rear to be treated, but now we were surrounded and would have to keep the wounded under our protection. There were from fifty to one hundred who would have to be left unburied. The dive bombers and artillery were taking their toll fast.

The squadron commanders began to arrive and, as soon as one came up, I assigned him a duty. I had not closed my hand on the map after the shrapnel hit my leg, and the map was lost. The first commander that I assigned a duty was to have the advanced guard. He said, "You mean a rear guard, don't you?" He had been using his own men's rifles and did not know that we were surrounded and would have to fight our way out.

I said, "Since this is on your mind, you form a rear guard." There was so much noise, shells bursting, rifles shooting at the dive bombers, and all the confusion of taking care of the wounded, that I did not have time for the fine points of the way an order should be given.

The squadron that was to have the advanced guard was to proceed out on a single trail leading from the southwest corner of the hill. They were to follow this trail to a heavy forest about one-half mile away. They were to deploy and put up a cover for the wounded and the rear guard if they were fired upon. They were to fight for the entrance to this forest. If we could get into the forest, the Japs could not flank us, because there were no roads or trails that intersected this single trail. The advanced guard was not to enter into a fire fight unnecessarily. The squadrons that were to carry the wounded were to follow the advanced guard; then the rear guard, Captain Kelley's unit, was to follow the wounded.

The stretchers that carried the wounded were all improvised from blankets or clothing. The fire was on the southwest slope of the hill and on top of the hill. The wind was from the southwest. The able-bodied men could run through the fire, but the litter bearers with the wounded had a struggle. The woolen blankets and clothing would catch fire and the bearers would have to drag them on the ground, with the wounded in them, to put out the fire. The wounded never groaned or complained when they were being dragged.

I went along in the rear of the advanced guard. Our trail was up a narrow valley between two ridges. It was about sundown and we could skylight the Japanese on the ridges to the east and west of us. The west ridge was casting a shadow across the valley, giving us some protection. The Japs on the ridges were marching south in the same direction we were. They were in single file. We had to march a little faster so we could get to this forest trail first. Also we did not want to get too close; they would recognize us. We wanted to secure the entrance to the forest before this happened.

I felt sorry for the litter bearers. Only two could carry a wounded man, and we had to ask them to walk faster after we spotted the Japs heading in the same direction.

They did not recognize us as being their enemies until our advanced guard had deployed near the entrance of the forest trail. Some fire came from the west of us aimed at the advanced guard. The advanced guard put down heavy fire on those on the east and west ridges. This slowed down the firing from the Japs but caused those carrying the wounded to hurry for cover in the forest. I did not know how many wounded men there were. We had to change litter bearers often and we hardly had enough well men who were not in the advanced or rear guard to make the change. Captain Sterling was in charge of the litter bearers and he had a hard time keeping the column moving through because the ones who had had to hurry during the most dangerous area were exhausted.

By sundown in this great and beautiful virgin forest, it was completely dark. We halted to let the advanced guard get out front again. We took this time to rest and change litter bearers. In the meantime the rear guard was picking up some enemy fire. The Japanese would have to follow us as there were no other roads or trails to our left or right. Some of the wounded were dying every little bit. At first the litter bearers would just lay them out by the side of the trail. When the Japs would stumble upon one of the bodies, they would yell like our Comanche Indians on the war path. Our rear guard would fire in their direction and the Japs would fire back. We could hear the noise and sometimes see the flash from the guns in the dark. Our rear guard would fire at them as long as there was anything to help locate them.

This trail was narrow and rambled through these big trees and bushes. It stayed on the ridge or high ground by going around the head of canyons or low places. It was so dark in the forest that one could not see his hand before his eyes. I had to lead the way because I was the only one who had seen the map of this trail and knew the direction it would take. I would walk in the trail until I could hear leaves and sticks breaking under my feet, then I knew I was out of the trail, also if I bumped into some bushes or trees. About 11:30 P.M., during one of our rest periods, a lieutenant who had been helping with the wounded came to me and said, "Our men are worn out and cannot carry the wounded any farther. We will have to lay them out beside the trail."

I told him, "We do not know where we are going and might be in the same predicament that they are in the morning. I have had no contact with anyone and all of the troops on Bataan are scattered. If your men cannot carry the wounded, we will just have to form a circle and fight it out." We did have longer rest periods.

A soldier from one of the units about one hundred yards to our rear came to me and said, "The lieutenant that was wounded wants to talk to you."

I went back where the lieutenant was lying on a litter. He told me who he was and said, "I can't live much longer. I am losing too much blood. Please do not put me out near the trail. The Japs are cutting the bodies to pieces and stomping those the Americans leave near the trail." He asked me to tell his mother where he had died, if I made it back home. His voice was very weak.

I told the captain in charge to lay those who died back away from the trail. As to how far would depend on the terrain and the bushes. In a short while the column started moving again. Soon I heard a noise that sounded like someone talking not too far from our front. I stopped the unit and sent someone ahead to see if it was a friend or foe. I went with them. We came to a clearing where several trees had been cut down and the stumps left. The moon and stars were shining through the foliage. There were five Filipino men sitting on the tree stumps near an old building. They said they were employed at a saw mill nearby. They were men of military age and, since they were up this late at night, I wondered if they were not deserters. They said no Japs had passed by where they were.

We went on past this clearing in the forest and soon were in another heavy forest. I was having trouble following the trail. It was so dark and it had not been traveled much more. I smelled fresh water. I thought at first that we were near Manila Bay. We could hear firing of artillery on our right and left, but not to the front. We had a Jap unit behind us that kept harassing our rear guard all night. Soon after I smelled the fresh water, my feet slid out from under me and I fell into a river that was over waist deep. I had a squad hold hands and move out single file into the river to check the depth and width of it. It took about eight men to span the river. They held hands and let the litter bearers carry the wounded across above them, so if the bearers fell or were washed down, they could catch the wounded men.

When we came out on the south side, we found a well-improved road. This helped our litter bearers because now four could carry a wounded man instead of just two. When we crossed the river, we were out of the forest and could see farther ahead so we could move faster. The moon had gone down. My watch crystal was broken and I could not tell what time it was. On the trip through the forest, no one had said anything, except the men that I had talked to. There was no unnecessary noise at this time. All I could hear was the rifle fire of our rear guard and the Jap rifle fire. The artillery shelling was constant. It all sounded much worse on the east of us near Manila Bay. We could tell that the Japanese were ahead of us and moving south. We had no artillery that I knew of, so this had to be Japanese artillery we were hearing.

The river and improved road ran parallel to the direction that we had been going. Instead of south, we started traveling east. This direction was toward the Japanese artillery, but I was in hopes the road would turn south again soon. Since losing the map, all I could remember was the single trail through the forest and we had traveled it. After going about three-quarters of a mile, we heard some jabbering in front of us. I took a squad of men to check it out. All of the men had their guns cocked, expecting the worst. We would move a few feet, then stop and listen. Suddenly we heard words spoken in English. Our corporal stepped out in front of one of the men and asked, "What unit are you with?"

He answered, "The 31st Infantry Regiment."

This was the unit under Colonel Brady that had been on our left, to begin with, the evening of April 8. I gave the Air Corps Regiment a rest period, and Colonel Maverick and I went to talk to Colonel Brady.

He had the walkie-talkie receiver to his ear when we first saw him. He slowly fumbled around with the receiver, hung it up and said, "That was a call from General King's headquarters. He said we are going to throw in the towel at nine o'clock in the morning. Our troops are to form a circle on a hill [he gave the number of the hill] and hold off the Japs until nine o'clock."

Colonel Brady asked me, "How many men do you have?"

I said, "I do not know, but we can count them as we have them march by so we can skylight them."

"Colonel Maverick and I can do that. General King asked me to send two officers to Corregidor to report our final location and how many men we have. I want you to go and take another officer who can be of some help to those on Corregidor. They are not going to surrender. General King said there would be a boat waiting for you at Cabcaben."

I told Colonel Brady I would have to rest a few minutes. I was still running a high fever and was completely worn out from two days and nights of fighting.

Colonel Maverick started our troops marching by in single file to count them. Two days before, we had had 1,400 men and now we had approximately 400. Two days before Colonel Brady had 700 men and now he had approximately 200. Captain Dorman asked me if he could go to Corregidor with me. I believe he had charge of the 19th Bomb Group. He left Lieutenant Maxie Chenault in command.

I told Colonel Brady that we would lie down in a rice field not far from where we were and rest for a little while. Colonel Brady said, "The Japs will be along soon."

The paved road that we were on turned south soon and so did the river we were following. Captain Dorman and I lay down in the first rice field we came to. The rice had been cut about two feet high. We went about fifty yards from the road and went to sleep almost immediately. This was probably about 2:30 A.M. We were awakened by a tremendous earthquake, or they were exploding ammunition that was causing the earth to vibrate. I could feel the water slosh in my stomach. I had not had any food in over two days.

Captain Dorman and I got up and started our journey to Cabcaben. When we started to cross the first stream, we found that the Japs had passed along the road while we were asleep and we were now behind the Japanese lines. There were two of our army trucks stopped at the edge of the water with two men in the cab of each truck. They were dead. Some were in a sitting position and some had slumped over. They had been shot at close range. On the other side of the water there was another truck with the driver dead also. Just behind this truck on the caliche road was an American soldier lying on his stomach with his head in a pool of blood. I turned him over on his side and he groaned. The blood came from his chest. He swallowed with a gurgling sound and lay limp.

The moon was full and made it easy to see that the white caliche road was in good shape. It was going in the direction that we wanted to go: southeast toward Cabcaben. We had traveled just a short distance when we heard the sound of a motor. We jumped behind some large trees and waited a few minutes. It didn't seem to be moving any closer or any farther, so we decided to investigate. We thought it sounded like the motor of a tank, but it turned out to be a large air compressor on one of our two and one-half ton trucks. The oil had been drained out so it would destroy itself. Steam was coming out of the radiator, and it was knocking as if the pistons were about to stick. It had been camouflaged with limbs and brush on top of it. I am sure it had been left there to slow down the Japs, making them think it was an American tank.

The Japanese had set fire to the forest a little farther to the east of us. We had to evade this area enough to stay out of the light from the burning trees. After we passed the fire area, we took a more direct route to Cabcaben. We could not believe that under these conditions there would be a boat waiting for us; but we had to try to make it. We were following a dim two-track road, when we noticed a squad of soldiers in single-file formation about one hundred feet ahead of us. They were dressed in khaki and all were small men wearing a different kind of helmet from ours. It was just getting daylight and we could skylight their shape and size. We were sure they were Japanese. They were going the same direction that we wanted to go. We jumped out of the trail into the brush but continued to follow them.

Soon we could hear a battle going on about one mile to our front. We could hear our .30/.30-caliber rifles and the Japanese .27-caliber rifles firing. Cabcaben was only one-half mile to our front and a little to the left. When we came to the turn leading to Cabcaben, we could see and hear an artillery ammunition dump exploding. We knew the Japs had taken Cabcaben and there would not be a boat waiting for us.

Our next plan was to get back on the American side of the battle again. From the sound of the rifles, our troops were on the south banks of the Real River and the Japs were on the north side, where we were at this time. From the sound of the battle, the Japs were trying to force a crossing on the river at a low place between some hills.

Captain Dorman and I checked the ammunition for our .45 automatics. I had three shells left and Captain Dorman didn't have any. We both still had our hunting knives. There didn't seem to be any fighting going on on top of the hill to our right, where the river had cut through and left a steep bluff on the north side. We went through the brush to the top of the hill. We could see our troops firing on a concentration of Japanese in the lower area. This would have been an excellent target for a trench mortar. The Japs had known for a long time that the Provisional Air Corps Regiment did not have any trench mortars on Bataan. Looking off this cliff into the water in the river, we saw five or six of our large buses that our troops had destroyed by running them over the cliff. They had formed a small dam and were holding some of the water back. The Japs were firing from the east and west sides of the hill at our troops on the south bank. We slid down the cliff that had been caved in when the buses were destroyed. We held onto the buses where the Japs could not see us cross the river. The buses were turned over in every position. The crankcase oil had spilled all over the buses making them hard to hold onto. We were trying to keep our heads above the water and out of the sight of the Japanese soldiers, especially to the east of us. We were pretty well hidden from the ones upstream on the west.

The sun was just coming up. This was the beginning of that historical day of April 9, 1942. We made it across the river and crawled into the high grass on the south side. Now we had the problem of getting into our lines without being shot by our own troops. Captain Dorman and I were both smaller than the average American and I had been mistaken several times in the dark as a Japanese because of my stature. We didn't dare charge our lines because our soldiers might think we were Jap soldiers making a forced crossing at that point. Our troops knew that there were friendly troops mixed up in this area, but being able to distinguish them was a problem. We decided to take our handkerchiefs and wave them above the grass until we were recognized. We squeezed the water out of them. We were wet and greasier than any mechanics you have ever seen, after wading through the oil-covered water.

We held our handkerchiefs about fifteen minutes before anyone said anything. I was getting afraid the Japs would start firing at us. The regular cadence of firing kept coming from both sides. We could not see any of our soldiers but could hear the firing of each rifle blast. We could see several Japanese soldiers firing into our lines, but they never did expose themselves except for a second at a time. The Japs, if they saw us, may have thought we were trying to surrender and did not fire at us. After what seemed like a long time, an American lieutenant yelled for us to come on across. Those were welcome words to hear. We crawled a little farther in the grass until it was too short to hide us, then we ran for our front lines and protection. It was only fifty yards and if anyone ever ran a hundred yards in ten seconds, we did. We came first to a deep trail leading up a slope at an angle. No one will ever know how satisfying it was to be back with our own troops and feeling a sense of protection.

The lieutenant that yelled at us met us. I was worn out from the dash uphill and was sick. The malaria fever was beginning to show up again. I had to lie down and was trying to vomit. A corpsman took my temperature; it was 102 degrees. The lieutenant said, "We saw you out in the tall grass but had to be sure it was not Japanese starting to charge our lines. Then we had to pass the word along the lines not to fire as you started toward our lines."

They had been expecting a charge from the Japs at any time and his men would have to repulse the attack.

I was on my feet again soon but had an awful swimmy head and a terrific headache. I looked back at Cabcaben with my field glasses. The ammunition dump was still smoldering and there was no boat to be seen anywhere along the docks. Cabcaben was just a small barrio of probably two hundred people. It was now on the Japanese side of the river, and the artillery ammunition was still exploding at intervals.

The only chance for Captain Dorman and me to get to Corregidor was to go down the coast facing Corregidor and try to find a way across. There were three miles of deep water and a swift current near Corregidor on the beach. This current went out of Manila Bay toward the China Sea. It would take a strong swimmer to cross the current after he had swum two and one-half miles. Many that had tried it were swept out to sea and drowned. Neither of us was an excellent swimmer. The only chance we had to get across was to find an old boat that we could fix up or a barrel that did not leak or even a dry log. We had been down on the coast about an hour when we saw a motor boat with several *boncas* tied on behind coming out of Mariveles. The Japanese fighter planes came down on them like hawks and strafed all of the boats. When they would see a Zero make a dive at them, they would lie down in the boats. Each time fewer and fewer of them sat up again. We could see that we would have to cross at night or we would find ourselves in the same condition as these boatmen.

About 9:30 A.M. a large group of Filipinos came running down to the beach to hide. They said that they had tried to surrender at nine o'clock, but the Japanese continued to fire at them. Several in their group had been killed. They did not think the Japs were taking any prisoners. This group still had their rifles and this may have been the reason they were fired on. They did not know how to surrender. They had tried to surrender in the area where General King had gone through the Japanese lines in a jeep with a white flag. These Filipinos surely did something wrong while trying to surrender. It made me even more anxious to get to Corregidor.

All day long Captain Dorman and I combed the waterfront of Manila Bay going toward Mariveles, trying to find a way to escape the thousands of Japanese infantrymen. Our anti-aircraft continued to keep the bombers flying very high as they came over Corregidor. Once in a while they would hit one of them, and it would angle off to the south toward their navy ships. This would give them a chance to be retrieved from the water if they parachuted out of the plane. The fighter planes were not swarming over the Bataan Peninsula and strafing as they had been so many days before. They were active over the water between Bataan and Corregidor. There were many small streams running into Manila Bay and we would take our clothes off and wade or swim across the mouth of these streams. We could make better time this way than by going upstream to where it was not so deep. Before night we were sun burned all over. The night of April 9 was very quiet. There was no artillery fire from either side as there had been for the past three and one-half months. We could only visualize what had happened to our troops and what was ahead for us.

During the night we could hear motor boats near the shores of Corregidor. We assumed that they were picking up men trying to swim to Corregidor. None ever came closer than a mile to the shores of Bataan. Captain Dorman and I slept on a solid rock ledge up over the pounding surf of Manila Bay. I was so tired and felt so bad that I slept on that rock as well as if it had been a nice mattress at home. When we awoke, Captain Dorman said, "I know where the Bataan bakery was. Let's go down there and see if there was bread or flour left that maybe the Japs didn't find." It was some three miles to the north. I had been to the bakery just two weeks before when I was begging for food for my starving men. I did not care to go with Captain Dorman because I did not think there was a chance of finding anything. That was the last time I saw Captain Dorman.

I rested a while longer on this rocky ledge. Soon I met Lieutenant Burns, who had four enlisted men with him. The lieutenant was a Texan. We decided to form a guerrilla unit if we could find a few more men. In a short time we were able to pick up eight more men who would go with us. If we could evade the first wave of Japanese that would be looking for the scattered enemy, we thought we might be able to find an old boat and go back up Manila Bay after the Japs had left the area. We went under the cliffs by wading and swimming to big holes in the cliff at water level. We found one large row boat that was half-submerged. There was a small pier along the shore where the old boat was located. We found a hole in the bottom and thought we might be able to repair it enough to keep it from leaking.

We were wading in water from waist deep to shoulder deep all this time and the waves coming in and out seemed to cause my fever to rise. We had most of the water dipped out of the boat and had one end propped up like a ship in dry dock for repair, when I got seasick and tried to vomit. I told Lieutenant Burns that if he would let two men take me back around the cliff to shore, I would have to leave.

He said, "We need to fill our canteens with fresh water and the two men could take all the canteens and bring back fresh water." The men had to hold my arms to keep me from falling into the ever-moving water. My head swam and I was so sick I was green. The men put the extra canteens on two sticks by running the sticks through the small chains secured to the tops of the canteens. They knew where there was fresh water up a draw near this place.

I first lay down on the beach in the shade of some bushes. One of the men came back and said there was a small nipa hut about fifty yards from where I was lying. I went to this hut. It was new and had never been occupied. It was built up off the ground about eight feet. I soon fell asleep. A Filipino army major awakened me and told me there was a twelve-man Japanese patrol up the hill about one-half mile that was coming this way. He said the Japs were torturing the Americans to death where they caught one or two by themselves. He said he lived on the island of Mindoro and was trying to get over there. I gave him my field glasses because I didn't feel like carrying them and I knew the Japs would get them when I surrendered. It looked as if that would be soon.

I was so dizzy I could not stand up without the aid of a cane or stick. The major gave me a stick. I told him that there were two American soldiers up the draw getting some water at a well. He said he would try to warn them as he went that way. I started up a trail going uphill to the west. I knew that I had to stay ahead and out of sight of the patrol.

The trail that I was on ran parallel to the coastline but was one-quarter mile from the coast and through dense brush. When I got on top of the first hill, I stopped in a clump of bushes for a brief rest and looked to see if I could see anything of the patrol. I looked down the hill and up the draw where the soldiers had gone for water. I saw the major running south from where he had been. The Japs were running toward the well or where I thought it was. I don't believe the major got to the well to warn the men before the Jap patrol arrived. I moved on over the hill toward Mariveles and was careful not to leave any tracks. Soon the trail led me near the shore of Manila Bay. There were Japanese flags stuck in the ground on their staffs about every quarter of a mile. The flags were about 3' x 5' in size. This meant that this was Japanese territory and that they had been there recently.

I stayed well under the cover of the brush all day. About one hour before sundown, I met an American sergeant and a corporal. They wanted to go in to surrender. I told them what the Filipino major had told me about Americans being tortured when surrendering in small groups. We decided that we had better try to surrender to a large group or where there was a Japanese officer to keep us from being tortured. We slept in a very heavy clump of bushes that night.

We heard a patrol come by within a hundred feet of us about ten o'clock. We assumed that it was the patrol I had seen at the well. At sunrise we started toward Mariveles. We came near the coast again and realized that we were in Japanese territory. If I were caught with fire arms two days after the surrender date, the Japanese would have cause to punish me. I took my .45 pistol, with the clips and holster, and threw them as far as I could from the cliff into the water. I also threw my hunting knife and scabbard into Manila Bay. I kept 120 pesos in bills in the cuff of my trousers and in the lining of my belt by folding the bills longwise. I put my two rings in the fly of my trousers. This left me with only a mess kit, canteen, and canteen cup. I had used all of my first-aid pack three days before. This was April 11, about eleven o'clock in the morning. We came over a hill, and about three hundred yards west of us was a large group of white tents. I estimated it to be the camp of one regiment of infantry troops. This was what we had been looking for so we could surrender.

9. *Our Surrender*

We tied our handkerchiefs on a five-foot stick, held it high in the air, and stepped out into the open going toward the camp. There were some bomb craters in our trail as well as some dead men who had been dead two or three days. We could not tell what nationality. After we walked around the craters, we saw a car start toward us from the tents. There were two Japanese officers and three enlisted men in the car. They drove up near us, in one of our U.S. Army reconnaissance cars. Of course, we were wondering all the time if we would be allowed to surrender or would be shot. It had been four days now since I had had anything to eat and my fever was still with me.

The Japanese came within one hundred feet of us. We were standing still, three abreast, holding our white flag and had one hand raised. The enlisted men jumped out of the car and were holding their rifles on us from a kneeling position. The officers first held their pistols on us. This was the first time I had ever heard Japanese speak Japanese; and, of course, I did not know anything they said. We were searched by the officers. They felt all over our bodies while we held our hands over our heads, but this group did not take anything from us. The officers motioned for us to get started toward camp. I thought they motioned for us to get into the car and I thought how nice it would be to ride after walking everywhere I had been for the last four months. I stepped onto the running board of the car and all of the Japs went into a fit. Even though I could not understand a word of their language, I could understand their motions and the displeased sound of their voices. I knew I was doing the wrong thing. They did not want me riding in the car.

We started walking down the road, with the Japs riding in the car, holding their rifles on us. This camp was about two miles northeast of Mariveles. I could see the main road that ran from Mariveles to Manila about a quarter of a mile on the west side of the Japanese camp. There was a continuous column of Japanese troops moving south. There were long columns of tanks, trucks, cavalry, and infantry men. They were loading their army on ships on the west side of Bataan to go farther south to take other islands. They did not know at this time that Bataan had held out long enough to let our troops in Australia and the Australian army build up enough to prevent them from landing in Australia. Their timetable had been interrupted to the extent that they could never land in Australia. They had been deprived of the use of the largest harbor and ship facilities in the Orient. This had been our objective on Bataan. This had been decided after so many ships had been sunk at Pearl Harbor that we had been completely blockaded and no supplies could reach us. We had reached our objective.

Never had an army of the United States done so much with so little furnished to them. We had no replacements or supplies after December 8, 1941. Some medical supplies had been flown in, such as quinine.

As far as my unit, the 27th Materiel Squadron or the Air Corps Regiment, was concerned, there never were any troops that tried harder to be obedient and to do a good job with what they had than these men. They never whimpered or fussed but knew that it was up to them to determine their fate. As I thought of what had just passed, I could not think of a single time that I did not do just what I had been trained to do, to the best of my ability. None of my men or officers shirked their duty but performed to their utmost. I felt badly that our men had to fight with insufficient weapons and under starving conditions with no medical help. It just could not be supplied by our nation, and we were ultimately starved into having to surrender.

When we came to the Japanese camp, one guard was sent with us. They motioned for us to go to the main road, where all the traffic was.

When we walked across the road and started toward Manila, I noticed a supply sergeant who had been at Nichols Field lying face down, with a hole in the back of his head. I took his blanket roll and covered him with it. The Jap guard was yelling at me trying to make me hurry on up the road.

I had been allowed to keep my stick to lean on for balance. There was a lot of dust along the road and the temperature must have been 100 degrees. We had to walk off the road on the left side because the road was so congested with troops and equipment. We were going north and they were moving south.

We came upon a brand new Plymouth passenger car stopped in the road. There were two Japanese officers trying to get it started. They grabbed me by the arm and pushed me under the steering wheel. I suspected that they meant for me to start the motor. I noticed the mileage on the speedometer; it had 98 kilometers, as well as I can remember. It was about that distance to Manila. One of the officers pointed at the ignition key. I turned the key and it started immediately. They had been trying to start it in gear. They smiled and I started to get out, but they stopped me. They wanted me to drive them to Mariveles, which was in the opposite direction from which I wanted to go. I jerked away from them and joined the guard and the other two men who were waiting for me.

When we had gone about one-half mile, we came to the end of an infantry column. There was a ragged slouchy soldier dragging along outside the formation, scavenging. He had on his back probably a hundred pounds of junk he had been looting from the American camps. There were others like him along the road. This particular one was hot and thirsty. He saw my canteen and pointed at it as if asking for a drink of water. I had to give him my canteen. He unscrewed the cap and smelled of the water. He turned up his nose, then held my canteen upside down and poured out every drop of water. Then he threw it down at my feet in the dirt. I felt like killing him. I did get the water out of the river, but I had chlorine flakes to treat it.

The chlorine did smell pretty strong and that's probably why he poured it out. He did not know what chlorine was, but with the high fever I needed a sip of water pretty often.

We had gone about a mile farther when we found a Japanese private in the middle of the road with one of our two and one-half ton trucks. The motor was running. He stopped us and talked to one of the guards. Finally he led me over to the truck and motioned for me to get under the steering wheel. He got in on the other side and shook the gear shift. He wanted me to put it in gear for him. This size truck has four speeds and the driver has to use the clutch to put it in the right gear. I realized I had an opportunity to do a little sabotage. Some of our people had erred in not destroying the truck before surrendering. There was a lever on the side of the gear shift that had to be raised before the gears could be shifted. To use the compound low, the truck would move very slowly but the motor would race like a car going sixty miles an hour, and yet the truck would be moving only ten miles an hour. I knew he would not know how to change the gear after he got started. I put the truck in compound gear and jumped out. The Jap got under the wheel and raced the motor. I am sure he burned it up in a few miles.

When I jumped out, he was smiling as if he was well pleased with his accomplishment. I am almost sure he had never driven before, from the way he was wiggling the steering wheel. The motor was already hot from his racing it trying to get the truck in gear.

We were close to the entrance of the hospital at Little Baguio at this time. There was an American corpsman standing where the road to the hospital led off the main road. I talked to him. There was a Jap guard with him. I asked him for some quinine and some bandages to dress the shrapnel wound in my leg, but he did not have anything. He was there to tell everyone that they could not enter the hospital. We met another column of Japanese cavalry and had to get off the road and across the bar ditch. Over on our left under the shade of a mango tree, there was a Filipino girl with nothing on but a black slip. She was lying on her back with the slip pulled up over both breasts. She had been bayoneted or shot under the left breast. The blood that came from the wound was still red and fresh. Apparently she had been raped and killed.

When we got to Little Baguio we were turned over to a group of Japanese that had collected about 2,000 prisoners. I did not know any of these soldiers. My Air Corps Regiment was not in this area when they surrendered two days before.

I was allowed to go down to the stream nearby to refill my canteen that the Jap soldier had emptied two or three hours before. I had had to have a sip of water pretty often and I appreciated the sergeant and corporal who had surrendered with me letting me have a drink from their canteens. Near the stream where I replenished my drinking water, there were some Japanese soldiers swimming and letting their horses drink, but I still had some chlorine flakes to purify the water so I could drink it. When I came back to the main area, Colonel Wickard had me lie down in an enclosure where I could rest and take a nap.

Most of the soldiers were sitting or lying on the ground. They were all very tired and hungry. They had not washed or shaved for days. Their clothes were stiff and dirty from perspiration. Their faces were stoic. They looked like walking dead men. Little did they know or realize that the worst was yet to come.

The Japanese had supposedly planned and prepared to take care of us after the surrender. General Homma had had a meeting of his staff, and two of his officers took the responsibility for getting the prisoners to the first prison camp. This is the way it was divided: Colonel Tashimitsu was responsible for the first assembling of the prisoners at Balanga, some nineteen miles from Mariveles. He and General Homma reasoned that the prisoners could furnish their own food that far. (They did not take into consideration that the Bataan troops had been out of food four days when they surrendered, also that the Japanese soldiers would have taken the food or anything else away from the prisoners, if they had had anything.)

Major General Yoshikada Kawane was to take the second phase from Balanga to the first prison camp, which was Camp O'Donnell. Major Hisake Sekeguthi was to take care of the sick and wounded at Balanga and San Fernando and maybe set up some field hospitals in between. The civilian prisoners and military prisoners were kept in different columns. Most of the civilians rode in trucks to the prison camps. It was said that General Homma was ignorant of the starved and diseased condition of troops in our area, but they had tried to tempt us into surrendering by dropping propaganda leaflets depicting all kinds of good foods just a few days before the surrender. He must have known we were starving.

We stayed at Little Baguio a day and a half. I think it was to let their troops use the road to Mariveles and on west where they were loading troops and equipment to ship farther south. They also wanted to leave the prisoners of war in the area so they would not be fired upon from Corregidor until they could get their artillery into position to return the fire. They were sure our artillery would not fire into the area as long as there was a heavy concentration of our troops on the lower Bataan Peninsula.

The night of the eleventh, they brought in some beautiful cavalry horses. One of them was a dark bay Arabian horse that was very sick. He had suffered from heat exhaustion. The Japs did not know what to do with him or how to doctor him. I believe I could have kept him from dying had it been my responsibility. While I was looking through the fence at the sick horse, I noticed a footlocker that had been ripped open and rummaged. Upon looking closer, I found that it was my footlocker. We had sent it to the rear by our supply officer on April 6. The wind had blown some of the papers from my 201 personnel file up near the fence where I was standing. They had my name on them. So I knew how and where my footlocker with my personal effects had been left. Our regimental files were buried near here in a deep hole. They had been dug up and the papers scattered everywhere. On the twelfth, Colonel Wickard, from Chicago, arranged for me to lie down in the shade with three other sick men. This was my first night of real good rest in two weeks. I had been making counterattacks, marching, and fighting most of the time. Nothing was ever said about our getting to eat. The last, light meal we had had was on the night of April 6.

10. *The Death March*

On the morning of April 13, we were awakened early by the Japanese. About sunup I was sitting on a stump talking to a Japanese lieutenant. He spoke English very well. He told me he had come from Singapore to Bataan in March. He had come down through China and had helped capture Singapore from the British and Australians. He said that this was not the first time he had been under artillery fire. I asked him how many troops came to the Philippines from Singapore. He said about 100,000. All at once he grabbed an enlisted man's rifle and hit me over the head with it. He drove my steel helmet down to my ears and bruised the top of my head. He said, "Throw that helmet away. Prisoners of war are not supposed to wear helmets. You talk too much."

I threw the helmet away and looked around. I was the only one who had been wearing a helmet, but I had not been told that it was not permissible. Some were wearing garrison hats, fatigue caps, or sailor hats. Those who had been on the front lines and had had no chance to get anything else were bare headed. When he told me that I talked too much, I thought that he was the one doing too much talking. He was not supposed to tell how many troops had moved from Singapore to Bataan, especially to the enemy. He may not have known but was guessing. He was part of what they called the Shanghai Division that was used to take our area.

The sun was searing hot after it came up. I needed something to wear on my head to help keep the fever down (after having to throw away my helmet). I could have found something in some of the abandoned camps that we had come through from Mariveles to Little Baguio if I had known I could not keep my helmet. The Japs began to get us lined up in columns of fours. We knew we were going to be moved somewhere. General Clifford Blumel passed the word to the prisoners for the sick and weakest men to be near the front of the column. General Blumel was in the first rank of the columns of fours. He was the first on the left side of the column. This position would set the pace. I was in the second rank behind General Blumel. The general was to set a pace slow enough so the sick could keep up with the column.

When we lined up in this column, none of us doubted that we would be treated in a decent and humane way, according to the international law dealing with prisoners of war. You could hear the guards shouting at the men as though they were on a cattle drive, headed for the cruel slaughter pens. They were beating the men with the butts of their rifles and jabbing them with their bayonets to get them in place in a hurry. They were giving orders in Japanese and no one could understand them. After we had marched a short distance, the lead guard came to the front and tried to get the front ranks to speed up the march. General Blumel told the Americans in the ranks to continue to keep the pace down so our weak men could stay with us. The Japanese guards continued to yell and threaten the men in the ranks with their bayonets. I looked back down the column at the men's faces. They were glassy eyed, expressionless, and stunned looking. They had gone unshaved for days, they were dusty, and their clothes were caked from salty perspiration and dirt.

I stepped on what looked like a piece of khaki cloth. I slipped back as if in mud. It was human flesh that we were walking on. We could smell decayed human flesh all along the road where men had been killed, their bodies left where they had fallen. The columns of tanks, truck, and cavalry horses had run over them, pulverizing their bones into pulp. I thought, "These men have given every ounce of strength for their country." We did not know what our fate would be, but we were not very optimistic.

Now seven days without food, I was weak and hungry; my head hurt and I could not shake the fever. Many were in the same condition. It was hard for me to stand up, my head was so swimmy from the fever.

When we had marched from Little Baguio to Cabcaben, the Japanese artillery started pounding Corregidor from every direction on Bataan. We probably were the last group of prisoners to move out of this peninsula. The Japanese had purposely held us on Bataan the eleventh and twelfth of April so they could set up their artillery positions to fire on Corregidor. This was a breach of the international law, to hold prisoners in a combat zone; we should have been moved out immediately. Though the artillery spotters on Corregidor could see the Japanese moving their artillery pieces into position, they could not fire on them because of the danger to the American prisoners.

Soon our artillery began counteracting the Japanese artillery fire. About the second burst of our artillery, I saw a Jap artillery piece bounced up out of the ground by a direct hit. The American barrage first started over us, then began to lower. I told a Japanese guard who was marching along by me (he could understand English), "We had better hit the dirt, hadn't we?"

He said, "Hell, no! If you didn't want to die, why did you join the army?"

I told him, "I have something to live for." About that time a large shell burst near us and to the rear of our column. Everyone scattered into the bushes looking for a ditch. This guard got into a road culvert. In a short time the guard began to blow a whistle to get us back into formation. It was reported that the shell had exploded so close that some of our men were wounded.

We had some large mortars on Corregidor, but they did not have enough range to help us on our front lines. There were some fourteen-inch guns that could fire far enough to help us, but they could not be turned in our direction to help us on the front. They could keep the Japanese navy fourteen miles away from the mouth of Manila Bay. They were especially set for the defense of Corregidor or Manila Bay.

About five o'clock that afternoon, we stopped the march for the day. This was near Pilar. Pilar was between our main line and the Japanese main line that we had left April 7. There were two small artesian wells that had spigots on them for us to get water. The farthest well was near a sugar cane field. Since there was a long line waiting at the first well, I went to the one near the cane field. It was not so congested. I had filled my canteen and started back. I heard some Japanese guards shouting. I looked back and there were some Filipino soldiers who had gone into the cane field to get some sugar cane to eat. The soldiers came running back toward the guards. They shot the first two, and the others ran back into the cane field. One was wounded. The Japs kept firing into the field. I suppose the others got away. There were seven or eight who went into the field, and mostly because they were so hungry.

When we got back to the main camp, they had lined the prisoners up and were running them through a tent where they were being questioned by Japanese officers who spoke English. They were supposed to be getting the name, rank, and serial number of each man so they could be reported as prisoners of war to the American Red Cross. The Red Cross would then send the names to the United States. This way they could notify each man's family that he was a POW. When I came before the table, I gave my name, rank, and serial number.

The officer said, "Where is that Norden bombsight?" This was the most accurate bombsight in the world at that time. We had only two in the Philippines and I knew very little about them. They had been destroyed and thrown into water over two hundred feet deep between Bataan and Corregidor. I had three men who were on a crash-boat detail in Manila Bay and they had helped destroy these bomb-sights. I had never seen them but had heard of them.

I told the questioning officer, "I have given you my name, rank, and serial number and that is all I am supposed to give you according to the international law concerning prisoners."

He said, "We only comply with international law when we see fit."

I replied, "I comply with international law, and two wrongs don't make a right."

He told me, "You are going to talk." Then he took his sword off his belt with the leather case on it and said, "Where is the bomb-sight?"

I said, "I have told you everything that I am going to tell you and all I am required to tell you." He tried to hit me over the head with the sword, but I dodged it by moving out of his reach. He called two enlisted men into the tent. They had bayonets on their rifles and he ordered them to place the bayonets under each of my shoulder blades. They pushed me against the table where the officer was standing.

He said, "Where is the bombsight?"

I did not reply and he hit at me again. I could only partially dodge that blow and it hit the right side of my head and skinned my ear. He hit me a stunning blow to the left side of my head and knocked me cold. They were dragging me out of the tent when I came to.

He said, "You wait outside; you are going to talk."

When we got on the outside of the tent, there were two lieutenants being guarded by two Japanese soldiers. Both of them were bleeding all over their heads and one of them had his ear half torn off. They had been beaten worse than I had. I could feel the blood running down the right side of my neck where my ear had been skinned.

I told the lieutenants, "We can't take it this way, can we?"

One of them asked, "What can we do?"

The Jap guards were leaning on their guns and I could tell they didn't understand what we were saying. There were about two thousand prisoners milling around us. I said, "We can run into the crowd and get lost."

One of the lieutenants said, "What if they call us back?"

I told him, "We will have to change our names."

The lieutenant said, "If we change our names our folks won't know we are prisoners."

My reply was, "I had rather it be that way than to be dead."

The other lieutenant, who had said nothing until now, said, "What are we waiting on?" He started running toward the crowd of prisoners. We knew if we were going, we had to do it soon. Just as we got to the edge of the crowd, the Japanese guards jerked their rifles up and yelled, "*Kora*," which we did not know the meaning of. It would not have made any difference if we had known. The guards came charging into the crowd to find us. They had on steel helmets, with rifles on their shoulders and fixed bayonets, so they were easy for us to spot in the crowd and evade. They looked for us until dark and I doubt if they could have recognized us except for the blood on our heads. We got to the water faucet as soon as we could and washed off the blood. There was a long line waiting to fill their canteens; but when they saw the blood on our heads, they let us get to the water first. We were never called back or questioned again. My name was not reported to the United States as being a POW for two years.

That night I slept in a sandy furrow. My head ached from the two knots on each side, and the shrapnel wound in my leg throbbed. Dust and sand drifted over me during the night and my hair and body were caked with dirt the next morning.

When morning came we were lined up facing the sun with an open field in front of us and a grove of trees to our backs. We knew we were going to get the sun treatment. The guards wanted as many of us to die as possible under these conditions. They kept us facing the sun until a lot of our men began to faint and fall out on their faces. They would let two men drag them under the shade of the trees, but they had to return quickly to the ranks without even being able to wet their faces from their canteens.

It must have been about nine o'clock before we started on the march for the day. Some of the guards told us, "Tonight you eat." That did not happen.

About four o'clock the next morning, the officer who was bunking with me awakened me and said, "They are feeding some in line." We ran over about fifty yards and got in line. It was a false alarm or they were feeding their own troops, because they didn't put out any food after we got in line.

The next morning it was harder to get up and prepare for the long march. I was sicker and much weaker. We stood facing the hot sun again, until some began to faint. We started the march with more holding onto each other's belts to keep their balance. I was holding Captain Mannersmith's belt. He was a 31st Infantry captain. He tried to help me all he could and was always encouraging me. When we would have to stop because of narrow bridges, I would drop down on my knees to rest; and he would get me by the hair of my head when we were to move up, and say, "Let's go! It's just a little way farther."

Captain Mannersmith had found a small, dirty towel to put over my head. One time when we stopped, there was some water in a ditch along the roadside and, while I was on my knees resting, he went over to wet the towel for my head. I noticed where he wet the towel; there was a dead man lying face down in the water. He had the top of his head blown off and his blood and brains were scattered over the water. I'm sure this was not an easy thing for the captain to do, but he got the towel wet and it was a great help to me.

We passed an artesian well, with lots of cold water squirting out, about one hundred feet from the road. A few of the men from the front of the column started running out to get water for their canteens. The front guard shot three of them before they stopped running for the water. There were already seven or eight bodies lying around the well. My fever was so high and I was so weak, I hardly remember that day. Just before sundown the head of the column started turning into a barbed-wire stockade. During this day's march, I had drifted back close to the rear of the column. I was about fifty yards from the gate when the column slowed down. It was very hot and dry; no wind was stirring. I fainted or blacked out. Captains Mannersmith and Abney put my arms around their necks and dragged me inside the gate to the shade of a tree. Someone filled my canteen with water and bathed my face. I came to, but my head hurt so badly I could hardly stand to open my eyes. I lay there all night. An officer came to me the next morning and said, "If you can't make the march past one o'clock, you had better not start because they are not leaving anyone alive on the road."

We had heard that the guards had received orders not to leave any men alive if they fell out of the column of march. I did not feel as though I could walk even five miles, but I didn't know how to keep from leaving when the others did. I knew I was with friends and countrymen, but they could not help themselves, much less me.

We were lined up and counted. Just as we started out the gate on the march for the day, a large group of POW's started coming into the stockade. I took a chance and jumped into the column coming into the stockade, so that I could stay another day. I knew I could not make the march past one o'clock and stay on my feet. I stayed under the same tree that I had been under, for the rest of the day and all night. My fever seemed better, but we still had not been fed. I knew that I was getting weaker every day that I went without food, so I decided to try the march the next day.

When we started the march the next day, I still had to hold on to someone's belt as did many others. About ten o'clock that morning, I felt death near me and I just didn't think I could go any farther. I noticed a buck sergeant in front of me staggering along and holding someone's belt in front of him. He turned loose of the belt and staggered out of the column to the right. The front guard turned around and shot at him like someone shooting at a bird, just half aiming. The bullet hit him in the chest and the sergeant rolled against the curb on the street. The guard saw that he had not killed him, so he pushed out his rifle in one hand, like firing a six-shooter from the hip, and shot him again. This time the bullet hit the sergeant in the pit of the stomach. Then the guard rushed up to him and ran his bayonet through his chest. He then put his foot on the sergeant's body and pulled the bayonet out. He took his handkerchief out as he was trotting back to the front of the column. He wiped the blood off his bayonet. After seeing all this, I was determined not to fall out of the column.

I think we were somewhere between Hermosa and Lubao on a gravel road, and it was about eleven o'clock when my knees just would not work. I was pulling too heavily on the belt of the man in front of me. He didn't complain, but did all he could to help me keep going. I became numb all over. I could see ahead about one quarter of a mile. There were two or three nipa huts with some shade trees. I was going to try to make it to those shade trees, but I fell down in the column. The soldier that I was holding on to got me by the hair of my head and said, "Come on. Try to make it. It's just a little farther." My knees buckled. Two men tried to carry me with my arms around their necks. I could not move my legs to help them. They were falling behind in the march and I asked them to let me go. I did not want them to get killed trying to help me. I pulled myself from them and fell on my knees on the gravel road with my hand beneath my forehead. I could hear the crunching sound of the gravel from the shoes marching by me. I tried to rise up again and I saw a Japanese officer with boots on, some thirty feet ahead and a guard running at me with a bayonet. The officer shouted something at him. The guard just jabbed me and did not follow through with it as though he were really trying to kill me. I felt the grinding of bones and a streak of fire in my right side. I passed out. Then I had a dream or vision. Evidently I thought I was dying. I saw my wife, Ethel, in tears, saying, "Don't leave me with these children." Then my daughter, Lennie Lou, who was ten years old when I left the states, appeared in a light blue dress, with her hair done up in pigtails. Tears like dew drops were running down her cheeks. She said, "Daddy, don't leave me." Then my son appeared. He had his two front teeth out, just as I had left him (he was six years old) and in an excited tone, he said, "Daddy, don't leave us." Each of them appeared one at a time. I could see them from the waist up and they seemed very close to me.

It was in the afternoon about four o'clock when I regained consciousness. When I moved, I felt something on each side of me and I was under a tree. I had a terrible headache and my side was burning. I tried to raise up and I noticed I was between two men. I moved my arms over against them. They were stiff and cold. I waited just a minute, thinking that some Jap might see me move and try to finish killing me or recapture me. I raised up slowly, looked around and discovered that I had been carried about one quarter mile from where I had fallen. There were the two nipa huts and the grove of trees. One of these men I was lying between was a Catholic chaplain. He had his rosary beads on his chest. The other man was a soldier. I realized I had apparently been left for dead.

My mouth and throat were so dry that my throat felt swollen. I could not have talked at this time. I looked for a water well near the nipa huts, but noticed an artesian well out in the field about one hundred yards. There was a trail leading to it. There were no trees near the well and I felt conspicuous going out there in the open. I did not have any water in my canteen, but I did not remember using it that morning. I went out to this cool, soft-water artesian well; I cupped my hands and drank all I could hold, then filled my canteen. I was enjoying this so much, I washed my face and hands, then took off my shoes and washed my feet. The shrapnel wound in my left leg had bled into my shoe and dried. It smelled like a decayed animal. I tried to wash my shoe out and I did wash my socks and put them back on. I did not wash the shrapnel wound because I did not have anything to dress it.

I pulled my shirt up to look at the wound in my side. When I breathed, bloody bubbles would come out and I was afraid that my lung had been punctured. I tested it by taking a deep breath, holding it and seeing if the pressure escaped and the bubbles continued to come out. There were no bubbles as I held my breath. I assumed the bayonet had gone below my lung and into the cavity near my liver. My diaphram going in and out as I breathed would draw in air then let it out when the wound was not covered. I had never washed the wound because I had been told that the blood was purer than any water I might find.

I felt somewhat better with the good, cool water on my face. I decided to wet part of my shirt to help keep me cool. One-half mile down the road was a small barrio, or village. We still had not gotten back far enough from the lines to where civilians lived. To the best of my memory, it had been nine days since I had eaten. I saw this little village and thought I might find a cat, dog, or pig that had been overlooked by the Japanese. I could eat them some way, raw or cooked. I walked slowly at my own pace to the barrio.

It was just about sundown when I got there. I started around a large cement stucco building that had been shelled or bombed. It had been an old store building. Just as I started around the back corner of the building, four Japs jumped out in front of me, with fixed bayonets. I didn't try to run. I put my hands up over my head. They searched me, but did not find anything on me that they wanted. I could not speak one word of Japanese and they did not speak English. They would give me orders by motioning and I would do what I thought they wanted me to do.

When they were searching me I took my hands down. One of them put his finger on my bloody shirt and then looked at the blood that stuck on his finger. I pulled my shirt up to show them the bayonet wound. One of them pointed to the tip of his bayonet and I nodded my head. They talked for a few minutes, then motioned for me to go to the front of the building. This was where the main road was. All four of them came with me. Two of them motioned for me to go down the road in the direction I thought the column that I had dropped out of that morning had gone. These two Jap soldiers went with me. They were very reasonable, letting me set my own pace, which was slow.

This was a very cloudy, dark night. Not any lights could be seen anywhere. The only noise to be heard was the crunch of our feet on the gravel road. We would pass houses or nipa huts along the road, but no lights could be seen. The guards talked to each other, but at no time did they bother me. About ten o'clock we came to a large camp at a sugar plantation in which there were a few lights on tall poles. It had a high barbed-wire fence built all around for an enclosure to keep prisoners. After I entered the compound, I recognized these soldiers as being the ones I had started out with that morning.

All over the ground in this compound was a thick carpet of sugar cane pulp that the soldiers ahead of us had chewed up and spit out. They had been allowed to have some sugar cane stalks to chew, but the new group had not. The next day all the prisoners built more barbed-wire fences to hold more prisoners. The Japanese officer who was in charge of fence building did not make me work after he saw the blood on my shirt and I motioned to my head like I had a bad headache. He let me sit near where they were working.

I slept on my right side that night, thinking it would stop the bleeding and help the blood to clot. I felt better the next day, after resting the day before, except for following the work detail around. I was still weak, but did not have such a bad headache. It was pretty cloudy that morning and not as hot as it had been. It was a relief to know that we could not be given the sun treatment as long as it was cloudy. Soon after the march started, we went through a small town. The civilians were lining the streets. Most were old men and women, with a few children. They stood and looked at us with tears rolling down their cheeks. I noticed an elderly lady to the right of our column who was holding out an egg to anyone who would come out and get it. The guards would not let the civilians get near us. I moved to the outside of the column and when I got about even with her, I ran out and she gave me the egg. The guard at the front of the column looked back and saw me just as I was getting back to the column. He took after me and I ran from the right side to the left side of the column. He aimed his rifle at me just as I entered the ranks. He could hardly see me, so when I saw him coming through the column after me, I stooped down, cracked the egg on the pavement and swallowed it. All this time I was running from him. I threw the egg shell over my shoulder and it hit his helmet. When he saw what it was he stopped chasing me.

All that time I was having trouble keeping the egg down. When I swallowed it, it hit the bottom of my stomach and bounced right back like a rubber ball. I put my hand over my mouth and swallowed it again. This time I kept it down. I do not know if it was a Filipino balut egg or not. This is a duck egg that has been set for twenty-one days and then boiled. The Filipinos use these quite a bit. The reason I think it might have been a balut egg is that, when I swallowed it, it felt like a solid lump at first but did not feel like that when it came up. Also the egg shell was harder to break than on an ordinary egg.

Before getting into the populated area, out of the battle zone, we saw dead soldiers all along the highway. We noticed this was especially true around water wells along the road. After we got into the towns where people were living, the Filipinos must have buried the bodies because there were none visible. The ones that we did see along the road had been killed recently. The road from Lubao to San Fernando was churned into a powder by the tanks, artillery, trucks, and cavalry that had passed over it.

On this last day's march, the guards were shouting, clubbing, and having trouble keeping the column moving at a regular pace. The men's feet were swollen to about twice the normal size. Many had cut the strings in their shoes to allow for more room and comfort. I saw one major who had cut his shoes into leather strips and the flesh still protruded. He fell down on his knees and a Jap guard stuck his bayonet through the fleshy part of the major's arm. He pulled the bayonet out and the major got up and stayed with the column in the march. Many had dysentery from drinking bad water that hadn't been chlorinated. I saw one man leave the column to defecate and a guard shot him. Some were bayoneted.

I had made this day's march without a high fever, although I was weak and tired; but I did not hurt any special place. My salty shirt had rubbed the bayonet wound raw and it did burn a little. The Filipinos would stand off at a distance with their arms full of sugar cane, but the guards would not let them come close enough for us to get any of it without being shot.

Just before sundown, while it was still very hot, we came into San Fernando. At this time, after traveling about seventy miles, I did not know where we were, the day of the month, or the hour of the day. I was near the rear when the column slowed and I noticed it was turning into an area with large tin buildings. I was so weak and tired from the heat that I blacked out and started to fall. Two men pulled my arms around their necks and helped me into an arena where they had cock fights. They wet my face with water from my canteen before they left me. I sat up and noticed ten or twelve other men lying around me. Some of them were naked and unconscious. They had dysentery very badly and could not control their bowels. This was just a place they left men to die.

11. *Some Relief from Misery*

I crawled out of this place into an open yard at the back. It was fenced to keep the prisoners in, and I slept on the bare hard ground that night. When I awoke the next morning, there was quite a commotion going on in one of the buildings. A friend of mine came to me and said, "They are feeding the prisoners some very thin rice." I got in line and got my first taste of Japanese cooked rice. It tasted like the starch my mother used to make to starch the clothes. At first I could not eat it. I could not keep from vomiting. I noticed a lot of the men were having the same problem. I knew I had to eat to live, so I tried a little harder to keep it down. This kind of rice was called *lagou* and we were served about one cupful. Many could not keep it down. Part of the trouble was due to the fact that we had gone so many days without food.

Soon I had to go to the latrine to defecate. This was a large trench dug out in the ground. There were 2″ x 6″ boards across the center. The odor was awful and there were so many maggots crawling so thick three feet away from this pit that no one could get close to it without slipping on them. The excretion in the pit was mostly blood.

My bowels had not acted, that I could remember, in six or seven days. My bowel action was white, just like the rice I had just eaten. The gastric juices had gone out of our stomachs, so the food was not broken down for the body to assimilate it. This made me worry. Could I live after being without food for thirteen days? I went back to the building and some of the men could not eat all of their rice, so I tried some more. This seemed to help my strength. The malaria had left me and I was feeling better.

The Japanese were preparing to move us out to some other place, I heard, by rail. I also heard that other prisoners were staying at other places in San Fernando, like the pottery shed, the Blue Moon dance hall, the vinegar factory, and various other places. I was in the main tin building, sitting on the ground near a wall. I heard someone knocking on the wall from the outside. I pulled the corrugated tin apart, so I could see out. A Filipino was standing there with two large duck eggs to sell me for one peso each. I traded with him and gave an elderly colonel one of them. (Five years later I saw him in San Antonio, Texas. He recognized me and told me how much he had appreciated my giving him one of the eggs.) Both eggs were boiled.

We were loaded onto a narrow-gauge train with small boxcars. They were seven feet high, thirty feet long, and eight feet wide, 110–115 men were crowded into each of the boxcars. There was only standing room; then the doors were closed.

It was unbearably hot. Some of the soldiers in the back began to yell, "Give us some air!"

Finally the guards opened one door and roped off a lane crossways of the car, from one door to the other. This made it more crowded, but when the train began to move, it gave us more air. We stopped one place for a short while and the Filipinos tried to get the guards to let them give us some sugar cane. This was not permitted, but they did give some of us water in soda pop bottles. I was afraid to drink any of it because of dysentery. Before we got to Capas, which was a three- or four-hour ride, several soldiers in the back of the cars fainted from overheating or lack of oxygen. They were pulled out between the doors and some regained consciousness, while others died.

When we got off the train at Capas the guards made us leave the dead in the boxcars. From here we made an eight-mile hike to Camp

O'Donnell. This was the first time that I had felt completely free of fever and pain on this whole trip. I had lost a lot of weight, but I made the last eight miles in good shape, even though exhausted. This was April 21, 1942. It was also Texas Independence Day. When we came into Camp O'Donnell they had us sit down in a group so the commandant could talk to us. He spoke through an interpreter. He was introduced as Captain Tsuneyoshi. The interpreter told us that the commandant was very disappointed in us because we did not stand when he came out to greet us.

The commandant said, "You are mine. You are my enemy. You should be grateful to the great Japanese Imperial Army for sparing your lives. Our children will fight your children for hundreds of years and we will banish the white man from the Orient. You will die from old age under our command. We have laws here that you must obey. Anyone involved in attempting to escape will be given the death sentence. We have drinking water, but it is a death penalty to use the water to bathe."

We could readily see from his demeanor and tone of voice that this prison life was going to be bad. We knew that the suffering would continue indefinitely or until we could bear it no longer. I do not know how the American wool blankets were rationed or where they came from, but I was issued one wool blanket after the commandant made his speech. We had started from the Bataan Peninsula on April 13 with 2,000 men in the group. I changed groups by staying in the same camp two days. I suppose there were 2,000 in this group when they started, but less than 1,500 finished the march. The others were shot or bayoneted when they fell out of the column from weakness or sickness. Some became overheated, fainted, or passed out, and were bayoneted. Some escaped by jumping out of the column when we made a turn where there was brush near the side of the road. None were left alive on the road if the guards knew about it. Most of the time the guards marched in front or near the rear of the columns. At all times we marched in columns of fours.

When we came to Camp O'Donnell it was about one hour before sunset. After hearing the rules and regulations from the commandant, we went to the mess hall. Here we ate thin rice seated at tables with benches. This was the first time in a long time that we had sat at a table to eat. My last time was that one day on Corregidor. I found out that prisoners were fed two light meals a day. There were about 7,000 prisoners here when we arrived. I slept on the ground with a clump of grass for a pillow that night. What few buildings there were in this fifty-acre camp were already filled with prisoners.

The next morning I met Captain Mike Ushakoff, who had been my first roommate at Nichols Field, and Captain J. (Jimmy) Y. Parker, who had been our executive officer at Nichols Field. Later I met Colonel Bill Maverick, who had been with me the last two days on Bataan. He had been the most loyal and helpful officer I had ever known. He was the commanding officer at the Nichols Field Air Base; also, he was in command of the 1st Battalion of the Air Corps Regiment during the last month of fighting on Bataan. In the prison camp he had been put in charge of all air corps personnel. Colonel Maverick asked me if I would be his executive officer to take roll call every morning and get out the necessary work details the Japs requested. These work details would be burial details, wood details, water details for the kitchen, etc.

I told Colonel Maverick that I would take the job if he would let me rest a day or two. My feet and ankles were swelled up to my knees and I had developed a bad case of dysentery. He told me to get a place to sleep in an old building that was close by where he was staying. I went into this building and it was well occupied. It had a wooden floor and a nipa roof. There was a strip across the roof, near the top, about one foot wide, that was not covered. The building was about sixty feet long and thirty feet wide. Everyone slept on the floor. There was not any furniture of any kind in the building, not even a table or chair. I crowded in between two officers that I knew, Captain Munton, who had worked in the post office in California, and Captain Abney, who was from Texas. I felt sorry for them because of my odor, but I could not help it.

I had not had a bath or a change of clothes since the second day after I surrendered. Now it was a death penalty to take a bath or use excess water. Even sponge baths and washing clothes were not allowed. My clothes were stiff from sweat, dust, and blood from the bayonet wound. My left shoe had an odor like a dead horse, because of the blood that had run down into my shoe from the shrapnel wound. In a couple of days the odor had caused those who were near me to move away from me. Not one of them said anything to offend me or complained about the smell. This gave me more room.

I went to an American doctor and asked him what could be done about my dysentery. He said, "If you can get some sulfathiazole tablets it would stop the dysentery." He did not have anything to dress my wounds. He did give me some burned shingles to eat to slow down the dysentery. It did slow down my trips to the latrine, but made my whole stomach sore. When my bowels would act, it was like sandpaper; it took the lining of my stomach with it, causing excessive bleeding.

I went out into the camp area to see how many of my old 27th Materiel Squadron I could find and to see if I could find any sulfathiazole tablets. I would ask each man if he knew where I could get some of these tablets. The next day, Donald Stover, who had been my runner for the 27th Materiel Squadron, brought me five tablets. Then Sergeant Rodgers brought me five and one-half tablets. I gave them two pesos for each tablet. They had taken them off dead men at different times. The doctor had said I would need twelve tablets, but since this was all I could get, he said for me to take four twice and two and a half the last time and I do not remember how far apart I was to take them. This dysentery was wrecking my whole body, but the tablets stopped it.

It was a depressing sight to see how our troops were living. They were staying in buildings that had fallen down, with the roofs still intact. They would crawl under these roofs to sleep and try to stay out of the rain or even the heavy dews. Some had holes dug in the ground and some would crawl under the floor of old buildings. They had sore throats, bad colds, malaria, and dysentery. I talked to Master Sergeant Felix. He had 2,000 pesos and wanted to lend me 500 pesos. He said he was afraid someone would steal it from him. I told him I would take 250 pesos and maybe Colonel Maverick would take the other 250 pesos. We would give him our IOU's as security. This we did. (About three years and six months later I received a notice from an ex-POW in Colorado with my IOU. I sent him $125.00; Sergeant Felix had died in prison camp.)

The first morning that I took the roll call for the Air Corps Regiment was depressing. The condition of these once healthy and proud soldiers was pathetic. Not a single one of them was well. They weighed from 80 to 120 pounds. Their clothes were as dirty as mine and their hair and beards were matted from sweat and dirt. They were pale and under their eyes the skin was puffy. Many could not wear their shoes because of the swelling in their feet and legs. Many were too sick to get to the formation for roll call and I would have to go with the first sergeant to find them. They would be under the old buildings or in a hole without any covering to keep them warm at night. Those who did report to the formation were the ones we had to make a rotation roster from for the many work details the Japanese asked for. The burial detail did not have to walk as far as the wood or water detail. Those who were the least able to walk were used most of the time to dig the graves and bury the dead.

A man might be on the burial detail one day and be buried the next day himself. In Camp O'Donnell there were never less than fifty to die every day. Sometimes as many as seventy would be buried. The Japanese organized what they called a hospital, but it was just a place to die. They never gave any medicine or extra food to those sent to the hospital. The hospital was built about four feet off the ground.

They would put the dead under here for the burial detail to pick up every day. The Japanese would not let our chaplains have a regular funeral service; in fact not a service of any kind was allowed. All the graves that I know about had at least ten buried in them. A mound of dirt was placed on them to keep the dogs from eating them and to keep the bodies from floating out of the graves in heavy rains. One day a grave that had been dug in a low place filled with water during a heavy rainfall and three bodies floated out of the grave. We had to put them back in the grave. Our grave registrar tried to keep up with who was buried in each grave. I noticed at first that there were many marked "Unknown" because the Japanese had taken their dog tags for souvenirs. They had no other means of identification. We required everyone who did not have dog tags to make one out of bamboo. This helped to get all the dead identified.

Most of the dead were buried naked and most of the time the Japanese would cut their stomachs open. They said this was to determine the cause of death. Everyone knew that starvation brought on disease and death. We learned that the swelling was caused from a deficiency of Vitamin B. It was called beriberi. More men died from dysentery than any other one thing. Starvation caused them to be too weak to throw off any kind of disease.

I had been administrative officer for the Air Corps Regiment about two weeks when I received orders from the Japanese that I was to have charge of a two-hundred-man detail to go to Clark Field to work. They gave me three days' notice. I really did not like the idea because I knew they would want these men to do hard and heavy work cleaning up Clark Field. It had been badly bombed and burned up. I knew they would not feed these men enough to exist and the Japs would press me to make the enlisted work harder. This would cause trouble, because I would not expect the men to do hard work if they were not properly fed.

The day before we were to go, I took a malaria chill and had a very high fever. I was not able to go. They sent Captain Kirk in my place. He had been in command of the Headquarters & Headquarters Squadron in my battalion on the front lines on Bataan.

Our water supply in the prison area was very limited. We could fill our canteens once a day by standing in line for a long period of time. The water used in the kitchen had to be carried about three quarters of a mile from a river. I had to serve on the water detail one day, and as we passed the Japanese headquarters on our way to the river, there was an American soldier stripped to the waist tied to a post with his hands tied behind him. He had been whipped with a wire. His body was bloody all over and he was hanging limp. I am sure he was dead.

When I returned to camp, I inquired about this soldier. They said the night before he had walked out the main gate of the prison compound and was caught walking down the center of the street in a little village about one-half mile from camp. He was running a high fever and was delirious. Someone had seen him about ten o'clock that night inside the prison, just walking around. They asked him, "Where are you going?" He had replied, "I am going out to my mother's farm."

Our senior officers had tried to reason with the Japanese officials that morning and had tried to get him released, but could not. To try to escape was a death penalty, and according to them, he was trying to escape, when in fact he did not know what he was doing or where he was.

The next day I was checking out a group to go on a wood detail to bring wood for the kitchen. We were in front of the headquarters building waiting for the trucks to take the detail out when one of the enlisted men fell down and began to scream and have a fit. He seemed to be choking. He was foaming at the mouth and chewing his tongue. I put a stick crossways in his mouth to stop him from chewing his tongue. I had two other men hold the stick while I went into the headquarters office. There was only one person in the office, and from the insignia on his uniform, I thought him to be a doctor. I could not speak Japanese and he could not understand English, but I tried by making signs to get him to come outside and help this man. He got out of his chair and escorted me to the door and kicked me out the door on my face. I got up and went back in the office. I could see the Jap officer was very mad from the sound of his voice and his actions. He was ordering me out again, but I got behind him and grabbed him around the waist and pushed him to the door. He looked down and saw the soldier lying there with the stick in his mouth, then he relaxed and I turned him loose. He went out and took a closer look at the soldier and went back into the building. I looked in the office and he was preparing a syringe. He came back and gave the man a shot; he soon relaxed. He did not go on the work detail.

I met this man several years later at an ex-POW convention in Albuquerque, New Mexico. He came up to me and said, "Were you an officer at Camp O'Donnell?"

I said, "Yes, I was."

He asked me, "Do you remember one morning on a wood detail when an enlisted man had a convulsion in front of the Japanese headquarters?"

I told him, "Yes, I remember."

He said, "I am Sergeant Julius J. Krick, and I have been looking for you since I got out of prison camp so you could verify my actions when I had that convulsion. I am still in the service, but I do need a statement from you, so they won't think I am gold-bricking when I fall out on a full-pack march."

I wrote a statement for him and heard from him later, saying he had an office job.

The Filipino POW camp was west of ours. They buried their dead in the same cemetery that we used. Their death rate was higher than ours because they had more men. We had around nine thousand in the American camp. Their death rate ran from three hundred to four hundred a day. They would file by on the south side of our camp carrying their dead from about nine o'clock to eleven o'clock in the morning. Their corpses were carried by two Filipinos at a time. Their litters were made of bamboo poles with a blanket tied on them near the ends. The dead were in such poor shape the weight was not a problem. There was a POW barbed-wire fence between our camp and the road that was about five feet away, but we could not get closer than four feet of the fence or the guards would shoot us, so we could not talk to the Filipinos that passed by.

This horrible episode at Camp O'Donnell continued from April until sometime in June. Most men died from dysentery or pneumonia. There were too many damp, foggy, or rainy days that kept the men wet from lack of proper shelter. They took colds that usually turned into pneumonia. They tried to stay dry by digging holes like animals or using the old buildings to crawl under. This camp was truly a hell on earth.

12. *Changing Prison Camps*

About the middle of June 1942, the Japanese decided to move us to Cabanatuan. We were moved down to the hospital area at Camp O'Donnell late one evening. We were put in the hospital barracks in very crowded quarters. There was a slow rain all night, but we were dry. I was awakened about daylight by a soldier who came to tell me one of my men was running around outside naked. He said this man was going around looking in the barracks windows, trying to steal some clothes, he thought. He did not know the man's name but had been told that he was with the 27th Materiel Squadron.

I went outside to see if I could find the man. When I found him, he was huddled in a corner trying to stay warm. He was Staff Sergeant Charles W. Thomas. I had used him as my first sergeant. I had not seen him in three weeks. He had been sent to the hospital with malaria and dysentery. He was delirious and I could not get him to talk. He just stared into space. He would do what I asked him to do, but his mind was blank. He was so sick and weak he could hardly stand up. I had been given a pair of coveralls that had been taken off a dead man, but I had washed them when I went to the river on the water detail. This was all the clothing I had, except what I had on.

I gave the coveralls to him and he put them on. He still had his shoes on, but they were wet. I took him back to the barracks with me. I tried to get him to tell me where his bunk was and how long he had been out there. He couldn't or wouldn't talk. I had him lie down until the Japanese started loading us on the trucks for the trip to Cabanatuan. I estimated it to be about seventy miles. The trucks were very crowded. When I tried to get Sergeant Thomas a place to sit by me, one of the guards yelled at him and started hitting him with a stick. I moved over against the guard and said, "*Nai, nai,*" which meant "No, no," in English. The guard didn't hit him again. The guard was trying to make him hurry. Sergeant Thomas leaned on me most of the way, because he was too weak to sit up by himself.

The Cabanatuan prison camp was built before the war near the foothills of the Sierra Madre. This is where most of the prisoners who were captured on Corregidor were taken. There had been a United States agricultural experiment station there. The camp alone covered about one hundred acres. There were many army barracks here that had been built for a Filipino army division. The roofs were made of cogon grass and the walls were closed in with nipa. The floors were made of bamboo slats. There were cracks between the slats to allow for air circulation, which made it much cooler than a solid floor. Each of the barracks had a hallway in the center. The sleeping bays were up off the floor about eighteen inches. There were bays on each side of the hallway. Several guard towers were at intervals on the outside of the camp. The prison compound was enclosed with a high barbed-wire fence.

When we began unloading at Cabanatuan, they formed us in columns of fours. The sergeant and I got on the inside of the column, because I did not want the guards to bother him or ask him any questions. He had dysentery very bad and when he had to defecate he would just start out of the column without saying anything to the guard. I got permission to go with him. He would just pass blood, as he had not eaten enough to show in his stool. I would bring him back and we would take our place in the column. It took the column a long time to start moving since there were about 7,000 of us. When we did start moving, we were moving in columns of twos. I traded places with one of the men on the outside, so I could move up in the same column with Sergeant Thomas. He would sit down when the column was not moving. The guard did not like for me to trade places with the outside man. He could not understand English, but I finally convinced him that I was trying to take care of a sick man. We moved up several hundred feet and a Jap officer came along and took Sergeant Thomas out of the column, with some other sick men. He would not let me go along to help the sergeant. They took them to a long barracks that had one wall; the ends were closed in, and the floor was dirt. When we moved by this building, I could see through the open windows and doors on our side. There were no hanging doors or windows.

All of the POW's that were moved from Camp O'Donnell were located in the west side of Cabanatuan prison camp number one. We found out that Corregidor had surrendered on May 6, 1942, about one month after the surrender of Bataan.

I was put in charge of the barracks in which I stayed. There were about one hundred men. The next day about noon, Colonel Bill Maverick, my old commanding officer at Nichols Field, came to me and asked if I would take charge of the barracks I described above, the sick bay, where Sergeant Thomas had been taken. Colonel Maverick told me to take as many men as I needed to help me with this detail. I did not know what to expect, nor could I have imagined it. I appointed eight men to go with me.

I was stunned beyond description when we got to this sick bay and looked in. There were about ninety men lying on the ground in the dirt, naked and unconscious. They were skin and bones. Most of them were lying on their backs, some were on their sides. Their hair and beards were a tangled mess, soiled by their own excretion. Their mouths hung open and their eyes were half closed. They all looked like dead men. I could not recognize a single one of them. I tried to find Sergeant Thomas, but could not. I learned later that he had been taken to the hospital.

Most of the men who had dysentery had defecated just as they lay. The only thing we could do was to remove the soiled dirt and replace it with fresh soil. We tried to drop water on their lips and into their mouths so they could swallow it, but if we tried to drop it down their throats they would strangle. I tried to find out some of their names, but was never able to get any of them to utter a word.

These ninety unconscious men who had been moved from Camp O'Donnell were the final aftermath of the horrible, inhumane death march. These men had suffered the agony of an unheard-of tragedy in a civilized world. This treatment of the death march and imprisonment at Camp O'Donnell is beyond the imagination's ability to comprehend. If there ever was a hell on earth, this was administered to the 7,000 souls of some of the bravest and most devoted of our military personnel. Day after day they were in agony, seemingly blotted out in memory by their nation. They suffered under the burning tropical sun, on starvation rations, with little water to drink. They could not even wash the filth from their bodies or clothes, matted hair, and beards. They were mentally depressed, had swollen limbs from beriberi, unhealed, festered wounds that were never treated. They also had distended stomachs, bloody dysentery, and raw, sore mouths from pellagra. Even a drink of water would cause their mouths to burn. Everyone had stomach worms that would sometimes find their way out of the body through the nose. No attempt was made by the Imperial Japanese Army to furnish any kind of medication to alleviate the suffering. The International Red Cross tried to give them medicine, but the Japanese government refused to let it help in any way.

These young men, in the bloom of life and born in the image of God, with the earth for a bed and the clouds for cover, had no law to protect them. Now they withered and trembled in weakness and pain, with no civilized medication to help them. They were far away from family, friends, and the nation they loved. They had given their all for her. It was hard to realize and harder to accept that it should end like this.

This was the worst detail I was ever to serve on and I went back to talk to Colonel Maverick about the limited help that we could give these pitiful men. He knew they were beyond help. He had tried to get medicine from the Japanese, but they would not help in any way. He said, "They just take the dead out about four o'clock every morning." All of these ninety men were dead within four days.

In this new camp we were having problems getting enough water to drink. I would appoint a detail from our barracks to take ten canteens and stand in line at the water faucet until they could fill the canteens. Sometimes it would take five or six hours to get the water. I would have to send men to relieve those in the water line if they could not get back by meal time. Most of the time it would be eleven or twelve o'clock at night before they could get back.

One night it was twelve o'clock before the detail returned. To prevent wakening those in the barracks, they left the canteens just outside the barracks on the stick used to carry them. My bunk was the first bunk near the door. About half-past twelve, I heard these canteens rattle. I looked outside and saw a man taking a canteen off the stick. He was stealing a canteen of water that belonged to some soldier in my barracks. Neither he nor I was strong enough to scuffle, so I jumped out the door on this man. He fell to the ground and I held him there until someone identified him. He was from a barracks near us.

There was no law in the camp unless a group would vote or suggest it. I had appointed group leaders in this barracks. We discussed what we should do in this case before we let him go. We decided that he should not ever come over to our barracks again. Should he be caught stealing again, we would give him ten whacks with a board. If this ever happened anywhere in camp again, we never heard of it.

The Japanese guard towers were equipped with spot lights. They required the American prisoners to guard the inside of the compound at night, and if anyone escaped, those on guard would be shot before a firing squad. Most of the breaches of their rules carried a death penalty as punishment.

After we had been in Camp Cabanatuan two weeks, we came out of quarantine. My unit was moved to the east side of the prison compound. I told everyone who was assigned to my barracks that when we moved to the east side into the new barracks we must stay together, in the same barracks, so we could keep all of our roll calls correct. We moved down to the east area that afternoon. Each person was allowed twenty-eight inches of space on the bay where we slept. Then there was what we called the "cat walk" up above the second bay, near the roof or gable, that was twenty-four inches wide, on which someone had to sleep. This catwalk ran lengthwise of the barracks.

After we were released from quarantine we were able to visit with our friends from Corregidor. They told us what the radio (Voice of Freedom) on Corregidor received regarding the fall of Bataan. These reports came from all over the world. This was the only English-language broadcast that we could receive while we were blockaded on Bataan, except the propaganda reports from Tokyo Rose. Some quotations from these reports are as follows:

Fall of Bataan

The weary men have at last been overpowered by superior forces on Bataan. The praises of their countrymen will be cold comfort. They would have preferred a chance to fight the Japanese on something like even terms. The chance was denied them. We know from what Stimson told us that a few successful efforts were made to supply them through the Japanese blockade and thanks to their efforts the men were never short of ammunition, but this and luck was all they had. They lacked guns and heavy air support. The delaying action they performed with gallantry will take its place forever in the traditions of Americans. Bataan has been lost but it will be remembered generations from now. The men of Bataan have given the world a wonderful legacy. The gratitude to those gallant men must close our ranks and we must do our duty.—*New York Times*

It is impossible not to feel saddened by the end of the gallant fight.—*New York Herald Tribune*

April 8, 1942: "It makes me feel proud"—President Roosevelt

The Bataan forces went out as they would have wished, fighting to the end of their flickering, forelorn hope. No army has ever done so much with so little and nothing become of it more than its last hour of trial and agony. To those weeping mothers of its dead I can say that the sacrifice and halo of Jesus of Nazareth have descended upon their sons and that God will take them unto Himself.—General MacArthur

Bataan has fallen but the spirit that made it stand is a beacon to all liberty-loving people of the world that will never be forgotten.—Voice of Freedom

I have nothing but praise for the men who conducted this epic battle. Our troops outnumbered and worn down by constant fighting, exhausted by insufficient rations and diseases have had their lines broken down. A long and gallant defense has been overthrown.—Secretary of War Henry L. Stimson

Tonight we must close with a note of sorrowful pride. Britain has been moved almost beyond words to learn that our defense of Bataan is ended. They have written a story which will never be forgotten.—Radio London

Our debt to the men of Bataan must be paid. It must be paid by the mightiest devotion and upsurge of energy of every man and woman in the nation.—*Oakland Tribune*

Tributes of words seem inadequate and empty. It is enough merely to say that the Bataan defenders will be immortal.—*St. Louis Globe Democrat*

No defeat can dim the glory of the Bataan defenders. No reverse will lower our pride in lifting them to the ranks of America's greatest heroes. America's regard for them is an emotion too genuine to shout, too personal to parade. Bataan is America's badge of those who fight without fear.—Washington D.C. Radio News

13. *Near Execution*

There were three cooks in my barracks. They would go to the kitchen early in the morning and stay until after dark. We did not have any lights in our barracks, so when I went to breakfast, I would check to see if these cooks were present. I checked the roll like this every day. After about two weeks, one of my men told me that one of the cooks was staying in a barracks across the street because there was more room. I talked to the captain in charge of that barracks and he said he had picked him up on his roll about a week before. All this time I had been reporting him to our camp adjutant as I had been told to do when we moved into this barracks. We were not to drop anyone or pick up anyone on our rolls. I knew that this meant the report that our adjutant was making to the Japanese was showing one more man than we actually had. The prisoners were not reported by name or number, but just as a certain number of prisoners. This could mean the death penalty for me and the other captain. I immediately went to the American camp adjutant who received our reports every day and explained to him what had happened and asked him to get it corrected. He said, "My God! I can't do it now! The Japs are mad at me and I would get shot or beaten up if I caused them any trouble. I will report it just as soon as I think it is safe." I reminded him every week for a month before he reported it.

The Japs sent two guards down to the barracks after me when he finally reported the mistake. They handed me a note that read, "The commandant wants to see you."

They also sent two guards after the other officer. I was sure the commandant wanted to see us about reporting the one too many men, but I told myself it could be something else. The commandant had a milk goat and it had come up missing. Then he had a fat dog that had disappeared. I did see where the bones of the goat had been burned, but I did not help eat the goat or the dog, nor did I know anyone who had. It was about eleven o'clock in the morning and very hot. It was August. The officer and I arrived about the same time at the commandant's office. We were escorted to this large room in which there was a round table and three chairs. No other furniture was in the room. We both bowed and said, "Ohayō," which was "good morning" in Japanese. There were two Japanese captains and an interpreter seated on the south side of the round table. They did not return our greetings. They asked us our names, through the interpreter, as they did all of the questions. They told us to stand at attention at all times because we were prisoners.

The interpreter said, "You are American officers and do not make this kind of mistake in your army; therefore, you have intentionally and purposefully reported one man too many on your roll to make it possible for a man to escape. Why did you do it? You know it is the death penalty to help anyone escape."

I held up my right hand asking for permission to speak to the captain. The interpreter nodded his head in approval. I said, "In the American army men are carried on the roster by name and serial number and each officer can check and see if there is a duplication. They also have the authority to transfer men from one barracks to another if there is more room for him to sleep in another barracks. It is mathematically impossible and I do not know how it would be possible for one man to escape as long as we were showing one man too many. If we had reported one less, this could be; but since we both were carrying the cook on our roster, it would always show one man too many."

The three officers talked among themselves, during which time the interpreter called us to attention several times in a very angry voice. We would relax and try to put our weight on one leg at a time.

They did not like this and considered it disrespectful to the Japanese officers. Prisoners were to stand at rigid attention.

There were no windows or doors open and it was unbearably hot. Perspiration was pouring off both of us. After about fifteen minutes of jabbering among themselves, the interpreter said, "You are American officers and you know better than to mix them up on their roll-call reports. This report has gone to the Manila headquarters and in this camp they are held directly responsible for its correctness; therefore, you will be punished by going before a firing squad at eleven o'clock in the morning. This will set an example and prevent its happening again."

The officers went into the adjoining room and left the door open. The two guards kept us at rigid attention in the large room. The guards motioned for us to back up into the corner of the room. I asked the other officer, "Can you think of anything that we should tell these ———— ?" About that time the guard next to me backhanded me, slapping me across the nose. The blood from my nose ran off my chin. This was my way of finding out that we were not to talk. We stood at attention in the hot corner for about thirty minutes. We could hear the Japanese officers talking loudly in the adjoining room. At times it sounded as if they were talking on the telephone. The interpreter came back into the large room and sat down behind the table. He called us up before him and said, "We do not know how you could arrange for a prisoner to escape by showing too many on the roll-call report. If this is a trick, you will die the next time. This time we will not shoot you; next time we will." The guards escorted us back to the entrance of the compound and dismissed us.

I went immediately to the American headquarters and to the camp adjutant to get him to appoint someone else to take charge of my company. I could not take a chance of something happening again that would cause me to be brought before the camp commandant. If that happened, it would mean certain death for me. They had no summary court or court-martial. One was not allowed to plead his case. The adjutant said that, if I were replaced, I would have to pull guard duty or work detail. I told him that I could not take the chance, that I had been warned that one more mistake would not be tolerated. I realized that even though it might not be a mistake on my part the

Japanese would say I was connected with it, and I would be put to death. The adjutant found another officer to take my place.

I was moved to another barracks that was not so crowded. This one was near the entrance of the camp and only officers were in this barracks. I had been in the new barracks about a week when the Japs decided to divide us into groups of ten in what they called "blood brother" squads. If one of the ten in your group escaped, the other nine would be shot before the firing squad. Since I was the ranking captain in this barracks, I got my pick of who I wanted in my group of ten. I chose five chaplains, three married captains, and a lieutenant that I had used as an adjutant. His name was Lieutenant John A. Goodpasture. Every night before I went to sleep and every morning when I awoke, I would check to see if the other nine were there. We made an agreement that, if any of us decided we just had to try to escape, we would tell the others, so they could try to escape too. They were not to tell anyone outside the blood-brother squad.

A lieutenant colonel and a navy lieutenant from another squad tried to escape one night about half-past ten. They were caught trying to get under the barbed-wire fence. They might have pleaded innocent had it not been that they had a pack with them full of extra clothes, etc. They brought them to the brig near our barracks. The Jap guards would throw them against the ground and whip them with ropes until they got up. I could hear them groan when they hit the ground. The next morning they were tied to the gatepost at the entrance of the compound. Every hour or so a guard would come by and hit them across their shins with a board that looked to be a 2″ x 2″. The navy lieutenant had his left eyeball dangling from its socket down on his cheek. Their heads were bloody all over. That afternoon about four o'clock a truck drove up. They were taken down from the post, but still had their hands tied behind them. A rope was placed around their necks and they were tied behind the truck. The lieutenant colonel said, "I demand a fair trial. Uncle Sam will make you pay for this."

The truck started down the road fast enough that they had to trot to keep up. They would fall down and the truck would stop long enough to get them up. In the back of the truck were two grubbing hoes and two spades. They went east to the main road, then turned south around the corner of our compound. The lieutenant colonel fell down again. The Jap officer who was riding in the cab of the truck took his sword out of the case and hit the lieutenant colonel just above the shoulders, cutting off his head. They threw his head and body into the truck and drove on out of sight. In about thirty minutes we heard a shot fired, then in fifteen minutes the truck came back. About three days later we heard dogs fighting where we thought they had buried the two officers.

A few days after this incident, the Japanese came marching along the north side of our camp singing some kind of song. They were marching in line by platoons. Just back of the first platoon there were three Japanese, one on each side of a standard bearer. The standard bearer held a long bamboo pole over his shoulder with a man's head swinging from the end of the pole. The head was tied to the pole by its hair and had been embalmed. After they marched the length of the camp and back, they hung the head on the pole at the corner of our camp fence. This was on the main road leading to the other villages. They put a sign up in English which read, "This is a bad man from the mountains." We found out that this was the head of a mayor of a village some twenty miles away. Guerrillas had been operating in this area, and the Japanese took the mayor's head and burned the village as an example so the Filipinos would not harbor any guerrillas.

14. *Camp Routine*

The Japanese had employed some Filipinos to dig a well in the east part of the camp. They had dug about fifteen feet when a lieutenant came to me and said, "One of the men digging the well wants to see you." I arrived at the well and a man who was emptying a five-gallon bucket of dirt each time it was drawn to the top said, "In the next bucket of dirt will be a note for you." When he drew the next bucket of dirt from the well, he set it on the ground and motioned for me to dig in the top of the bucket for the note. I scratched around in the top of the dirt and found a small piece of paper that was folded four times. The Filipino walked away as if he did not want to have anything to do with it and I put the note in my pocket. I left without looking at him or speaking.

I went back to my barracks and there was no one near my part of the barracks, so I opened the note and read it. It said, "There will be a motor boat with five gallons of gas waiting for you at the mouth of the Pandan River." It was not signed, but I recognized the handwriting to be that of a woman who had done my laundry while I was on Bataan. She was also the schoolteacher who had wanted to marry me for the duration of the war. Back on Bataan I had thought that she just wanted to marry an officer as it would enhance her chances of getting more food, but this note made me believe that she was a loyal friend to me and to the American people. She was taking a big chance of being killed if the note had been intercepted by the Japanese. At first this made me feel good to know that someone would still try to befriend me.

I hated to let this chance go by and had I not been tied to the blood-brother squad, I probably would have tried to make a run for freedom. The mouth of the river emptied into Manila Bay near Orion, which was about 160 miles away. I had been having malarial fever with about three weeks to a month between spells. My throat and mouth were sore from scurvy, and I was so weak I could not run if the enemy had chased me. There were no signs of how long we were going to be POW's and it looked even more as if we were all going to starve to death, be punished to death, or die of some disease. The chance to escape was hard to pass up, because it was so hard just trying to live.

Two days later I was called to the well again. This time the man emptying the dirt took off his large straw hat and dried the sweat from his brow and inside his hat band. Then looking around to see if anyone was watching us, he took a note from the band of his hat and rubbed against me as he bent to pick up the bucket to empty it, putting the note in my hand. He didn't say a word and neither did I.

Again I went back to my barracks to read the note. This note was inquiring about a buck sergeant of mine and his whereabouts. The sergeant had tried to marry a Filipino girl a short time before the war was declared and I had persuaded them to postpone the marriage, at least for a while. The sergeant had been very sick and had been taken to the hospital area. I wrote a note back to her on the margin of her note and told her where the sergeant was. I folded the note the width of a hatband and gave it to the man who had been delivering the notes. He wiped his brow again and quickly put the note under his hatband.

The small amount of food that we had been getting had deteriorated in quality until it was almost impossible to eat. For example, there were so many weevils and worms in the rice that it was half weevils, worms, and rocks. One day at noon, I decided to count the number of weevils and worms in my cup of rice. I counted eighty-two insects in this single cup of rice. I knew if I did not eat insects and all I would have very little rice, so I just put them back in the rice and said to myself, "That's all the protein you will get anyway."

Some men who had been on a bridge-building detail at Lagoona were sent to the Cabanatuan hospital, and they reported that my battalion runner, Private John Dudash, had been shot by a firing squad at Lagoona. One of his group of ten had escaped. He was shot June 12, 1942. Then through our underground telegraph, I was told that my platoon sergeant, Alva M. Rogers, was shot before a firing squad while working on a bridge-building detail at Clumpit. The Clumpit bridge was the highest bridge on the route from Bataan to Manila. It had been destroyed by the American demolition squad when we withdrew into Bataan. On July 14, 1942, Donald Stover, the runner who had been with me all during the defense of Bataan, died at Cabanatuan of beriberi. Actually he had starved to death. News of this kind always hurt, because each of these men had been so faithful and loyal to me. They had been excellent soldiers.

I visited Lieutenant Morton Deeter, my former adjutant. He was staying in a barracks in the east end of the compound. He was about as sick and weak as I have ever seen anyone, to still be alive. He had yellow jaundice and malaria, but he survived. Lieutenant Deeter was my most trusted patrol leader as well as an excellent adjutant.

In July we began to get some quick hard rains. Up to now we had not had a bath since we left Camp O'Donnell. When it rained we would take off our clothes and stand under the eave of the buildings where the water ran off the roof and, in this way, take a nice cool bath.

An epidemic of diptheria broke out in camp. I had had diptheria when I was in high school. Several died before they started to give any vaccine. About 125 died before the epidemic was over.

A group of American civilian prisoners was brought into camp. As we watched them go by on their way to the quarantine area, where they would be kept for two weeks as all new prisoners were, I saw Sergeant Edgar U. Meredith in the group. He had been one of my platoon sergeants back on Bataan. I spoke to him, but he did not recognize me. He sent word to me that night asking me to tell all of the 27th Materiel members not to let on that they knew him. He had gone to the mountains near Baguao when Bataan fell and had been working in a gold mine as a civilian. The Japs had not connected him with the military. In as much as it meant a death penalty for all military men not to surrender by a certain date, he needed to keep his civilian status. He later told me that the going on the outside was so rough that he had to surrender. He said the Japs had made the Filipinos afraid to harbor an American. He had a large plug of Tinsley chewing tobacco that he started to throw away. It had been wet and had molded. I told him I could use it if he did not want it. He gave it to me.

My dry beriberi was causing me lots of pain. I had never chewed tobacco before, but I started taking little pinches of this and found that it stopped the pain for several hours. My barracks adjutant, Lieutenant John Goodpasture, had beriberi so badly that I had to bring his food to him. He walked like a chicken with frozen feet. I gave him some of this tobacco every evening before bedtime. It relieved his pain also. Since we found that this was an important medicine, we tried to be economical with it. I had four or five officers who came to my barracks each evening for just a pinch of tobacco. When it became scarce, they would almost cry for me to give them just a tiny pinch of the tobacco. I quit using it myself and gave it away a pinch at a time to those who had beriberi much worse than I had it.

I never did get to tell Sergeant Meredith how valuable his plug of tobacco was. Even now, thirty-two years later, smoking or chewing tobacco once a day prevents those lightning-like sharp pains from hurting my feet at night.

The improvised latrines consisted of a large pit covered with boards, with two or three seats on top. The prisoners passed so much blood that the flies and maggots were numerous. There were so many maggots that they would undermine the walls of the pit until the wood platforms would fall in when the walls gave way.

I heard of only two men who took their own lives. This was soon after they issued one razor blade per month. They cut the veins in their arms.

August 20, my birthday, I was given a pair of shorts by one of my captains in my blood-brother group. This captain was from Fort Drum, near Corregidor, and was a West Point graduate in artillery. This was like giving someone a suit in normal life and I appreciated this gift very much.

15. *To Japan*

November 2, 1942, about fifteen hundred of us were checked by a Japanese doctor, who was an eye, ear, nose, and throat specialist. He said I had a fungus growth in my ears. Then on November 4, 1942, the same fifteen hundred were told to wear our best clothes to the ball park. I did not have a choice to make because what I had on was all the clothes I had. When we got to the ball park we were stripped of all our clothes and given a blue-denim jumper and trousers. Then we were told that we were going to be taken to Japan on November 6. When I returned to my barracks, I began to take the Filipino pesos out of their hiding places. At this time I had 220 pesos and I knew they would not be worth anything in Japan. I went to a Japanese sergeant to see if he would trade me yen for pesos. The actual value when the war started was two yen for one peso, but the best trade I could get was to trade even. We had been able to buy some fruit on the black market here at Cabanatuan and some canned food and some coconut brittle candy at Camp O'Donnell. It was against the rules to buy anything on the black market, so the prices were very high when we had a chance to buy anything.

There were some prisoners who wanted to trade places with me to go to Japan. I thought surely we would get better treatment and more food if we were in the Japanese homeland. I did not believe that the Japanese people would sanction the kind of treatment we were being subjected to if they knew about it. Early the morning of the sixth, I went down to Colonel Maverick's barracks to tell him good-bye and I gave him twenty yen as he had no money at this time. He expressed his appreciation to me for being his most trusted officer and said that had been the reason he had used me for all the counterattacks as well as putting me in charge of the Air Corps Regiment the last two days of fighting on Bataan. He wished that he had been selected to go to Japan, but he thought they would soon move all prisoners to Japan. (Colonel Maverick was put on a ship in late 1944 to be taken to Japan. It was sunk by our bombers. He survived the sinking of the ship, but took pneumonia and died. He was buried on the island of Taiwan, in a mass grave, with 480 other Americans.)

The morning of November 6, 1942, we were shipped by rail in boxcars from Cabanatuan to Manila. They marched us through the main streets of Manila from the railway depot to the pier. While we were making this march of about one mile, a Filipino band was playing. The Japanese were trying to show us off, but after we had marched a short distance, the band started playing "God Bless America" and at first everyone yelled; then there was silence. Tears were streaming down our faces. It was gratifying to know that the Filipino people were still loyal to us. The band leader could have been executed for this, if the Japanese had known what he was playing.

When we arrived at Pier 7, we were loaded onto a ship called *Nagato Marue*. This ship had been sold to Japan in 1935 by the United States as junk. There were three compartments on this ship and five hundred men were put into each one. The three compartments took up most of the bottom of the ship. When we entered the hatch, or head of the stairway going into this hold, the heat was unbearable. It was stuffy and very hard to breathe. When I got to the floor of this compartment I could tell that horses had been shipped in it. The smell of urine and horse dung was still very strong. They had built bays about four feet off the deck so prisoners could get in them sitting up. There was not room for all to lie down at the same time. We had to take turns to be able to lie down to sleep. All life belts were taken away and there were four life boats for fifteen hundred Japanese crewmen and fifteen hundred prisoners.

We left the dock about ten o'clock the morning of November 7. There were twelve ships in the convoy with one destroyer escort. When we passed Corregidor, a Japanese orderly threw out a waste paper container that had a wreath of flowers and an American flag in it. When I saw that American flag in the water, I could have cried. On the top deck the Japs had a small monkey tied on a leash. This

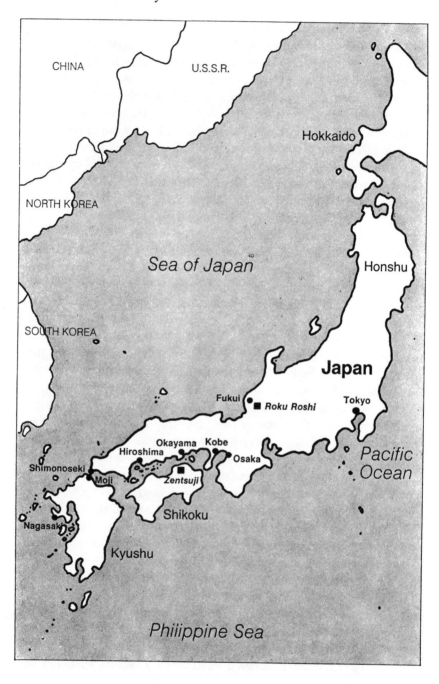

little monkey was already seasick and trying to vomit. You could tell he was sick by looking at the color around his eyes and mouth.

At ten o'clock the morning of the eighth a detail was sent for our breakfast of rice and soybean soup, a small amount for each prisoner. At three o'clock in the afternoon we were fed rice and fish. We received a small serving three times a day. We would get the leftovers from the Japanese soldiers' meals. Six men were allowed on deck at the same time to smoke, if they had anything to smoke. Sometimes a Jap guard would give us a cigarette. There were three urinals for each five hundred men in the hold and five hundred Jap crewmen. The Japanese were to be first. There was no bathing or washing.

By November 9 there were many seasick and there were no places to vomit. The sour smell was putrid. The Japs were allowing about sixty men out of each compartment on deck at this time. They put an air funnel down into the hold, which helped some. We had been organized into twelve-man squads. Major Martin from Montgomery, Alabama, was my squad leader and I was second in command. These organizations were to be used for such details as feeding, emptying the "honey bucket," etc. Everyone who felt like climbing the stairs wanted to go on details just to get some fresh air. Tropical ulcers and prickly heat soon appeared. It was easy to get an infection from the dirty, sweaty clothes.

One evening while I was taking the empty rice buckets back to the galley, which was on the top deck, I heard a loud noise like an explosion. The Japs tried to hurry us back to our hold. I saw the destroyer speed up and begin circling the convoy. When I returned to the hold, they were taking the air funnel out. They battened down the area overhead with a canvas cover. The guards said it was a submarine. We could hear the destroyer dropping depth charges. Since we were below the water line we could hear the depth charges exploding. Our ship did not have any markings on it to show that it was a POW ship. According to international law it should have been marked. It was about two hours before they took the canvas cover off and put the air funnel back into the hold.

The guards sat on a gunny sack at the head of the stairway coming out of our compartment. One day when the sun was shining just right on the gunny sack and the guard was not sitting there, I could see crabs crawling around on the sack. We got body lice and crabs from the soldiers on this ship. November 10 we anchored at Tykow, Taiwan. There were about two hundred freighters in this port. There was no blackout here. The harbors were lighted for night work. On the twelfth there were five more ships that came into this harbor. On one of these ships there were some English and Australian prisoners. They were wearing those broad-brimmed military hats. At night there were a lot of anti-aircraft search lights on, but most of the time they were just practicing with the search lights.

On the fifteenth everyone was sent below deck and the ship moved out of this harbor about eight o'clock in the morning. Several of the men in our hold died and were buried at sea. Weights were put on their bodies so our submarines could not trace the convoy. On the sixteenth we anchored by an island that had an airfield on it. I think the name of the island was Hoko. The twentieth we anchored at a quarantine station at about eight o'clock in the morning. The twenty-fifth we went into Moji, Japan. There were a large number of our men too weak to climb the steps to get out of the hold of the ship. We just had on the blue-denim jumpers and trousers we had been given and we were wet with perspiration. As we came off the ship, we were what they called deloused, by their spraying us until we were wet. They had frost that morning and a cold breeze was blowing off the water. I don't believe I have ever felt so cold in all of my life, just coming from the tropics and with no extra clothes. They counted us off into groups of four hundred, and each group was sent to a different camp. We were lined up on the pier so they could inspect our personal belongings. Some had several packs of Adobe cigarettes and would have to pay import duty on all over two packs. Those who had more than two packs would pass them to others around them before the inspecting officer came by, and after he passed, the owner would take the cigarettes back.

We were hauled out into an open lot and given a small box of food that had been donated by some welfare organizations. The box contained a small cup of rice in the center of a small wooden box. In each corner were some pickled *daikons* (radishes), cheese, a small raw fish about the size of a minnow, a slice of orange, and a roll of kelp seaweed. This was a morale builder. It looked as if we were going to be fed well during our stay in Japan. There were many who did not get the boxes because they did not give us time for everyone to be served before they started moving us out.

16. *Work Camp in Japan*

We were ferried out across the bay to Shimonoseki. Then we marched one kilometer to an underground railroad station. Signs on either side of the ramp going down to the station said "Bomb shelter." Several of our men were too weak to make the trip from the boat to the train and were picked up by the Japanese. We were put aboard a train and allowed to ride in chair cars. Before, it had been in boxcars. There was no heat in the coaches and our teeth chattered all night. I was too cold to sleep. After riding all night and part of the next day, we arrived at Osaka at half-past two in the afternoon. Then we took an interurban to a small station on the outskirts of Osaka. We marched about three kilometers to the Yodogawa steel mill. We were issued one rice bowl, one soup bowl, one fork, one spoon, and a pair of chopsticks. We were given five very light-weight cotton blankets, and one pillow stuffed with rice husks. We were put on half rations until work started. We slept on the ground with a straw mat for a bed.

On November 28, Thanksgiving Day, there was a frost on the ground and we were issued a coat and a pair of pants made of something resembling closely knit gunny-sack material. Most of the men had bad colds and were sick. The body lice and crabs began to become numerous and there was no heat in the open building. Two days later they put one stove in the building to serve four hundred men.

The name of this camp was Yodogawa Bunshaw, which was a steel mill. They made fifty-gallon drums, motor blocks, ten- and twenty-gauge sheet iron out of fifty-foot-long slabs of steel one-half inch thick and eight inches wide. These slabs of steel were shipped to the factory on canal barges. The factory had large overhead cranes. It was in operation day and night. The furnaces were heated with powdered coal, which was blown into the furnace with an electric fan to make it burn. The air around the factory was always polluted with heavy smoke. It was hard to keep our clothes and bodies clean; then there was always the noise of the factory.

I was given POW number 374. I used this number all the time I was in this camp. My name, Captain Coleman, was written in Japanese.

The first day we went out to work, each man was assigned to a crew. My first job was loading coal cinders on a car mounted on steel rails. We used a scoop to load the cinders into the car; then we had to push it about one hundred yards and dump it into an old slough that had water in it. Four of us worked with one car. I worked on this detail about three days, then I was put in charge of a detail of 140 men inside the factory. This detail had various jobs; some handled with tongs the white-hot slabs of steel that were rolled out to make the ten- and twenty-gauge sheet iron; some cut the sheet iron into strips four feet by nine feet on steel cutters; one man oiled the large motor in the center of the factory; others picked up scrap metal that the steel cutters trimmed off to make the sheet-iron strips. My duty was to make a report twice a day on how many men were working on my detail and what they were doing. This was done in Japanese on a particular form, and I was the only American allowed in the office to fill out this report.

December 3, Second Lieutenant Francis Gurney Smith died. He was the first casualty from this group of four hundred. He died of malnutrition, beriberi, and pneumonia.

We were moved to a new place that the Japanese had prepared especially for prisoners. It was farther away from the factory, but the noise of the machinery could still be heard. Our sleeping quarters were about fifteen feet up over part of the factory storage area. The rest room was on the ground floor. There was only one entrance into our quarters and that was through the guard room, then up some stairs to the sleeping quarters. There were two bays, the first was about two feet off the floor; then four feet above it there was another bay. Each bay held from twenty-eight to eighty men. We had to climb a ladder to get to the upper bay. We had to take off our shoes when we came through the guard room before going up to our quarters. We worked eight hours a day, seven days a week. There were straw mats on the bays where we slept.

On a Saturday, sometime in January, after we came in from work, they told us to take off all our clothes and just to put on overcoats, that we were going to be allowed to take a bath. It was freezing cold. We were allowed to unlock a back door and went down steps to an opening near the main office building. We went into an area that had a board fence around it, but no top. There were two tanks about twelve feet long, ten feet wide, and three feet deep. They were filled with very hot water. They told us to take a small bucket of water and pour it over ourselves until we were wet enough to soap ourselves well, then pour water over ourselves to wash off the soap. After this we could get in the water and stay about fifteen minutes. While I was in the water, I looked up at the windows of the three-story office building next to us, and the women secretaries were sitting in the windows watching us take our baths. It was embarrassing at first. When we got out of the water our bodies were pink from the hot water. This really was a treat. We were allowed to take a bath every Saturday afternoon. They were the first we had had in three months and we really did enjoy them.

One evening we were asked to answer some questions that they had passed out on sheets of paper. One of the questions was, "Which did you fear the most on the battle field, bombs that were dropped by our planes or artillery shells?" Most of us answered that we feared the bombs most; but actually we feared the shellings most, because we could not see the shells before they hit, and the bombers could be seen, and this gave us a chance to get to cover from the bombs. Another question was, "Are you related to the President or any Senator or Representative in the United States?"

Two days later a guard told me that I looked like President Coolidge, and just to be talking, I said he was my uncle. The guard said, "Why didn't you say so on your paper?"

I said, "He is not President now." I found out later that the guard entered this on my record.

He said, "The Japanese liked President Coolidge."

A Japanese came to me several times and questioned me about our military organizations. He would be eating peanuts or tangerines and offer me some to eat. He asked me how many armored divisions the United States had and I would tell him that I did not know. Then he would say, "About how many would you guess they have?" I would answer that I had no idea. He did not work in the factory and I knew he was sent to get military information. I could tell by the wording of his questions that he was a military man and probably was a military intelligence agent.

The men on my detail who handled the hot steel with tongs used gloves or mittens. A pair of these mittens would last about two days. I would have to take the worn-out mittens to the supply department and exchange them for new ones. There would be an armload to exchange every other day. A girl about sixteen or seventeen years old waited on me in the supply department. I could say only a few words in Japanese and the only English word she knew was, "OK." Her parents worked at the same counter. They were Protestant in their religious belief. This little Japanese girl was very sympathetic toward me. When she would give me a stack of men's gloves in exchange for the old ones, she would point to a certain glove in the stack. I would take them and go behind some stacks of steel and look at that particular glove. Each time she would have a needle, safety pin, or pinon nuts. The first needle she gave me I took back to camp, and the men used it night and day to patch their clothes. I found part of a nylon rip cord from a parachute that we used for thread. We unraveled the rip cord. The safety pins came in handy in many ways. I would thank her by saying "*Arigatai.*"

I soon learned Japanese well enough that they could understand what I was talking about and I could understand them most of the time. One day I asked one of the Japanese men, "Where are the rest rooms?" He pointed to a building just outside the door. I went out there and two women were coming out of the building that he had directed me to. I thought the man was trying to get me in trouble, so I went back and watched until I saw some men going into the building. I had to go, so I went inside. There were about ten individual stalls on the side of a hallway and a long cement urinal at floor level on the other side. I opened one of the stall doors and a woman was squatted over a hole in the floor, facing me. I closed the door and said, "Pardon me," and she said, "*Hai*" which meant "Yes." She did not seem the least bit flustered. She probably did not know what I had said in English. From then on I was a little more careful when I opened a rest-room door because I found out that the men and women all went to the same rest room.

There was a kitchen in the southeast part of the factory in a separate building. They brought out some burned rice in a woven bamboo basket to see if the prisoners would eat it. They gave each man a handful; we ate it and liked it. They brought it out every day for a week. The prisoners ate it so well that the Japs started eating it and we no longer got it. They issued us some dried grasshoppers in a cellophane bag. They had been dipped in soy sauce. They were brittle like crackers, but the hind legs never got soft enough to keep from scratching your throat when you swallowed them.

Most of the Japanese employees were nice to us. There were eight Japanese women who worked in the same area that my group of prisoners were working in. Some of our prisoners would get into the kitchen garbage barrels. They would get fish heads, cabbage stems, etc. The Japanese women would come to me, patting themselves on the rear and say, "*byōki,*" which meant "sick" and then they would point at the prisoners. Sometimes they would tell me in Japanese that the garbage would give the men diarrhea. I told them that these men were starving to death and had rather die with a full stomach than an empty one.

I took a malarial chill one morning while working at the factory. I asked one of the foremen if I could go back to the camp. He could see that I was shaking all over and I told him it was a malarial chill. He asked, "Do they give you any quinine in camp?"

I said, "No. The guards say they do not have any quinine."

He said, "Tomorrow I bring you some. I will have it tied up in a red hankerchief with my lunch pail. I will leave it in the bottom right-hand drawer of the desk in the office where I work. If you get caught getting it, you will be stealing it from me and I will not admit favoring a prisoner."

I went back to camp, which was about one hundred yards from the main factory, without being escorted. I was still sick the next day, but I didn't want to miss the chance of getting the quinine. The problem now was deciding how I was going to get it back into camp. We were searched every day at noon and every night when we came back to camp. I had a metal safety-match box about the size of my middle finger. I got a strip of adhesive tape from the corpsman, Mr. Oburn. I had noticed that when they searched us they felt under our arm pits, but never out over the ends of our elbows.

I found the quinine where the Japanese foreman had said he would leave it. It was in a small round paper tube. I quickly took it from the desk drawer and went to the rest room. I packed the powdered quinine into the metal match box and with the adhesive tape stuck it under my arm near the elbow. I talked to the Jap foreman who had brought it to me and asked him about how much that amount would cost. He said, "I gave this to you, but if you want more, that same amount will cost 20 sen." He would bring me all I would leave the money for. I ordered more of the same quantity because it was just the right amount to fill the match box. The Japanese army began to pay us according to the international law. Prisoners were paid according to their rank, in the Japanese army. A captain received 220 yen per month. They gave me 60 yen and put the rest in what they called a savings account, without my permission. I paid them back 30 yen for food. If I received a pair of socks or a G-string, I would pay them the cost of the item. I took up a collection in camp among the officers and bought about 2,000 yen's worth of quinine over a six months' period.

When the Japs began to pay us according to our rank, they took us out in the yard and had us take off all of our clothes and take everything out of our pockets and place it on top of our clothes in front of us. They checked through all of our clothes and made a record of how much money each of us had. This was to cut down our buying on the black market, which was against the rules. I had 180 yen that I had brought from the Philippines. The first sergeant announced that "Tai Coleman is the richest man in camp." They gave us some small notebooks and we were to keep a record of what we spent our money for. They thought this was a sure way to keep us from buying black-market items.

17. *Misery Continued*

Our prisoners would buy anything they could eat. Sometimes they could buy dried squid, peanuts, canned milk, canned peaches, etc. One of my men was caught bringing a bottle of catsup into camp and they punished me for letting him bring black-market food into camp. They slapped me in front of the men they were searching. They told me to search every man on my detail before leaving the factory. I told them that these men were desperately hungry and I was not going to interfere if they could find some food. The guards said that my detail brought in more black-market food than all the other details. I think this was mostly due to the fact that they worked where it was possible to get the food.

One of Lieutenant Haupman's Japanese friends whom he worked with brought him a raw beef steak. To cook it, he put it in his mess kit and covered it with the sand where they were heat-treating some steel sheet iron. I noticed a Jap foreman holding his nose in the air as if he smelled something unusual. They located where the odor was coming from and waited until the owner came to get it. Lieutenant Haupman was caught and beaten unmercifully. He was unconscious and both eyes were swollen closed. He completely lost the sight in one eye and partially in the other. Vitamin deficiency had something to do with it also. After about two weeks of recuperation, he came back to work. The same Jap that had befriended him before gave him some cans of condensed milk. He smuggled these into camp by taping them to his scrotum. Lieutenant Haupman did not tell the Japanese who gave him the beef steak.

When I brought the quinine into camp, I gave it to Dr. Richards, who was the only American doctor in our camp. He would give the medicine to those who were the sickest with malaria. I took a fourteen-day course of quinine and it held my malaria off for two months. Most of those who took the fourteen-day treatment quit having malaria. Then the Japanese doctors would say, "We knew you would quit having malaria after you became acclimated." They did not know, of course, that we had been getting quinine into camp.

We received some Red Cross packages in camp that were packed by the British in Africa. They had cigarettes, chocolate bars, cubes of sugar, and rice pudding in cans. The Japanese thought they would use it to reward the hardest workers, thereby getting more work out of the prisoners. We had a work inspection by some district officers and doctors. The inspecting officers had us line up and hold out our hands with the palms up. They would go along in front of each person and feel the palms of his hands to see if there were any corns or rough places on them. When they felt my hands, they hit the palms of my hands with a wooden paddle as hard as they could. It came as a shock to me because I had not noticed they had a paddle. They held it behind them until they were ready to use it. They did not know that I was the foreman of a large work crew and did office work. When they awarded the prizes for the hardest workers, from the Red Cross boxes, some would get three or four cans of food. I only got five lumps of sugar. When we got back to the barracks, this was all collected and reissued equally, without the Japanese knowing anything about it. The Japs kept the cigarettes and chocolate bars for themselves. Once in a while the guards would give us an American cigarette.

Since we had to leave our shoes down in the guard room when we went to our quarters upstairs, it was easy to get our shoes mixed up. Several decided to mark their shoes by cutting their initials in the leather. Captain George Maxfield asked me to cut his initials on the inside of his shoe top. I cut G. M. up near the top. When we went to work the next morning, the Japanese sergeant announced, "No prisoners shall mark their shoes." They noticed the marking of Captain Maxfield's shoes and punished him for doing it. That evening we were ordered out into the prison compound and stripped naked and made to kneel down on the cinder-covered yard. We were not allowed to move from this position. The temperature was about 40 degrees. They said someone had sold a pair of leather shoes to a Japanese and the one who sold the shoes must confess or we would have to spend the night out in the cold. They took all of the money out of each person's pockets. They did not find any evidence there. Then they brought out the Jap who had bought the shoes to identify the one who had sold them to him. He said he could not identify any of us. They beat him again in front of us.

We had been kneeling in this position about one and one-half hours when the Japanese decided to bring all of the sick and bed-ridden men out and put them in the same position that we were in. A bed-ridden navy Chief Bird confessed to selling the shoes to the Jap, so the rest of us would not suffer any longer. He said he sold them for 150 yen. His closest friend said that the chief still had his shoes and confessed just to stop the Japs from punishing the men. They made him kneel in a balanced position on a wooden saw horse. He could not keep his balance on the 2 x 4 saw horse without help. He was in such poor shape that every vertebra in his back stood out as he bent over. They took a stick and beat him across the back until blood ran off his back. Our men carried the chief back into his barracks and put him in his bunk. Before we were allowed to stand up, the guards would hit anyone who moved across the back with a big stick. When they dismissed us, we had stayed in the kneeling position on the cin-

Captain John S. Coleman, before he embarked for the Philippines in 1941.

Men of an anti-tank company shown holding their position on Bataan, 1942. *U.S. Army*.

General King surrenders Bataan, April 9, 1942, at Cabcaben, P.I. *Left to right*: Colonel Everett C. Williams, Major General Edward P. King, Jr., Major Wade Cothran. *U.S. Army*.

Japanese escorting a U.S. surrender party, Bataan, April, 1942. *U.S. Army.*

POWs with their hands tied behind them just before starting the death march out of Bataan to Camp O'Donnell, April, 1942. *Defense Dept.*

Prisoners guarded by Japanese troops with fixed bayonets on the death march out of Bataan to O'Donnell, April, 1942. *Defense Dept.*

Japanese troops with captured Americans march along a jungle road on Bataan to a collecting station before the death march, April, 1942. *U.S. Army*.

Japanese guard prisoners sorting out equipment captured at Mariveles, P.I., April, 1942. *U.S. Army*.

A large number of American soldiers just before the death march from Bataan to Camp O'Donnell, April, 1942. *Defense Dept.*

Starting out of Bataan on the death march. *National Archives.*

POW detail being guarded and worked by Japanese. *National Archives.*

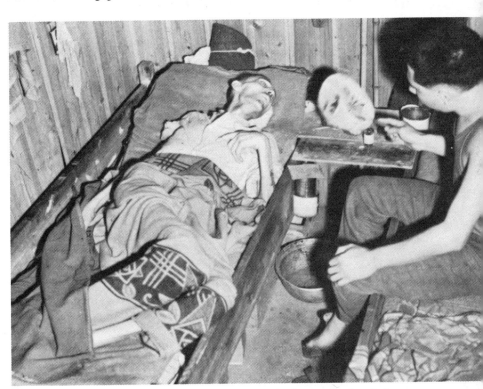

Attending a sick buddy in a sick bay somewhere in Japan. *National Archives.*

Graves of Americans found by American soldiers near Camp O'Donnell after the liberation of the Philippines, 1945. *National Archives.*

A burial detail at Camp O'Donnell, P.I. *National Archives.*

A view of Camp Roku Roshi, Japan, September 8, 1945. *U.S. Army.*

At a POW camp in Japan the day prisoners were liberated, September, 1945. *National Archives.*

A group picture the day Coleman and his fellow Americans were liberated, September 8, 1945. Coleman is fifth from the right, wearing a cap.

Eating rations that were dropped to the POWs September 2, 1945, at Roku Roshi, Japan.

On September 8, 1945, just after liberation, former prisoners wait for a train at Fukui to take them to Yokohama to be shipped to the United States. Coleman is being served by a Japanese Red Cross woman; across the table facing the camera is Lieutenant Morton Deeter.

ders so long they had cut through the skin on our knees. It took us a long time to be able to straighten out our legs, they were so stiff and it was hard to get to a standing position again.

The next morning after this incident, the Japanese ordered us to turn in all of our leather shoes. They said the prisoners could not wear better shoes than the Japanese tax payers. They issued us some canvas and rubber shoes. Very few of them fit. One prisoner who had a small foot got a pair of number tens. He doubled the toes back over his instep and tied them so he could walk easier. The Japs saw this and beat him for making fun of their shoes. Later we saw some of the guards walking around in our leather shoes.

Several of us had one wool blanket. We heard that they were going to require us to turn them in, so we tore them in strips about three feet wide and wore them around our bodies under our clothes. It was about zero temperature and we had no fire to keep warm and very few clothes. I gave two strips to friends. When the guards came around to take up the blankets, everyone was wearing them under their clothes. They never did know what happened to the blankets.

One morning when one of the steel cutters was broken and they were repairing it, all those who worked when it was in operation were just standing around or sitting on the ground waiting for it to be fixed. There was a wooden box near by and I asked one of the women, in Japanese, "Would you please have a seat?" I pointed to the wooden box.

She said, in English, "Did you say, would I please have a seat?"

I was very surprised that she could speak English. I told her, "You speak English very well."

She said, "I used to be an English instructor in the University of Tokyo, but when the war started, English became very unpopular and I had to look for another job."

My hair stood on ends! We had been talking around these women not knowing that any of them understood what we were saying. I went around to the American prisoners who worked with her, and told them not to say anything around her that she should not know because she could speak English better than we could. I was sorry and embarrassed for some of the things we had said in her presence.

The next day I had to go back to the area where she worked. She was counting sheets of steel in each stack that we had run through the cutter. There was not anyone near her, so I apologized for what we had said around her. I told her that we did not know that she could understand English. She was very nice and put me at ease by saying, "You did not say anything that Japanese men do not say." I pretended to be helping her count the sheets of steel. She was telling me about the war news, especially what the newspapers were reporting. This was the first time we had heard from the outside world since we left the Philippines.

When we got back to camp that night, I called nine leaders together and told them what I had found out. They went back to their details and told as many as they could. We could not have a meeting of more than ten at a time. I told Major Reardon and other officers. Each day I would talk to this lady and at night there were many wanting to know what was happening. The Japanese had had some naval problems in the South Pacific that their people were worried about. The Russians were making some progress against the Germans. She told me that she did not believe all the papers and she believed it to be far worse for them than the papers were reporting. She did believe everything in the "Emperor's Column." The Emperor did not commit himself to anything questionable about the naval or aerial victories.

One morning before I went to work, the Japanese First Sergeant Hirose asked me to tell those on my detail that a woman who worked with our detail had been raped, and he wanted the one who did it to raise his hand. He told me that the woman had been caught in the rest room at the factory. She was raped from behind. I asked him, "How did she know it was an American?"

He said, "Because he used some English word and shoved her down and closed the door, so she did not see him."

I told my detail as they stood in line waiting to go to work that I was going to ask them a question about who raped a Japanese woman, but for them not to acknowledge it, even if they were guilty. We knew what the punishment would be in our country.

The sergeant could not understand English. He told me to "ask them now." I made the question loud and plain as if I expected an answer. Of course, no one held up his hand. The sergeant stood on his tiptoes and looked through the ranks, waited about two minutes, and said, "Ask them again." I repeated the question and again no one responded.

When we got back in the factory to work, I told the woman who understood English about the sergeant and what he had asked me to do. She told me the Japanese woman was lying. She said the day before she had wet in her pants before she could get to the rest room. When she came back with wet clothes, the women on the detail teased her about it and she got mad, went into the office, and told them that she had been raped.

The next morning the sergeant asked me to question my men again about who raped the woman. I asked them again as I had the morning before and again no one responded. The sergeant did not seem angry or disturbed about it. I told him that these men were so starved and weak that they did not have the strength or desire to rape a woman even if she asked them to. That night a couple of my sergeants jokingly said to me that I should go ahead and admit to raping the woman, that they knew I had done it. We never heard anymore about it from anyone.

Every day or two some of our men would die due to pneumonia, beriberi, or dysentery which were all caused by starvation. We would have to sit up with the body to prevent the rats from eating it. One night while I was asleep, a big rat nibbled at my cheek. I slapped the rat from my face and it hit the wall and fell to the floor addled. I got up and went down the ladder from my upper bay to the floor. A prisoner had picked the rat up, torn its insides out, skinned it, and eaten it raw. He said, "Damn, I'm hungry."

All of the men who died in this camp were put into wooden boxes that were always too small. They would be doubled up and stuffed into the box. They would take the body to be cremated. They took the bodies to the crematory on a hand-drawn cart. If we were in from work, we would form two lines and they would bring the bodies between the lines while we held a salute in respect for our dead comrades. Most of the time the Jap guards would grin at us to show their disrespect. They brought back the ashes to our camp in a white urn about one foot square.

When we first came to Yodogawa camp the Japanese would take those who had beriberi very badly or had had their feet frozen to the hospital in Osaka. In the hospital they would amputate a foot or maybe both feet. We would never hear of these men again and they would never come back from the hospital, so our men began to refuse to go to the hospital. When their feet would swell up and gangrene would set in, they could not sleep for two days; then the flesh would start sloughing off the bone. Bloody water would start seeping from the decayed flesh; then they would become easy and could sleep all night and all day, they were so completely exhausted from so much pain.

These men with half a foot gone would get one piece of gauze to dress their foot. The gauze would soak up all the bloody water in one night. Sometimes the gauze would come off at night, and fuzz from those old grey cotton blankets would hang on the protruding bones and live flesh. The well prisoners would take time to wash the gauze and dress their feet every morning. After the open wound healed, they would have the patient put his foot on a chair with the bleached bones exposed and they would trim the bones back even with the good flesh. They did this with bone nippers. The bones would be bleached out after the fever left them. From the best that I can remember, there were twenty-nine men lying in the bunks at one time, with half of one foot gone. I was never sure if it was caused by beriberi or if their feet had frozen. We did not have heat in the building except twice, and the weather was zero degrees.

In February 1943, about nine o'clock one morning as I was checking to see where each man was working, I went by the number-two steel cutter. A man was holding a sheet of steel getting it cut into a nine-by-four-feet piece and he asked me, "What is wrong with the prisoner who has been picking up the trimmings from the back of my machine?"

I told him, "*Ashi tokson byōki*," or "His foot is very sick." He told me to have the man let him see it. The flesh on this man's little toe had come off in his shoe the day before, leaving the bone dangling and held together only by the cartilage. After sitting down, the young soldier started to take off his shoe.

I went down the aisle between the stacks of steel. In a few minutes I heard this prisoner screaming as if he was in terrific pain. I ran back. This big fat Jap was holding the prisoner's foot and kicking his sore toe. The prisoner was lying on his back, trying to pull away from him. My blood just boiled. I grabbed the Jap by his chin and the back of his head and gave him a quick jerk with all the strength I had. His neck popped, but he twisted around out of my grasp. He picked up a half-mooned-shaped piece of steel about one and one-half feet long and came after me. The foreman stopped him before he hit me. He told the foreman, "I'm going to have him [me] arrested and have him put in jail in Osaka."

I assumed he would have this done and my case would be tried in a civilian court. He went for the factory police. The policeman could speak English and he said to me, "You are under arrest, come with me." I told him that the Japanese military were supposed to punish us if we needed punishing and that the civilians were just to work us. I asked him to call my Jap Sergeant Hirose, who was in charge of our prison camp.

The police and the contending Jap talked for a few minutes, then took me into the office where I did my book work. They called Sergeant Hirose at the prison camp office. He told them he would come after me. After they hung up the phone, the police and the Jap talked again for a minute and the Jap went into another office just outside the factory building.

He came back with a cord that looked like a sash cord from a window shade. He measured it around my head and tied several overhand knots in it. I thought at first that he was going to whip me with it, but he put it around my head just above the eyebrows and tied it in the back. Then he took a small stick and started to twist it. He twisted it so tight that every knot seemed to break through my skull. The circulation of blood seemed to be cut off from my head. The pain was so excruciating that I fainted.

When I regained consciousness Sergeant Hirose had just arrived. He told them that the military, not the civilians, were supposed to punish the prisoners. I could understand only part of what he said. The sergeant was standing over me, and the policeman and the Jap were standing about two paces in front of me.

The Jap twisted his neck and said, "But he tried to break my neck."

I said, "*Nai, nai*, I was pulling you off the prisoner's sore foot." Really, if it had been in my power, I would have broken the Jap's neck. All of the prisoners were sick and weak and did not deserve such treatment.

Sergeant Hirose said, "I will take him back to camp, and if he needs punishing, I will punish him." He walked along beside me for a few minutes, then as we neared the camp he walked in front of me. He was very pleasant and jovial. He said, "They think they can punish prisoners, but they can't do that." He seemed as proud of me as a little boy would be over a little red wagon at Christmas time. We did not discuss this problem again.

It was about half-past eleven when we got back to camp. The sergeant brought me a big bowl of rice, which was the most I ever received in any prison camp. He kept me in from work one and a half days. This was my punishment. This was the first time I had realized there was friction between the civilian and military departments. Some of our prisoners told me the civilians were mad at the military because the civilian food was rationed and the military could get all of the food they wanted.

My head was sore and swollen where they had bruised it. When I went back to work, they had signs up in the factory, in Japanese, stating that the civilians were not to punish the prisoners. It was to be left to the military. The Jap that I had the trouble with never spoke to me again.

Sometime later the number-one steel cutter's motor went out, and this same Jap was trying to fix it. He had on large gloves. There were several cogs that had to mesh just right to get the right speed. When they were turned to a certain point, the weight of the knife on the cutter would automatically roll them down into position. I told the Jap that he was about to get caught in those cogs with the gloves on, but he acted as if I had insulted his intelligence.

He said, "I have done this work before." A minute had not elapsed when the weight of the cutter blade started to roll to the down position. His glove was caught, pulling his hand into the meshed cogs. They called two other Japs to get his hand out. All the time he was grimacing in pain. In about two weeks he came back to the factory just visiting, and he had his left hand in a sling, wrapped in gauze. The Jap foreman told me the cogs had crushed a bone in each of his four fingers.

The Japanese military asked us to write a short thesis on what we thought about the safety devices in the factory. I wrote in my thesis that the factory did not protect the workmen. The drainage troughs were about four inches wide and twelve inches deep, running the length of the factory at floor level. Some places had covers and others did not. Workmen could step in the uncovered part and sprain or break an ankle. They also did not furnish prisoners with eye goggles to protect them while handling the white-hot iron when they reached into the furnace to take it out. I told them that, in the United States, one factory could produce as much finished metal in one week as this factory could produce in one year, and that it would take fewer workmen to do it.

The main aim of the Japanese at all times was to show on the records a maximum number of men at work. As a result the decisions of our Dr. Richards were constantly overruled or ignored and men went to work who were hardly able to walk. In a few cases we rolled them out to the factory in wheelbarrows. These men could not stand up for very long at a time, so they were allowed to sit and chip mortar off the bricks. The men did their best to go to work, because their rations were cut in half if they did not work. A human could not live on the meager half rations. For this reason, diseases and ailments not normally considered serious were aggravated to such an extent that they became fatal.

No attempt was made to protect the men from occupational hazards. As a result, injuries occurred daily. Such was the case of the men who worked on the sand-blasting detail. Goggles or masks were not furnished and casualties in this department were very heavy. Many cases of lung trouble occurred. Lieutenant Todd, my bunk mate, was on this detail. He contracted pneumonia and almost died. He had arranged for a Japanese workman to bring him some canned peaches before he became sick. When he could not go to work the next day, I contacted the Jap and he let me have a pint jar of peaches. I would take one-half of a peach to Lieutenant Todd, in the sick bay, twice a day. He was so sick he could not eat his rice. I traded it off to another prisoner and he was to pay it back in half a ration at a time when Lieutenant Todd was well enough to eat. The detail assigned to make the fifty-gallon drums were susceptible to pneumonia, since they were never given enough clothes to go outside to stack the drums. They worked on the inside where it was very hot, then had to go outside to stack the drums and it was very cold. This sudden change in temperature caused them to catch cold and it would go into pneumonia. The Japs made mass punishment a practice. The smallest infraction of the rules caused severe physical violence to the individual who broke the rule and to all on his detail and sometimes to the whole camp.

Our men kept having outbreaks of dysentery, as well as beriberi and edema. One night I was passing by a bay that was supposed to be a well bay. One man was standing on his head with his toes touching the floor of the bay. About three inches of his colon were protruding from his anus. He was rubbing his stomach trying to get his colon back into his body. The colon did not look swelled or irritated. He finally did get it back inside. He said his stomach would cramp and he would have an elimination and the colon would come out again. He died in about two weeks.

One night I made a trade with a Jap to pay him two yen for a pound of butter. He brought me the butter the next night and I gave Sergeant Anderson, from Canadian, Texas, part of it. He was in the sick bay. I also gave others in the sick bay part of the butter. The guard had promised to get me a pound of butter every other night. I was in hopes I could help those in the sick bay to get more calories. The guard moved from our camp the next day. We were allowed to buy some fish meal in small boxes. It smelled like rotten fish, but there was some protein in it. We put this on our rice because we could not eat it without mixing it with something. I think I gained a few pounds until they quit letting us buy the fish meal.

Major Reardon, our senior American officer, tried to get the Japanese to continue bringing the fish meal into the camp, but they would not. They brought in some whale blubber for our dinner. We could smell this rancid tallow before we got to camp. The blubber was cut into one-inch squares and boiled. It was served as a soup, but actually it was just hot water with those squares floating in it. It surely was not appetizing, but we did try to eat it. Mess Sergeant D. C. Massey always served the best food that could be made out of what the Japanese let him have. He didn't get to order anything. The Japs brought him what they wanted him to have and he just had to make the best of it.

The language barrier between the Japanese and the prisoners had begun to disappear. Most of the prisoners had learned enough Japanese words to understand what they were ordering them to do in their jobs. Some of the prisoners disliked the Japs so much that they would not try to learn the language. We were handicapped by the Japanese not letting us have books to help us learn the language.

One day in March 1943, a group of fifth-grade school pupils came with their teacher to the factory where I was working. The teacher said, "These children are in a language class and they want you to read the English translation of *Snow White and the Seven Dwarfs*." They had their books with them and I read the story in English. When I started reading, the children's eyes lit up and they thought I was very smart. They thanked me and said they would be back the next day. I supposed they would have some other translation for me to read. When they returned the next day the teacher told me they wanted me to translate *Snow White and the Seven Dwarfs* into Japanese and then read it. I looked at it, but there were too many words I could not find a Japanese word for, so I told the teacher that I could not read Japanese as well as his fifth-grade students. The children looked very disappointed. I invited them back and told them I was very glad to have met them. They came back one more time, just to hear me speak English.

18. *To a Better Camp*

When we came in from work, July 31, 1943, twenty-five officers received verbal orders that we were to move to another camp. We were not told where, but were told to get our belongings together and report on the outside in the prison yard. This was about five o'clock in the afternoon, and, of course, we were surprised to know that we would be moved so suddenly. I would have liked to have had time to tell my Japanese friends that I worked with in the factory good-bye. Major Reardon and I talked it over while I was getting my things together. He said, "Maybe where you are going they will feed you better. Surely it can't be any worse. The working conditions could be better and, at least, you will be getting out of this factory smoke and can get a clean breath of fresh air."

Since June the death rate had declined to about one a month. There had been eighty-seven deaths since we came to this camp in November 1942. When we came here there were 400 prisoners, and of these there were 46 officers and 354 enlisted men. Those who remained were in very poor condition and had all kinds of vitamin deficiencies. There were 30 men confined to the sick bay. This was a close-knit bunch of men who would help each other at any time as much as they possibly could. We had gotten rid of our body lice, but the crabs still remained.

In preparing to leave, no one had anything to take, except that a few had a canteen and mess kit. I had a canteen, a mess kit, a dictionary, a notebook, a haversack, and two needles. We felt more like animals than men, with nothing more valuable than the clothes we were wearing. They gave us back our leather shoes and took up the canvas shoes and skivies. We lined up in columns of fours about six o'clock and marched one and one-half miles to an interurban station. We went from there to a railroad station at Osaka. Here we waited about an hour, standing in formation. A crowd of Japanese started gathering to look us over. They stared at us as if we were some kind of wild beasts. The Japanese officers roped off an area to keep the crowd of Japanese from getting too close to us. They set up two machine guns and brought in more guards. The Japanese guards were continually telling the crowd to stay back or they would use the machine guns.

It was dark here, except for some spotlights and a few small electric lights. We could look into the faces in the crowd and see individuals who looked as if they would like to kill us. There were some who just came out of curiosity to see what an American soldier looked like. The officer in charge had a megaphone and constantly told the crowd to move back. They would come up to the rope and push it out as if they were going to break it. The guard would push them back, threatening them with bayonets. The civilians would yell back at the guards and at times they were making so much noise that it sounded like a mob. After about forty-five minutes of this commotion, we were moved upstairs and boarded the passenger train. The crowd followed us upstairs, yelling and threatening us.

It was a relief when we entered the coach. It looked as if we were going to be mobbed in spite of how hard the guards tried to keep them away. These people who were so bloodthirsty toward us probably had had a son or close relative killed by our army. They were bitter and we could see it in their faces.

When we pulled out of Osaka we did not know where we were going or how far. We had been so confused by traveling in the dark and by the mob problem that we did not even know the direction we were going. The shades were drawn on the coaches and a guard was at each end. We could tell when we went through a town by the lights reflecting on the drawn shades. We stopped at a few towns during the night. The guards would not tell us where we were going, only that we were going to another camp. We were hoping that it would not be a coal mine or another factory.

Having to make this move and not being able to talk to the woman who worked on my detail at the factory, I realized I was losing my contact with the outside world. At this stage of the war, General MacArthur's forces had been making some good advances on his comeback in the South Pacific.* However, they were having to take the secondary place of importance as far as the war was concerned. Priority was given to the European theater as far as materiel, ships, airplanes, and troops were concerned.

About daylight the train came to a halt at a small seaport called Okayama. Here we got on a small boat, similar to a ferry. There were many Japanese civilians on the same boat. Some of them were moving their belongings with them. That did not consist of much. They had straw mats, three or four cooking utensils, a small bundle of clothes, and about one-half gallon of rice. They carried all of this on their backs. These people did not seem as curious or full of hate as had those in Osaka.

The boat came in sight of a large landfall that had more trees and vegetation than where we had been. There was no factory smoke hovering over the horizon or along the coast. When we tied up to the pier, there was no one waiting for us or any of the passengers on the boat. After the passengers got off, we started disembarking. We started marching east from the pier and I noticed a sign that read, SHIKOKU. I could not read all of the sign, but I assumed that to be the name of this island. We had been marching about thirty minutes when we came to a large stockade with high board fences and on top of

* The Japanese had been pushed thirteen hundred miles closer to Japan in one year. The U.S. forces had taken two islands near eastern New Guinea, Munda Island, and the Gilbert Islands and were bombing the Marshall and Caroline Islands.

the fences were sharp bamboo sticks. We went through a large gate with high posts on each side. On one side was a guardhouse. The streets were graveled and there were large two-story brick barracks. A large number of prisoners were milling around and came out to see the new prisoners. They all looked in much better shape than the prisoners at Yodogawa. I recognized some that I had known before. Captain Jimmy Parker, who was second in command of Nichols Field, also executive officer for a while of the 1st Battalion on Bataan, was there.

We marched inside the compound about fifty yards and halted, then formed a platoon front facing one of the large barracks. A group of prisoners following us took up a like position on our left. These were Dutch prisoners from Java. The commandant came out and told us what the rules of this camp were. He also told us that if we did not agree to abide by camp policy not to try to escape we would be put into solitary confinement. He asked for a show of hands of all who would agree not to try to escape, but very few of the Dutch prisoners held up their hands. The commandant became very angry and threatened to punish them one at a time. One of the Dutch officers, who was a captain, stepped forward with his hand up, asking for permission to speak to the commandant. He said, "Sir, you have been speaking in English and my men do not know what you are saying. If you will let me interpret the English into Dutch they may agree not to try to escape." The commandant had been using an interpreter to speak English, but had not thought about the Dutch prisoners not being able to understand. He began to cool off and agreed to let the Dutch officer translate into Dutch what he had said. The commandant would speak a sentence in Japanese, then the interpreter would tell the Dutch officer what to tell his men. They did agree not to try to escape. Everyone laughed and the tension eased. The commandant did not know how to take the laughter; he thought they were making fun of his question. They told us where our quarters would be, that we would be issued rice bowls, blankets, etc.

All of the American POWs immediately had a get-together with the ones we knew in this camp. We had not seen these men since leaving Cabanatuan in November 1942. They told us this camp was called Zentsuji, that it was a detention camp and there was no heavy work. We were called in to be given our room assignments and to sign for our property. We had to sign for this before we received it. We signed for five cotton blankets and two rice bowls. Most of the new prisoners were assigned to one barracks, with twenty-eight officers to a room. In my room there were two Dutch captains who had been taken prisoner in Java; three British captains, captured in Singapore; one Canadian officer who had been captured by a submarine after his commercial ship was sunk in the Indian Ocean; two Australian captains, who had also been taken after the fall of Singapore; two American officers who had been taken when Guam fell; and one officer who had been taken prisoner when the USS *Houston* was sunk in the Java Sea. The USS *Houston* prisoner, Lieutenant Commander Bill Wilson, had been a language student in Japan for the three years before the war and was a lot of help to us later. All of the others in my room were taken in the Philippines, but I had not known any of them before. They were all captains or equal to this rank in the Navy.

We had been on the train all night without sleep, except for a catnap now and then. We had not had any lunch. About 3:00 P.M., Captain Parker brought me a small loaf of bread, which was a big surprise since I had not seen any bread in several months. He said the prisoners were allowed some milk at times and that bread was served instead of rice from time to time. It seemed that this was going to be a much better camp than the one we had just left. Captain Parker and I had a good long visit.

The skies were clear and free of smoke and everyone had clean clothes free of soot. There were several drinking fountains and a nice wash rack where a person could scrub his clothes and a line to hang them on to dry. They even furnished us soap and a brush to scrub our clothes. There were 743 prisoners in this camp. Prisoners were allowed to play games like bridge and dominoes. At Yodogawa camp we were not allowed to play any kind of games. One Sunday at Yodogawa eight of us had decided to play bridge. On Monday morning we were called into the infirmary to be punished for playing bridge. There were no guards in the area while we were playing, but someone had told them. We were lined up in a circle and told to slap the man on our right as hard as we could. The guard said that if you slap your man too easy, you will be hit with a bento stick.* The first man to slap the man to his right pulled his punch a bit and the guard knocked him down. The others did not try to pull their punches.

Our living quarters consisted of two bays, one on each side of an aisle about ten feet wide. The bays were one and one-half feet off the floor. The floors of the bays were board with thin straw mats covering them. In this room of twenty-eight prisoners, each one had a space seven feet long and thirty inches wide in which to sleep. There was a one-foot shelf overhead against the wall that ran the length of the room. This is where we put our personal possessions. I had a Webster's dictionary, a safety razor, a shaving brush, a notebook, a toothbrush, a canteen, a mess kit, a haversack, and a few sheets of toilet paper on my part of the shelf. I brought some of this with me from Yodogawa and some of it had been issued after we arrived at this camp.

The socks that were issued to us cost three yen. They were made of a heavy coarse cotton and were just a tube with the seam across the end. They did not have a heel, and when we wore a hole in the place where the heel was supposed to be, we would just turn the hole up on the instep and wear it like this until another hole came in the heel part; then maybe we would get another pair.

August 1, 1943, in our new camp, the evening meal consisted of one small loaf of bread instead of rice, soya sauce, and soup, which was a much more appetizing meal than we had been having. The next day we were issued twenty Kinchi cigarettes per man. These cigarettes were about one-half the size of our American cigarettes. I did not smoke, but I thought I could smoke twenty cigarettes a month, just to have something to do. On August 3 we had a really good lunch, with noodles, beans, and a pint of milk. Each individual had to pay for his milk. There was never enough food to satisfy anyone. Most of the time we received between 1,200 and 1,400 calories per day. August 6 we received a Red Cross food box, and this was my first time to receive a complete Red Cross food box. We turned the canned food in to the kitchen to be used by all. The next day we were served beans, vegetables, tea, and gravy with corned beef.

Those who had edema, where their kidneys would act twelve or

* A club made from bamboo slats about one and one-half inches thick; each end was covered with rawhide leather. It was used to discipline prisoners.

fourteen times a night, became better with the small amount of protein we were getting. Usually every morning when a prisoner woke up, his face and neck would be swollen. His eyes would be so swollen he would have to use his hands to open them. The protein that we received in the Red Cross boxes was Spam, corned beef, and tuna. It was a life saver for our men. If they had had to go into winter with their health in such bad condition, many would have died.

The first night at Zentsuji, we were plagued with a heavy infestation of bedbugs and some sand fleas. To combat the bedbugs we made traps out of our canteen cups. They would fall in the cups and could not get out. This helped some, but we found out the best way to get away from the bedbugs, sand fleas, and mosquitoes was to tie a pair of old socks over our hands and the end of our pajama sleeves and leave our socks on our feet and pull them up over the bottoms of our pajama legs. This would keep them from getting inside our clothes. For a while we made fly swatters and would turn on the lights after the bugs had had time to come out and everyone would swat the bugs as fast as they could. We were issued long underwear that we used for pajamas. We had been using G-strings for underwear.

The Japanese had two projects going that involved the prisoners. One was raising rabbits. They had a large house with lots of hutches in it. They had about four hundred breeding rabbits. The agreement with the prisoners was that when we raised this number of breeding rabbits up to five hundred, the prisoners were to get three-fourths of all over five hundred that we were able to raise. Our job was to forage for food for the rabbits. This would be done every day by the prisoners' gathering clover, grass, dandelions, lambs' quarter, and other palatable rabbit food.

The other project was that the prisoners would raise a vegetable garden and they would get all they raised. These two projects sounded all right, but we later found out there were lots of loopholes.

In September, when the sweet potatoes were harvested in the neighborhood, we would get all the sweet potato vines and throw them across the prison wall to dry. This was to feed to the rabbits during the winter. As long as the vines were green the prisoners had sweet-potato-vine soup.

We received a Japanese newspaper one day by smuggling. It was dated September 10. It carried the news of the Italian surrender. It also stated that the Americans landed in Italy on September 9.* This really gave our morale a boost. Some of the navy and marine personnel received mail on September 13, and this was the first time that we had been able to believe that the Japanese had reported the names of those who had been taken prisoners by them.

The guards were telling us that the Italian soldiers were no good. We knew why they thought so: because they had surrendered. The navy Lieutenant Commander Bill Wilson, who had been a Japanese language student, would read all of the newspapers that were written in Japanese. He would burn them as soon as he had read them and then he would tell us what the papers were printing. When the Japanese thought we were getting news from the outside, they would come into our room where Commander Wilson's bunk was and look through everything he had. They would take up the straw mat and boards under his bunk. They would throw his things out on the floor and leave them there. They knew that he had been a language student in Japan before the war, and sometimes those he had made friends with in Japan would come to see him. After each of their visits the guards would search his personal property.

I was put in charge of a detail that went out of camp, sometimes a mile away, to get clover and grass for the rabbits. Most of the time there were about fifty on this detail. They were all volunteers and all were officers. This detail found wild onions and dandelions that we could use to make a salad to eat. Soon I could get more volunteers than were needed. At first we would put the onions in the sack with the rabbit food; then when we took the sacks to the rabbit house, we would take the onions and greens out and put them in our shirts. This went on for several months. When the rabbit food became scarce in February and March, it took much longer to find food for the rabbits. Those on the detail were spending too much time foraging for themselves and less time trying to find food for the rabbits. Every prisoner who went out had a sharp bamboo stick to dig up the onions.

* The North African campaign was completed by June 3, 1943. Troops landed on Sicily on June 13 and on Italian soil on July 9. Italy surrendered September 3, but the Germans continued to hold the northern part of Italy until they surrendered in 1945.

19. *Foraging for Food*

One morning the guard reprimanded me very hard for allowing the men to take so much time digging onions. Those on the detail were told that they would not be allowed to dig onions. There was one guard who would go with us most of the time. We had to pass a Shinto temple on our way to get food for the rabbits. We marched in columns of twos, and when we came to the temple, the guard would have me halt the column, have them left face, hats off, bow, hats on, right face, and forward march. The guard would do the same. He would stand next to me when he bowed. He could not look down the line to see if the others were bowing and it finally got to where no one was bowing except me and the guard. One day a Japanese civilian happened along on a bicycle; he stopped and bowed before the temple. He noticed that the guard and I were the only ones bowing, so he came over and told the guard that the other prisoners were not bowing. The guard gave us a good dressing down in Japanese. We could tell he was mad, but most of us never knew what he said. When we were dismissed to get the rabbit food, I told the men what he had said as near as I could understand. When we got back to camp, the guard told his sergeant that the prisoners were not bowing. The sergeant talked pretty hard to us, and before he dismissed us, he went down the line slapping every man in the detail. From then on when we stopped in front of the temple, the guard did not bow until he saw that all the prisoners were bowing.

There were six of us sent down to a Japanese home where they made *tōfu* out of soybeans. They would soak the beans, then crush or grind them, put them in what looked like a flour sack, then put them on a wooden block and put a limb from a tree on top of the sack so the juice could be mashed out. They had a tub of water under this to catch the juice. To put more pressure on the sack, two Japanese women would get on the limb. The ground soybeans would be boiling hot when they put them in the sack. When the juice would drop into the tub of cold water it would go to the bottom and gel. This substance was white like curdled milk. When we brought it back to camp on a cart, they kept it in cold water and it stayed white until it was served. If allowed to stay out of water for a while it would deteriorate and turn brown. To serve it, they cut it into pieces like pie and it was very tasty.

On several occasions when we went out on small details we were allowed to walk on the sidewalk when we passed close to people. Once in a while someone would say, "Good morning" or "Good evening," in English, although they would not look at us when they spoke. Most of the time it would be on the day the women were allowed to wear western clothes. Once a week they could wear western clothes, that is, short dresses in bright colors. The greeting would always be from a woman. It was always good to hear a friendly voice. In this small town of Zentsuji, where there had been stores, very few were open. There was no display of merchandise. Usually there were vegetables growing on the sidewalk, and they would stack dirt next to the curb and plant a garden. When limbs and twigs would fall from the trees, Japanese women would gather them for fire wood.

The group of prisoners that had been in this camp, Zentsuji, before we came had planted one-half acre of sweet potatoes out to the north of our compound about one block away. A group of us went out to dig the potatoes when the Japanese told us they were ready to harvest. We each took a hoe and some baskets. The prisoners who had planted and cultivated the potatoes said the agreement had been that the Japs were to get one-fourth of the potatoes. When we got out there, half of them had already been dug. We asked the Japs what had happened and they said they had given the high school agriculture boys half of them. Of course, there was nothing we could do about it since we had no way of enforcing any agreement.

The first of December I had a severe attack of malaria. This chill seemed to last longer than those I had been having and seemed to hurt me more. I was never treated any better than those in my barracks treated me. They put their own blankets on me to keep me warm. There were ten blankets on me when I began to feel like sitting up. I had appointed Lieutenant Commander John Nester from La Jolla, California, to arrange to trade my ration of rice to some other prisoner, to be paid back one-half ration at a time when I was able to eat again. Most of the time it would be a day and a half before I could eat after a chill. They took me down to a Japanese doctor when my fever broke. He had me stretch out on a couch with my arms over my head, so he could feel under my rib cage to see if my liver was hard.

He said, "Your liver is not hard so you do not need any treatment." In the store room we had quinine and Atabrine that was sent by our Red Cross to the Japs for us; but he would not let me have a fourteen-day treatment of quinine to prevent the recurrence of malaria. Everyone in my room did all he could to help me get well. I was the only one in my barracks who kept having the chills every month or two.

At a later date, I had a very severe malarial attack and a navy corpsman, a Mr. Jones from Fort Worth, Texas, was working in the doctor's office. One of the officers in my room called him over to see me late one evening. The corpsman said he knew where the Atabrine was, but the wooden box had never been opened. They planned how they could cut the nails holding the first board and open it. By twelve o'clock the corpsman brought enough Atabrine tablets for me to have the fourteen-day treatment.

We were issued some overcoats September 20 that had been confiscated from the British. These were good heavy overcoats. The winter of 1943 was not as severe as the winter of 1942 had been at Osaka. My men were sick at times, but none died. This was the first camp that I had been in where several prisoners didn't die each month. This was a healthier climate, and we had more of a variety of food and were not forced to work during all kinds of weather.

The Japanese began getting in some technical books for a library, like Spanish grammar, psychology, and several books on agriculture. The demand to read them was so great from the prisoners that we decided to set up some classes for the ones who were interested. The prisoners selected three of us to teach agriculture. They chose Captain Jim Chisholm of Australia, Captain Cadmus of the U.S. Army from Oregon, and myself. We had only one book to be taught on each subject. The instructors would start with one book and go all the way through it, then trade with another instructor. According to the Japanese rules we could have a maximum of ten men in a class. The first subject that I taught was the fundamentals of fruit production. These classes were taught every day. I taught this class and took a class in shorthand. Before we moved from this camp, I had completed five courses in each agricultural subject. The other subjects were successful poultry management, agricultural economics, biology for every man, and soils. The subjects that I took were shorthand, Spanish, public speaking, psychology, and bridge by Culbertson. I would have taken a course in the Japanese language if we had been allowed their language books to study.

It was necessary to take some kind of work to keep a person's mind plastic and to keep from worrying. There were some who were losing their minds, going crazy from fear of punishment, starvation, and disease that might take their lives. Since we could not get any medical attention, to take this schooling helped to build our knowledge as well as being good for our health. We were allowed to buy one notebook. The courses were well organized, and each teacher put in a lot of time on each subject. All of the students took notes and were very interested in trying to get the most out of each subject.

In as much as we never had any heat in our barracks during the winter, we would wrap up in our blankets when we were in our room to keep warm. This was against the rules as far as the Japs were concerned. To keep out of trouble we would take turns watching for the guards, who were likely to come in any time. Usually our watcher would stand in the hall next to the door entering our room. One day I was on guard and leaning against the door facing. Bedbugs would come out of the cracks in the door facing and bite me. If we saw a guard approaching, the one on guard would yell "Tally-ho" to give those inside time to fold their blankets and get their beds in shape. Eventually the guards told the commandant about hearing us say "Tally-ho" and I was called into his office and he asked me what this meant. He said he could not find it in the English dictionary. I told him it was an expression that we used like "Ouch" or "Oh" if a bedbug bit us or we got a splinter in our finger while leaning against the wall.

The commandant later issued an order in writing and placed it on the bulletin board which read, "No prisoner will say 'Tally-ho' because it does not mean anything." We also had a camouflaged word for "newspaper": instead of saying newspaper we would always say "the rag." This was done because the guards were very snoopy. They would listen outside our windows or anywhere where several of us were together. Some of them could understand English but would never let us know that they did. We were never allowed a newspaper, but we had them smuggled in by paying a guard from 200 to 250 yen.

Most of the time they would bring them in under their cap band. It was unusual if we were able to get a paper every two months.

A British army colonel who stayed across the hall from our room kept having severe attacks of hemorrhaging from stomach ulcers. We could hear him groaning during the night. The Japanese doctor never attempted to give him anything to stop the bleeding. After four heavy attacks, he died.

The Red Cross representative visited our camp. The commandant called in our senior officer, who was a British colonel at that time. They didn't allow him an interview in private. The commandant had to be present at all times. The colonel could not tell the representative that we were starving to death, for fear of reprisal after he left. When we found out that they were going to inspect our quarters on the second floor, we decided that when they started up the stairs, we would single file down the stairs, forcing the Red Cross representative and the Japanese to form a single file coming up the stairs. In this way we thought we might be able to say a few words to the representative as we passed on the stairs. When we were close enough to him we would say, "We are starving to death." Three out of five of us were able to tell him this, and I think he could see it was the truth by looking at our physical condition as well.

In November 1943, the Japanese asked that one man from each room be selected to make a recording to be broadcast. There were twenty men in my room at the time and I was selected by my roommates to make this recording. It was a three-minute talk in which I gave the name and address of every prisoner in my room. I told where we were located and asked anyone in the U.S.A. who heard this broadcast to please notify these prisoners' families that they were alive and at Zentsuji prison camp. The Japanese said this would not be used as propaganda in any way. It was to be replayed over the radio. (Recordings of this were made by those who heard it in the States and a record was mailed to each family. My family received two records from different people, which was appreciated by me and my family.) This broadcast was not made until the spring of 1944.

During the winter our rabbit project had not gone well. The Japanese would not buy or secure any food for them. There was very little food that we could find for them to eat. We had about five hundred breeding rabbits just before winter, which was the number we were supposed to have before we would be allowed to have any of them to eat. They would die back to about one hundred before spring. They would not reproduce during food shortages and dried food was not good for them, but we had to feed them some during the winter.

The Japs bought four hundred Buff Orpington baby chicks for us to raise. The enlisted men took care of them. Someone stayed up with them all night for quite a while to see that they kept warm. The Japanese would buy food for the chicks, but not for the rabbits. They raised about three hundred of these chickens until they were laying size. These were all sexed chickens, so they were all pullets. They started getting eggs, but then they began to find large pullets that just dropped off the roost dead.

One morning the commandant called me into his office and asked me if I could find out what was causing the pullets to die. I went out to the poultry house and one had just died that night. I performed an autopsy on the pullet and found that the liver and ovaries were abnormal. I believed it was pullorum disease, but I could not be positive without making a stained-antigen test. I went back to the commandant's office and told him what I believed it to be and said that if he would get some stained-antigen we could make the test and be positive. He asked how I could tell. I explained how the test was made by taking a drop of the live chicken's blood and putting one drop of the stained-antigen on a polished surface. If the mixture stayed smooth it was free of the disease; but if the mixture coagulated, the bird had pullorum disease. I recommended that the test be made on every bird and those that reacted to having the disease could be separated from the well birds. This disease was not harmful to humans and those that were culled out could be eaten. He wanted to know if this was a sure test to identify pullorum disease and I assured him that it was.

In about two days the commandant had a pullorum testing kit, which consisted of a mirror marked off in one-inch squares. There were about twelve of these squares and a bottle of stained-antigen. The commandant said the prisoners could eat all that turned out to be diseased. I asked the commandant to come and watch the tests. I wanted him to be a witness so he would not think I was culling more than actually had the disease just so the prisoners could have more to eat.

This testing kit, like all others, had to have a quart of hot water put under the mirror to keep it warm, so that the test was sure to work. When everything was ready, the commandant came out and the test began. The kit had a needle that was sharp on one end and had a small loop on the other end. I stuck the needle in the vein in the wing and used the loop to get a drop of blood to put on the mirror. Then I put one drop of antigen on this drop of blood and stirred it to mix it. The first few tests showed the birds to be negative. The commandant seemed rather interested in the test. We picked up a reactor and I was able to show him the difference in the positive and negative reaction. He went back to his office while we finished the tests. He came back in about twenty minutes and we had eight reactors, all of them perfectly healthy-looking pullets. The commandant stopped us and told us to take those eight to the kitchen. We started testing again and three more tested positive. The commandant became very angry and told us to put them back in the pen and stop the test. There were too many testing out bad. I explained to him that it was a contagious disease, but he would not let us go on with the testing. We had tested just about one-half of the flock. Usually most chickens die soon after they are hatched with this disease, but the enlisted men had taken very good care of these and had had good luck with them until they became old enough to lay.

20. *Other Bargains*

We made another bargain with the commandant. This time we were to feed out a hog with the prison guards' scraps, to be supplemented by any green feed we could find. They brought in a large Duroc boar for us to feed out. He was about two years old. We took good care of him because we were to get three-fourths of the meat. We watered him twice a day and went out on detail to pull clover, lambs' quarter, and careless weeds for him to eat. To keep the meat from tasting strong and staggy, he had to be castrated a good while before the meat was to be used. The commandant asked me if I could de-sex the boar and I told him I could if I had a sharp knife. He told me that the camp doctor would bring me one of his lances. I told him that I didn't think the lance would be substantial enough because it would break too easily. This was a large, tough hog. The doctor thought the lance would do the job. I knew that one of the marine sergeants who worked in the kitchen had a one-bladed knife, so I asked him to get his knife extra sharp and to be out there when I worked on this hog.

The commandant decided that this should be done the next morning. When I got to the hog pen, I had a rather large audience. The Japanese doctor, commandant, and two office girls were on the fence to see that the job was well done. The marine sergeant and three other prisoners were there to hold the hog down. I told the sergeant to have his knife ready to hand to me because I knew I would need it. I thought about what I would tell the commandant if he should ask me where I got the knife, since prisoners were not supposed to have knives. The helpers caught this two-hundred-pound boar and put him on his left side. When I took hold of his large testicles, I could tell that his skin was rough and tough. When I started to make the incision, the lance broke off at the handle. The sergeant gave me his knife, already open, and I made an incision at least five inches long on each side. I gave these two large testicles to the sergeant. The doctor gave me some powder to use on the open wound that he said was sulfathiazole, which I had never used on an open wound. I poured this on the wound out of some paper he handed to me. Everyone began to leave. The show was over. I asked the sergeant to cook the testicles when he got back to the kitchen and I would give him half of them. I was to meet him out in the chicken house after dark to get my part; when I got there the sergeant had found some paper to wrap the meat in so I could take it back to my room. I had made a knife out of a spring from the sole of an old shoe and a handle from a bone cigarette holder. We cut this fried meat up in half-inch squares and gave everyone in my room a piece. It was cooked crispy and brown and was so very good!

For some reason the commandant decided to reshuffle the rooming arrangements of the personnel. All officers of each separate nation were put in a room to themselves. I was moved from the east barracks second floor to the west barracks first floor. I was the only captain in this room. The other occupants were lieutenants colonel or majors. Only two other officers and myself were given straw mattresses. A lot of other officers of higher rank, as well as my rank, wondered how a captain was allowed in the room with lieutenants colonel and given a straw mattress to boot. Their guess was as good as mine. I never knew and it was never mentioned why I seemed to be favored by the Japanese. When they first brought the mattresses in, they asked where my bunk was. I told them; they put the mattress down on my bunk and left. In a few minutes they brought in two more. I thought everyone was going to get a mattress, at least in this room.

A spotted Poland China barrow was brought into camp for us to feed out for meat as we had the Duroc boar. After we had been trying to feed the two animals for a month, the commandant sent word that these two hogs had to be butchered on a particular day. The interpreter said I was to make arrangements for this and it had to be done before 11:30 A.M. on that date. I inquired around to see if anyone had butchered hogs before so that I might know whom I could get to help me. One Australian captain said he would help.

On the day of the butcher, several thought we should save the blood to be used in soup; in fact they said save everything but the squeal. From the kitchen we got some pans that were flat enough to go under the necks of the hogs. We would use a sharp butcher knife to stick the animals in the throats as they lay on their backs; then we would turn them on their sides to catch the blood. We caught nearly one-half gallon of blood from both hogs.

We had scalding hot water from the kitchen poured on the hogs to make it possible to scrape off the hair. We hung them up side by side under the porch near the galley front door to dress them. In a short while one of our prisoners came to me and said, "A Japanese general has just arrived in camp." I had opened my hog all the way through the brisket and had removed the intestines. I noticed the Australian was having a problem getting the intestines out of his hog and I expected the Japanese general any minute. The Australian said, "How do you get the intestines, liver, and lungs out?" He had cut the belly of the hog down to the ribs as you do on a sheep. I told him he would have to open the hog up through the brisket and rib cage. Just as the Australian had his hog dressed, the general and his inspecting officers came by and our commandant was showing the general how well he was managing the camp and how much food we were getting. I understood now why the hog killing had to take place by a certain time on a particular day.

We took the carcasses down and put them on a table inside the kitchen. Now "Donald Duck," the Japanese guard who was our interpreter, said we must divide the meat as agreed with the commandant. He said he was a swine man and had raised and butchered them. I told him we would cut the hogs up American style and divide it as agreed. The commandant was supposed to get one-fourth of all the meat. We weighed both carcasses and divided it by four. The interpreter set the scales, which were marked in kilos, but I had to do a little figuring to get it right. First I gave him all of the leaf fat. That was not one-fourth. Then I trimmed the fat off the shoulder meat. It still was not enough, so I trimmed the jowls; by trimming a little more fat off the hams it made the one-fourth. The interpreter did not say anything about the liver, heart, or lights, so these were not weighed in. The hog that I had castrated and used the medicine on the wound had a bag of pus where each testicle had been removed. The medicine had cured the outside, but not the inside. I cut out all the infected part and showed it to the interpreter. This wasted about five pounds and was cut out before we weighed the carcasses. The hogs were not fat, but the commandant wanted them butchered to show the inspecting officers how well he was managing the camp.

That night we had the blood soup for supper and it was the most putrid-tasting soup that I ever tried to eat. The soup was black and very salty. That was the last blood soup we tried. They had cut our rations down even more and everyone was worried about our survival. If anyone even talked about food, his stomach growled. That empty, gnawing pain was always in our stomachs. Several times I would dream that I was at home sitting at the dinner table just loaded with dishes of fried chicken or steak. I thought I could not wait for the members of my family to be served. I would wake up hoping it was true. The saliva had run out of my mouth until it wet my pillow.

Early one morning a Japanese guard came up the stairs to the second floor, and the electric light bulb was not burning. He asked one of the lieutenants, "What is wrong with the light bulb?"

The lieutenant said, "It's out." The guard thought he was trying to be sarcastic and had insulted his intelligence. The guard had an artificial arm and hand. (He probably had lost it in battle with Americans.) He hit the lieutenant across the face with his steel hand, knocking him down to the foot of the stairs. He followed it up by kicking him all the way to the commandant's office. The guard told the commandant that the lieutenant had cursed him; and, of course, a prisoner had no law to protect him, nor a court where he might be heard. Naturally the commandant believed the guard. The prisoner had to kneel down outside the commandant's office for a short time as punishment. He was still bleeding from the cut on his face.

The garden detail had a good garden started. They had leeks, cabbage, beans, *daikons*, etc. The garden was fertilized with human excretion, as were all Japanese gardens. They had a large earthen jar under ground in the corner of the garden that would probably hold a hundred gallons of fluid. They would fill this jar about half full of urine taken out of the latrines. They would let this ferment about twenty-one days, and when it was ripe enough to use, it would be dipped out with a long-handled dipper that held one gallon. Two gallons of water would be added to this one gallon of urine and this would make a strong nitrogen fertilizer. We would dig a small furrow down the row near the plants and pour just enough of this fertilizer to make it wet in the bottom. If one drop splattered on the plant it would burn a hole in it and the spot would turn white in two days.

While we were working on the garden some of our men were very weak and could barely get to the garden and back. The guards were continually after me to make the men work faster, since I was in charge of this detail. We had fussed at the Japanese so much about wanting more food that they passed a regulation that no one was to bring up the subject of food anymore. When one of my men would get sick or give out, I would tell him to lie down and then the guard would come up to me and say, "What is wrong with him?" Although the guard could not speak English and I could not speak Japanese very well, I could explain well enough to make him understand what I was talking about. I would tell him that this man was weak. He would want to know what made him weak and I would reply that he was feeling bad. "What makes him weak?" he would ask again.

Finally I would say, "He doesn't have enough to eat to be able to work."

Then the guard would slap me and say, "You are not supposed to mention food." This was what he was trying to make me say by continuing to ask the same question over and over. He did not really care about the condition of the men.

One day I was in the garden and noticed that someone had

stolen two large cabbage heads. I reported this to Captain Hosetana, the second in command of our camp.

He said, "No, the Japanese people do not steal."

I told him, "It was Japanese tracks because they were wearing straw skivies. They took two large heads of cabbage and crawled under the fence on the west side of the garden."

He said, "Tomorrow I go out there with you." The next morning he called me into his office with his interpreter. Captain Hosetana could speak English. On our way to the garden he asked me, "Where were you taken prisoner?"

I replied, "Bataan."

He said, "Were you in the horrible march I heard about?"

I said, "Yes."

He asked, "Did they treat you very badly?"

I answered, "Yes. I saw many killed on this march because they were too weak to walk any farther."

He said, "That report embarrassed me and my people, and I am very sorry that our soldiers were so inhumane."

Captain Hosetana said, "We have some beautiful cavalry Arabian horses that are two years old. Would you castrate them for us?"

I said, "No, Captain, I cannot do that for two reasons. One, it would be aiding your war effort and, according to the Geneva prisoner-of-war international law, a prisoner cannot be required to do anything that will directly aid the enemy war effort. Two, if I worked on the horses and one bled to death, your people would think that I had done it on purpose and punish me for it. It takes special equipment to make sure none would bleed to death."

The captain did not seem angry that I had refused his request. It seemed that the commandant had asked him to see if I would work on the horses. When we got to the garden, I pointed out to him where the cabbage heads had been cut off and where the thieves had gone under the fence. He acknowledged that it must have been Japanese and that he would try to prevent it from happening again.

Captain Hosetana left the interpreter and me after we walked out of the garden. The interpreter and I walked back to camp, which was about one-half mile. On the way back, I asked the interpreter, "How well are the citizens fed?"

He seemed very bitter about it, and said, "I lost one child from starvation and have another that is suffering from malnutrition. The people are murmuring among themselves about it."

One day I was sent with a guard to the garden. We went to a low spot that had nothing but weeds growing in it. They wanted me to tell them if it would grow oats. This was a large grain oat that I was not familiar with, but they said it was the kind that rolled oats were made from. This was a little out of my line, but they said these oats would grow anywhere the regular oats would grow. I was looking along an irrigation ditch for some lambs' quarter to take back to camp for a raw salad. The guard had stopped at the garden gate and was just letting me wander around. There was a girls' school or college about three hundred yards from the back side of our garden. Their school had just turned out. All of them wore blue skirts and blouses. When two of them saw that I was a prisoner, they stopped and smiled. They were just across an irrigation ditch from me. They squatted down and urinated in the ditch, facing me. They did not seem to be trying to show themselves off. In fact, they acted as though it was a normal thing to do. The guard and I walked back to camp and I told the interpreter that the oat seed he had shown me would not germinate. The seed smelled moldy. The low place in the garden was suitable for any kind of plants. It did not hold water, so there would be no damage to plants from too much water. The oat seeds were planted, but they did not germinate.

We were given permission to plant a garden between the wire fence and the wooden wall that was around our prison camp compound. This was on an individual basis. Some prisoners were more industrious than others were and some just did not feel like working at anything extra. Normally, if you got between the fence and the board wall, you could be shot by the guard. The barbed-wire fence was about four feet from the wall. Some of our men took advantage of this more than just to plant a garden. They would dig deep into the soil near the wooden fence, so it would make it easy to dig a hole under the fence if and when the chance ever came.

There was a bakery just north of our compound about one block. When the wind was from the north and they were baking bread, the aroma nearly drove us crazy. We had a verbal agreement between the married and single officers that if the married officers would dig a hole under the board fence, the single officers would raid the bakery. The married officers would watch the guards that walked the beat to get an idea as to the time the guards would come by this particular place. One night it was quite dark and almost raining. I had to break out the light bulb above the place where the raiders were to go out. I had to do this when the guard was farthest from the area.

This night three single officers went on the raid. In about fifteen minutes after they had gone under the wall, they came back with a hundred-pound sack of sugar. They said there were no rolls or bread cooked. We had to eat the hundred pounds of sugar before daylight that morning. I don't know how many took part in consuming the sugar, but it was understood that no one would put any in his pockets because when the guards searched us we had to turn our pockets inside out in their presence. They would look in the seams of our pockets for bread crumbs, tobacco bits, and sugar. My part of the sugar to dispose of was about one-half pint, the same as all who were in my room. We would eat the sugar until all our saliva was gone; then we would take a drink of water and wait a little while, then eat some more. This process went on until all of the sugar was gone.

About daylight the next morning the guards mustered us all out for a shakedown. They had found out that the sugar had been stolen from the bakery. When they had us lined up, they told us not to empty anything out of our pockets until the guard had inspected them. The guard would stop in front of us and tell us to turn our pockets inside out. In a few minutes there was a commotion down the line about five men from me. One prisoner decided he might have gotten a few grains of sugar in his pocket accidentally, so he turned his pockets inside out quickly and dusted them. A guard saw him and knocked him down, but they didn't find any sugar on anyone. We were held in formation until all of the rooms were searched. They did find one prisoner, Captain Cameron Starnes, with bits of tobacco in his pockets and he was taken into the commandant's office and questioned. Major Jones had received a pound can of pipe tobacco in a package from home about a week before this happened. This officer told the questioning personnel that Major Jones had given him some of his pipe tobacco. They checked their records and found that Major Jones had received some tobacco from home in a package.

In reality we had bought some leaf tobacco on the black market and we cut it up in shreds with some small scissors we had. We could smoke it in our homemade pipes. One morning the commandant made an inspection of all of our pipes. He had everyone who had a pipe put it out on his bunk so he could see them. Most of our pipe bowls were made out of cherry tree roots. Mine was made out of cherry tree roots and had an Eversharp pencil barrel for a stem with a bamboo mouthpiece. The commandant was a pipe fancier and he thought mine was the best one he had seen and wanted to know if I would make him one like it. I told him I would if he would get me a knife to work with because it was very hard and slow to make one without a knife. He said prisoners are not supposed to have knives and that he could not furnish me one. Of course, it was a slow process without a knife, but I was surprised that the commandant did not suspect us of having a knife to make the pipes.

The commandant did ask, "Why do you need pipes when you have no tobacco?" I explained to him that we kept the snipes of the cigarettes that were issued to us; then at the end of the month when we ran out of cigarettes we would smoke the tobacco that was saved from the cigarette snipes.

One of the prisoners asked a Japanese guard what they would do if Americans were parachuted in here to take over the camp. He said, "We have orders to shoot the prisoners before we let them be repatriated." This gave us cause to try to arm ourselves by making knives and planning what defense we could use if this happened. From our latest information, we had retaken the Philippines.* I was talking to a prison interpreter one day when he was in the prison compound yard by himself. We were talking about the war and I asked him, "Are the Americans still coming back up from the Pacific?"

He said, "Yes. Do you know how they are doing it?" I shook my head and he said, "They just send a lot of planes over an area and drop many soldiers by parachutes; then they drop heavy machinery to level off an air field. Then the planes start coming in loaded with

---

* On October 17, 1944, a landing was made at Leyte in the Philippines, and within four hours the landing was secured. General MacArthur came ashore and made a broadcast using the signal corps microphone. He proclaimed, "This is the voice of freedom! General MacArthur speaking. I have returned. By the grace of Almighty God our forces stand again on Philippine soil, consecrated by the blood of our two people. Rally to me—let the indomitable spirit of Bataan and Corregidor lead on."

soldiers, artillery, and tanks. This is done so quickly, we cannot stop them. They will take Japan the same way." The Americans had begun to make a believer of him and, if he was thinking this way, there must be thousands of others who were beginning to reconcile themselves to the fact that the Japanese surrender was imminent.

21. *Self-Defense and Propaganda*

After the guard told us what would happen to us if paratroops tried to liberate us, I was on the lookout for material suitable for making a knife. I was in the rabbit house feeding the rabbits one time when the Japanese had a carpenter doing some repair work. He was working with a steel saw and put it on the table when he went to lunch. I took the blade out of the steel frame and slid it in a crack in the building where no one could see it. I thought I could make two good knives out of the steel blade. I heard that the carpenter was inquiring about his saw blade that afternoon. I felt bad about stealing it, but thought it might mean the difference between life and death for me. The carpenter finished his job in about three days, but I waited about a week to get the blade that I had hidden in the rabbit house. I took it back to my room and broke it in half. I gave one-half to another prisoner. We had a problem making a detachable handle because we had to be able to slide the blade in a crack in the wall to hide it. We sharpened what was the back of the saw blade on cement and honed it to razor sharpness with a red brick. This was a slow process, but we finally had a sharp, pointed blade on one side and a saw on the other. We made a handle out of hardwood with a detachable rivet that went through the hole in the blade to hold it securely to the handle. This would make these blades about four and one-half inches long. We kept the handles in our pockets and were never questioned about them.

By January 1944, the war was not going too well for the Japanese. They continued to have articles in the papers trying to boost the morale of their people. I am quoting word for word from the *Nippon Times*, dated Monday, February 7, 1944:

"FIGHTING SPIRIT OF JAPANESE INFLAMED AS FOE ATTACKS MARSHALLS," says Sayo Toyama, by arrangements with Ashi.

"No matter how many planes and battleships the enemy may array 'for show' in the Marshalls, the Japanese fighting spirit will make short work of them, fully making up in spiritual strength," declared Mitsuru Toyama, veteran nationalist, upon hearing the news of the American attack against the Marshall Islands.

To attack the Anglo Americans has almost been my business in the past," he said. "It is unfortunate at this very important time that I have caught a cold, but you should tell the people that I do not mind it a bit now at this moment when the enemy with his so-called civilization is coming near.

"What I wish to impress on the people is that Japan is a sacred land, which had been firmly established tens of thousands of years ago as a divine country. That is why every attempt of land grabbers directed against our country in the past has always been repulsed.

"That we are alive is solely due to the august virtue of His Majesty the Emperor. The mere fact of having been born in this country is something to be extremely grateful for. We Japanese are a blessed people.

"When it comes to materials, perhaps Japan does not compare with America, but even though Japan may be wanting in 'things' she has a strength that more than makes up for those shortages. That strength is strength of soul, which is more important.

"The enemy on the outside, who are said to have an abundance of machines, have now come to oppress us, revealing quite openly their true character. They have mustered a number of planes and warships for show. Now it is up to the Japanese to face this mechanical strength of the enemy with our human torpedoes.

"Besides our human torpedoes, we still have our divine torpedoes. This is something of which our enemies know nothing and they do not reckon with at all. It is a precious thing which only the Japanese have. We have that spirit which teaches us that 'it is a great joy for all subjects to die in loyalty or to die in filial piety.'

"Now that the enemy is coming close we must strangle him. No business of half killing. With our human and divine torpedoes we must destroy him.

"In such times the courage of the Japanese increases a hundred times. It is the true Japanese whose courage increases a hundred times and whose confidence rises in just such times. This is all that is needed."

This kind of information was a morale builder for the American prisoners of war. We could tell that the Japanese were weakening and we were gaining by taking long jumps at a time in the Pacific. We knew that, when the European war was over, it would not take us long to end the war with Japan. We believed that, if we could withstand the starvation and disease until the next winter, the war would be over. All of the time we had believed that the United States and our allies would win the war but did not know when. The prisoners were starved into surrendering, but we only surrendered our bodies. We were not defeated mentally or spiritually.

A propaganda report was printed March 31, 1944, in the *Mani-chi* and *Nippon Times* that read:

Atrocity Charges of U.S. Are Scorned.
                AMERICAN EDUCATIONALIST RAPS ROOSEVELT
                      GOVERNMENT LIE ABOUT JAPAN
SPECIAL:
    LISBON: March 31, Dr. Albert Palmer, well-known educationalist in the United States, speaking at a meeting in New York, assailed the U.S. government for having invented atrocity stories of alleged murders of U.S. soldiers and Filipinos, according to a correspondent of the *London Worker.*
    The correspondent quoted Palmer as saying, "The Japanese soldiers did not commit any atrocities," and stating that the Japanese were very clean and polite.
    Palmer said, "The Japanese are generally regarded as experts in the domain of children's education." The correspondent said, "The *New York Daily News* backed Palmer's statement and in editorials made slashing criticism of Roosevelt and his policy, which it declared was entirely dependent on Moscow."

Of course, we had been on the receiving end of these atrocities and had witnessed many more with our own eyes. We knew this to be strictly propaganda directed mostly at the Japanese people. We were glad to know that the American people had found out about the atrocities, whether they believed them or not. At the time the propaganda was coming out, the Japanese people had begun to ask, "Where is our navy? Where is our air force?" The back of the Japanese navy had been broken at the battle of Midway and during the landing of General MacArthur at Leyte, in the battle to retake the Philippines.*

---

* The battle of Midway was fought June 4–5, 1943. The Japanese lost four aircraft carriers, one cruiser, and two destroyers. In this battle the ships never sighted one another—all the damage was done by aircraft. This battle broke the back of the Japanese navy. It was the turning point of the Pacific war. In the battle of Leyte, October 17, 1944, there were 650 U.S. ships of every description involved. This battle gave General MacArthur and his troops a solid footing on the Philippine Islands.

22. *Letters from Home and Camp Routine*

In May of 1944, I heard that I had two letters in the Japanese office. In about two weeks the American office boy brought the letters to me. They were from my wife and had been written about six months before. She referred to some letters that she had written almost a year ago, which I did not receive. She told me that my niece, Della Faye Coleman, had joined the WAC (Women's Army Corps). None of us knew what that stood for, since there were no women's military organizations when the war started. Everyone in my room tried to figure out what this meant. My children were well and in school and Ethel was working in the P.M.A. (Production Marketing Administration) office. Although I had written her in 1942 and in 1943, she did not say she had received any mail from me. Soon after receiving these letters, I received a twelve-pound package from home. This was a big thrill for me. It had a jar of malt tablets that had melted and run together. They contained Vitamin B. There was also a silver teaspoon that was greatly needed and I carried it in my pocket at all times when it was not in use. There was some peppermint candy, which the Japs had sampled rather heavily when they inspected the package. There was a pair of wool socks and a deck of cards.

The deck of cards held a surprise for me that I did not find until July 31, 1944. The deck of cards looked as if the seal had never been broken, but on this day when I opened the deck to play bridge and began to shuffle the cards, two pictures fell out. They were pictures of my daughter and son. They had been taken two years after I left them. Words could not describe how happy those pictures made me. I made a folding picture frame out of a Red Cross box and trimmed it with tin foil and placed it on a shelf over my bunk. There were very few pictures in camp.

We had made an excellent garden in 1944. We had lots of cabbage, leeks, *daikons*, green beans, and some other greens. We ran into an unforeseen problem. We worked to make a good garden and thought that we would have access to all the vegetables we wanted to eat while they lasted, but this was not the case. It was true the Japanese had agreed to give us all that we grew in the garden, which was about two acres in size. Instead, they would weigh so many kilos for the whole camp, then deduct what they had been contributing to our rations. They would not let us have any more food than we had been getting. We only had a different variety of food. It always amounted to about 1,200 to 1,400 calories a day. This made the garden detail so angry that they took a vote on whether to raise another garden or not. They voted unanimously not to bother with another garden since it did not increase our rations at all. We had really looked forward to the good garden produce being an addition to our regular ration of food.

In November 1944, I received a typewritten card from my wife, Ethel. It had been censored rather heavily. When there was something in a letter or card that they did not want a prisoner to know, they would black out the whole word. As an example, on Ethel's card she said that Wood, my brother, was in ——— (this five letter word was blacked out). Then she said that Jesse (another brother) was in the Air Corps. All of us in my room tried to figure out what the five-letter word was that they had blacked out. We measured the width of the typewriter letters it took to write "Italy" and it measured out just right. When I had left the states, Wood was a major in the army.

As the winter of 1944 approached, about every prisoner continued to be affected by vitamin deficiencies. Swelling of the face and neck was common. One of my roommates, Lieutenant Colonel Scottie Satterwhite, had become incapacitated from a back injury. He had had three vertebrae broken before he was taken prisoner. Scottie could not bend his back enough to put on his shoes, socks, or trousers. He was in pain from rheumatism all of the time, especially when it was damp or cold. It became my duty to help him dress in the morning and undress at night.

The Red Cross had sent in a new shipment of parcels, but the Japs would not let us have them. On two occasions we found empty Red Cross cans in the trash barrels. We questioned them about using Red Cross food that was meant for the prisoners. Their excuse was that they had to see if it was fit for the prisoners to eat. About the last of November, they issued us a box of Red Cross food. When we ate the meat again our swelling ceased. Just a little protein would stop the edema.

The fifth of December someone in my room broke five rice bowls while washing them. We took time about washing the rice and soup bowls, which were all of our eating utensils except a spoon. We knew there was a penalty of two days and nights in the brig for breaking a bowl. We knew it was so near Christmas that if we made the Japanese mad we surely would not get anything extra to eat for Christmas day. We decided not to report the bowls until after Christmas. We borrowed bowls from our roommates. Each of us could skimp along until after Christmas.

When Christmas came, we did receive some extra food. Each one of us got a tangerine and in the middle of the afternoon some mango bean paste with hot tea. We had been receiving the hot tea regularly. The day after Christmas, we drew straws to see what order we would take to get our broken dishes replaced. I drew number one, so I would be the first to be punished. We were all anxious to see what kind of humor the Japs would be in, and what the punishment would be. We each put on all of the clothes we had, because it was cold in the brig. It had cement floors, a slatted door, and one small window with bars over it.

I picked up my broken bowl and started out. The others said, "We will see you in a few minutes." I went into the Japanese office and went through the first door on my left, which was the supply room. The supply sergeant looked at my broken dish and I tried to tell him it had been accidently broken while being washed. He went over to a file and pulled out a folder. I supposed it was a record of what we had been issued when we arrived at this camp. He handed me a replacement and marked something on the form. I stood there for a minute and the sergeant said, "That is all."

I said, "Isn't there some punishment that goes with breaking dishes?"

He said, "We are allowed a 2 percent breakage and this will go toward the 2 percent." Then he asked me, "Aren't you the one who is related to President Coolidge?"

This was the first time I recalled making that statement to the sergeant at Yodogawa Camp when he said I favored President Coolidge. Of course, I told the supply sergeant, "Yes."

When I got back to my room, all the others had on all their clothes and were prepared to go to the brig after presenting their dishes to the supply sergeant. They said, "What happened? Wasn't the sergeant mad?"

I told them he had been very nice to me and did not act as

though he were mad. They were all eager to take their dishes in while the sergeant was still in good humor. The next man, who had drawn the number-two spot, hurried into the supply room; but in a short while we saw a guard escorting him across the street to the brig. The other three that were left with broken dishes were really confused as to what to expect. Each of them took their turn and went to the brig. They were to stay two days and nights with soup and water to eat.

We would send their soup over to the brig in canteen cups. We would put their ration of rice in the canteen cups with the soup. It would settle to the bottom and could not be detected. We would write them a note once or twice a day and let them know what was going on. We would fold the notes a little smaller than the width of the canteen cup handle. The handle was convex in shape and held in place by a small slide fixed especially for that purpose. The note was easily placed into the convex of the handle groove and the slide held it in place extra well. We would take the soup to the guard that stood at the entrance to the hall leading to the cells. Each cell had a small opening so the guard could push the canteen in to the prisoners. These men served their two days and nights without missing anything. They got the same amount of food they would have gotten had they not gone to the brig.

Good rabbit feed was hard to find by the last of December. We had about five hundred breeding rabbits again. The Japanese still refused to buy any kind of feed for them and again they began to die from starvation. It looked as if all our labor rustling feed for them had been in vain. Those on the rabbit detail were unhappy about losing some of the rabbits so early in the winter. It would be about two more months before we could start getting green feed for them again.

I talked to Colonel Miller, who was our American POW officer at this time. I told him I could feed the rabbits a certain weed that would kill all of them in one night, if he thought it best. This would put us out of the rabbit business. He told me to talk to those on the rabbit detail and take a vote on it to see what they wanted to do, then let that be my guide. We got the detail together, when we had guards who could not understand English, and everyone on the detail voted to kill the rabbits. Only one argued that we would not have a chance to get wild onions and dandelions for ourselves if we stopped the rabbit detail. They finally said they had been trying to make a success out of this rabbit deal for two years, gathering feed in rain or snow, and for all the work only once did we get fifteen rabbits for 723 men.

I told Colonel Miller about the attitude of the detail. He told me to go ahead and try to dispose of them, but he did not have much faith in my plan. The next day we went south of the camp where there was some low land that did not drain well. I pointed out to the men a red-stemmed, sharp-leafed weed and told them not to get anything except this. I could not remember the name of the weed, but I remembered studying about it in the United States and it is very constipating to rabbits. The guard did not know one plant from the other and did not pay any attention. We got the usual amount of feed, but a different quality.

When we got back to camp, the feeders gave the weeds to all of the rabbits. The next morning when the detail came out to go for feed for the rabbits, the interpreter told us that nearly all of the rabbits were dead. There were three bucks and one doe still alive. The weed we fed them is not poisonous and normally a rabbit will not eat it unless forced to do so out of hunger. They become very constipated and die in a short time. This detail helped skin and stretch these pelts for the next two days. The Japanese took the rabbits that were still alive out of the camp. They thought they had some kind of disease. They never did ask me any questions about it; and I think they were ready to give up the project too.

After about two years we had exhausted the use of the library books and teaching our classes on different subjects. Now, without our garden detail and the rabbits to feed, the time became very monotonous. We played bridge in the afternoon to help pass the time on our hands.

23. *Another Project*

One morning the Japanese called about one hundred of us out for a special detail. We found that it was a land-clearing project. We were to grub the stumps and rocks out of an area of land to be planted for a garden by the Japanese. This detail was organized into squads and platoons. On this detail all were officers: American, Dutch, Australian, and British. I was put in charge of the detail.

There was a Japanese guard we called "Donald Duck," because he was very boisterous and short, and waddled like a duck when he walked. The tops of his leather boots came above his knees. He had all the prisoners out early several mornings to give us calisthenics. He said we needed exercise to keep us healthy, but after a few mornings he decided it was food we needed although he could no nothing about that. He and three armed guards would take us to the area where we were to clear the land. He would push us to work harder.

One morning when we were passing the guardhouse on our way to work, he came up to me and said, "You are a very fine officer. These men do what you tell them to do." I recognized the Japanese tactics and expected some special favor request to come up next. Before we got to the work area he said, "The commandant told me to tell you that, if these men will work harder, we will put beans in their soup."

I said, "Will you put beans in the soup of the men in camp who are sick and unable to work?"

He said, "No, just those that work hard."

I told him, "If you will not help the sick men, we will not work any harder."

Then he suggested that I take a vote among the detail to see if they would agree to work harder if beans were added to their soup. I told him, "No, we will not take a vote."

He said, "You must. The Americans are democratic and vote on everything."

I told him, "This is silly and we do not vote on silly things."

He said, "Before we dismiss the men for work, you must take a vote."

We were marching in columns of twos, and I halted them and gave them "right face" as we usually did before dismissing them for work. He said, "Vote." And I said, "No, we will not take a vote." He slapped me twice and told me to dismiss the men.

We had been working about an hour when he came up to me and said, "When they are called together for lunch, you have them vote."

Again I told him, "We are not going to take a vote."

He became very angry and agitated as though he were going to slap me again. Several of the men who were grubbing a large stump about fifty feet away, said in unison, very loudly, "Quack! Quack!"

That really made him mad. He ran over where they were working and said, "Who said that? Who said that?"

Everyone on the work detail dropped what he was doing and just looked at him. No one said a word. He looked around and saw that no one was working, so he left the immediate area. After about thirty minutes had elapsed, he came to me again and said in a loud voice, "You are going to take a vote at noon."

This time a group of Australians grubbing a stump some fifty yards across a draw yelled, "Quack! Quack!"

It seemed that he realized why they were calling him Donald Duck after the cartoon character and it made him mad enough to pull his hair and spit. He called two guards, with bayonets fixed on their rifles, to go with him across the draw where the Australians were working. He asked them several times, "Who said that?" No one answered. They just stopped working and looked at him.

When he looked around and again saw that everyone had stopped working and was enjoying a rest, he shouted, "Get back to work."

I had not had a chance to talk to the men to explain why he was acting this way. They only knew that he and I were having trouble. When we assembled for lunch, the beans were not mentioned. I did not try to talk to the men about this at lunch, because he was following me too closely and I did not need to agitate the Jap any more. That evening when we were passing through the gates near the guardhouse, he came up to my side at the head of the column and said, "You pig! You pig sty! I am going to tell the commandant that you would not take a vote to see if the others would agree to work harder."

I said, "You tell the commandant anything you want to, but this increase in rations will not be considered unless you include the sick and starving men who are not in any condition to work." I halted the column in the usual location and got them in platoon front. He counted them and told me to dismiss them. He went straight to the commandant's office. I didn't hear anything more about voting, but we did get beans in our soup. The sick and weak also got some beans. We poured the liquid off and counted the beans, then divided them equally. Each one got four beans.

When we had cleared about fifteen acres of land on a hillside, they did not take us back to clear any more land. They said we were going to plant squash and pumpkin. In my opinion the reason for not taking us back was that our air raids were becoming more numerous in the day time.

In April 1945, we were in formation taking roll call. It was just good daylight, but the sun was not up. We heard an air-raid siren and looked up and saw a United States B-29 glistening in the sunshine about four miles high. The Japanese guard said, "Don't look up." Everyone did look up and some shouted with joy. They were not punished for shouting. That beautiful, glistening B-29 looked like an angel in heaven to us. As we gazed at this beautiful sight, one of the officers next to me said, "That B-29 crew is having to eat Type C rations for breakfast this morning and griping about it, while we are starving, and Type C rations would seem like a feast to us."

When the bomber first appeared, Colonel Unrhue, who had been a B-29 pilot and was shot down in the Pacific and taken prisoner, was the first to recognize the plane as a B-29. This was the first B-29 that those of us captured in the Philippines had ever seen. This gave our low morale a big boost. The guards were very depressed and even seemed humble to us for a day or two. They could see the "handwriting on the wall."

The next day they told us to dig just so many foxholes. I asked them how did they want them dug? They said, "Like you dug them in the Philippines."

We dug them about three and one-half feet deep, not as deep as most foxholes. We were saving energy and did not think they would be using them very long. We counted the number they had requested and it figured out to be one for every guard and office crewman.

We had not figured what we would do during an air raid, but figured it would be every man for himself. We did not feel that we were in any danger, because our people knew where Zentsuji prison camp was located. There were no important factories or large concentrations of warehouses in this area. It was two weeks after we had seen the first American plane that the air-raid siren sounded again and continued to sound. Now we would find out what we were supposed to do. I looked just above the horizon in the northeast and counted twenty-eight heavy bombers coming in low. This was about ten o'clock in the morning. The Japanese came into the barracks shouting for us to get in our rooms and stay there. They pulled the black curtains over the windows and told us not to look out, then they ran and jumped in the foxholes. We were left in the building all on our own. We yelled and laughed watching the planes until they passed overhead. From the noise the powerful motors made, we supposed they were B-29's. After the planes had passed overhead, the guards came back into the barracks and started hitting those who were near a window over the head.

We had a heavy rain the next day that filled the foxholes with water. This being a sandy soil, it caused them to collapse. We had to clean them out and get them ready for the next raid. They had us fill the sand barrels and see that all the wooden shovels were in place. Since the Americans were using phosphorus bombs, they knew they would need the sand to fight the fires. These barrels were on the inside of the buildings. They had barrels of water, with buckets hung on them, outside the buildings. We were never taken very far from camp after the bombings started. When we would go about five blocks, after *tōfu*, I noticed they had dug foxholes at every residence and at what few stores were still open.

After these many months and years as a POW, you never forgot that you were in the hands of the enemy. Most guards continued to be hateful, and because they changed guards often, you had no chance to become friendly. They had been taught to hate us and they continued to do so. Becoming POWs suddenly changed our way of life from the modern to an almost crude way of life. The language barrier and the unpredictable and hostile atmosphere came as a shock to most of us. All POWs were powerless and without any influence to the extent that there were no laws to protect us from inhumane treatment. In order to live you tried to minimize the harassment by not fighting back, but remembering those things that were to you illegal and unwarranted. Although all of the prisoners were your friends, should you get into trouble, using them as witnesses or accomplices would not help since they had no more authority than you did. You knew the Japs would not believe you or the witnesses, unless it was to their advantage to do so. As far as I know, no American ever betrayed another prisoner, no matter how much he was punished to do so.

In order to preserve sanity, we tried to study whatever we had at hand, or to work on some project. We had to learn to tolerate disappointments and to minimize our troubles. After three years as a prisoner of war, the same old routines became habit. We even wondered how we would fit into society or civilization again. We knew there would be many adjustments and they would be slow. Our minds were not as alert and our physical health far worse than when we were captured. We could hear many sick men saying, "O Lord, how much longer must we suffer this agony?"

One evening when I had gone with a small detail after *tōfu*, I saw a one-seated airplane land within three-fourths of a mile of our camp. When we returned to camp, it was about sundown and the plane was still there. I reported this to Captain J. Y. Parker. They organized a group of pilots and then drew straws to see who would get to fly the plane out to Okinawa. We had a problem deciding how an airplane with Japanese insignia on it could land on an American-occupied air field. We found out that the Americans had secured one-half of the island of Okinawa. To be able to come in at night without a map was another problem. They finally decided to come in low from the Japanese side near the beach and land as near the American lines as possible. Anyway, they were willing to try. It was also decided that, even though it was a one-seated plane, two of them could go because they would be light in weight. We made a list of all the men and officers in Zentsuji camp and gave it to them so they could report to our people.

We dug under the compound fence, and after they were out, we covered it up so it would look natural. All of us were listening for the plane's motor and praying they would be able to take off. The plane was far enough away that we were not sure we would be able to hear its motor. They were given a lot of advice by all the other pilots before they left. None of them had piloted a Jap plane of any kind. Our main worry was their being able to get to the American lines without being shot down. They measured the distance on an old map we had in camp and were of the opinion that a plane could fly from Okinawa and back on the amount of gas they carried. About one o'clock these two pilots returned. They had checked the gas tank and it was empty. While they were on the prowl, they went by a bakery and brought back a tow sack full of "dog biscuits." This was one of the Japs' emergency rations.

On June 23, 1945, I think the Japanese again began to read the "handwriting on the wall." Our heavy bombers would come over every few days and were unopposed. They seemed to think they had better begin to get their house in order to be able to comply with the international law governing prisoners. They had officers of different nationalities in the same camp. They attempted to get this cleared up by ordering the American officers in the Zentsuji camp to a camp on the mainland called Roku Roshi, in the central part of Honshu, twenty miles from a large city called Fukui.

In our preparation to leave we were told only that we were going to another camp. We didn't know where when we left Zentsuji. We had to prepare to have an inspection of all our personal property, which was very little. When we left our rooms we were not to go back. We were lined up and given just so much space to spread our personal property on the ground. There were two Japanese officers who made the inspection. Our diaries were the only things that bothered us. We were afraid they would take them away from us, because we might have written something that would offend the Japs.

Those that had things they did not want the Japs to see would pass them along the line ahead of the inspecting officer and then after he had inspected a row, the articles would be passed back to them. Of course, this had to be done very discreetly so the Japs did not catch on to what we were doing. Sometimes a person would pitch an article ten or fifteen feet to another person. The inspecting officers attempted to read a lot of our diaries, and when they were through with them, they would stamp "approved" on them or keep them to be destroyed. I had some shorthand in mine that they never questioned. They could not read shorthand, especially mine, and some said they had an inferiority complex that kept them from asking questions about shorthand notes.

I had the only Webster's dictionary in the camp. It was about four inches thick and weighed around four pounds. I had covered the backs with cloth. It was used extensively, mostly to settle an argument about the spelling of a word or its definition.

All of our friends who were left there stood near our lines and waved good-bye as we marched out of the compound. Then it was about 4:00 P.M. We left friends from England, Java, New Zealand, Australia, Holland, India, and Canada.

We were loaded onto a ferry at Takamatsu at 6:00 P.M. and moved to the Okayama railroad station for the night. It was after dark when we came into this depot and it was very crowded with Japanese. We were put in a small room where it was very crowded with just prisoners. There was not room to lie down. You could sit down and sleep sitting up, especially if your back was against the wall. About midnight the air-raid sirens began to sound. We heard heavy motors. The windows lit up as brightly as if it had been broad daylight, from the bombs and fires. I went to the rest room in the depot, just to see what the Japanese were doing. The lobby and every room in the depot were crowded with Japanese sleeping on the floor. Men, women, and children were lying on the floor. Some of them were sitting up as if they were listening to the sirens. I had to step over those sleeping on the floor. No one ever noticed that I was a POW. The rooms were very dimly lit. Going into the rest room I had to step over one very plump Japanese woman; she opened her eyes, then turned over on her side.

After a short while another formation of planes came over and we could hear bombs exploding. I could hear the Japanese women and children talking in loud, excited voices. The city all around the depot was on fire. In my mind I could visualize what might happen if the Japanese civilians knew that we were in the same building with them. They could riot and cause a massacre if it should get out of hand. The noise and bright light went on for probably three hours.

It was very hot in the room without any windows open, and with all the commotion we did not sleep very much. About daylight the morning of June 24, we were hustled out of the depot and immediately boarded a train. The Japanese civilians seemed surprised to see us coming out of the depot. Most of them looked angry, as if they would like to kill us. The guards made them keep their distance from us. We could smell smoke from the burning buildings, but could not see any fires. When we were on the train, the shades on the windows in the coaches were drawn.

We were given a small box of food, called a *bentō* box, for breakfast. It contained a small amount of rice, pickles, small raw fish about the size of a minnow, and some pickled seaweed. Our lunch was the same thing. We went through Kobe and Osaka. Each time someone raised the window shade and peeped out, the guard would run over and slap him. While they were punishing the first man, others would peep out. In each town we could see where buildings had been burned down, but the depots were all left intact. This was done purposely by our bombers, as we later found out, so that when this country was invaded each depot could be seen easily as a target from the air, making it easier to destroy their lines of transportation. We went through some tunnels and the windows were opened to give us some fresh air. The smoke from the locomotive would boil into the coaches and almost choke us. It caused us to cough and our eyes to water. We were always glad to get through the tunnels.

We arrived at Fukui at 8:00 P.M. and took a tram car. We rode about two hours and came to Chio. It was raining a slow downpour. We had one man with one leg, on crutches, and some were too sick or weak to march. We were lined up in the street, in the rain, and no one had a raincoat except the guards. We put the one-legged man and the sick men in the front of the column of twos to start the march. Again we did not know where or how far we would have to march under these conditions. It was very dark and our guards wanted us to march faster. They tried to get us to go around these sick men in the front, but none of us paid any attention to them. We just let them yell. We let the man on crutches and the sick men set the pace.

Soon we were off the gravel road and onto a dirt road going uphill into the mountains. We could hear the water in the creeks and the rivers roaring with the sudden downpour of water. About every thirty minutes, we would have the guards halt the march to let the sick men rest. We would sit down on the muddy ground to rest because we were as wet as we could get anyway. It continued to rain all the way to this new camp, which turned out to be twenty long miles from Fukui. The officer on crutches never fell or stumbled during the entire trip. We were on rocks that were protruding from the road bed. The red clay and rocks were slippery and sometimes the column would slow down for those who were finding it difficult to walk. There was a lot of lightning and thunder during the night. The lightning would help us see where we were going; the night was as dark as ink.

We arrived in the new camp, Roku Roshi, at 3:30 on the morning of June 25, 1945. We were cold, tired, and wet to the bone. Our shoes were soaking wet and muddy. The Japs had a warm fire waiting for us, also an excellent ration of rice and wheat with a thin fish soup. We had not had any sleep for two nights. We were really suffering from fatigue. The fireplace was hollowed out in the middle of the floor and the fireplace walls were cement. It was about four feet by nine feet in size and three feet deep, tapering at both ends. The building had a high ceiling and on one side there was an attic-type floor, where one hundred bunks were. The top of the building was made of clay tiles. The outside of the building was 120 feet by 200 feet. It had bays one and one-half feet off the floor and they were one hundred feet long. The whole building would accommodate five hundred prisoners. When we measured off the bunk space for each individual, it allowed us twenty-two inches by seven feet long, in which to sleep.

We were allowed to sleep until about seven o'clock that morning. The windows and the doors on the front side of the building were nailed closed. A log fence, covering about two acres, was the enclosure of the prison compound. The guardhouse and the commandant's office were in the extreme northwest corner of the compound. A wood shed extended south of the commandant's office. The prisoners' barracks extended across the east side of the compound, with the kitchen between our barracks and the commandant's office. This camp was located high up on the side of a mountain. The small village of Roku Roshi was about one-half mile southwest of our compound. The population of the village was probably around fifteen hundred.

There was only one road to this camp and it came from Roku Roshi, with the camp at the end of the road. The morning of June 25, we were called to a meeting by the camp commandant. He told us what the rules of the camp were and what we could expect. This commandant was not as sure of himself as the first one we had had at Camp O'Donnell some three years before. He did not brag about what they were going to do.

We had all our clothes to hang out to dry. In the afternoon we were all weighed. I weighed 98 pounds. My normal weight was 145 pounds.

July 1 a large detail was sent out into the woods to bring in fire wood. It was put in the wood shed to be used in the kitchen stoves. On July 3, we started clearing land of brush for a sweet potato farm. When we had cleared about one-half acre, they started breaking the land with hoes and shovels. Potato slips were planted soon after the ground was broken. Some details were building walks out of rocks. These were cobblestone walks. There were 335 officers and 30 enlisted men in this camp. We worked two hours in the morning and two hours in the afternoon. By July 8 we had set out thirty thousand sweet potato slips. We had a hard rain that night, and the next day all details repaired the road to Roku Roshi from our camp.

25. *Blackouts and Gardening*

On July 9, 1945, we had our first blackout since arriving in Camp Roku Roshi. We had three alarms during the night. Each time we could hear the drone of each flight of our bombers as they passed overhead. They sounded good to us. Soon after the third alarm, I went outside to the rest room. A guard was standing just outside the door of our barracks, probably listening to what we were saying. I could see billows of black smoke and flames shooting upward from the cities that were burning some twenty or thirty miles away. I said, "Ugh, rising sun?"

He said, "*Hai.*" This meant "Yes."

I pointed to another city burning and said, "Rising sun?" Again he said, "*Hai,*" only a little weaker this time. Then I pointed to the third town that was on fire and said, "Rising sun?" He jerked his rifle off his shoulder, and, with his bayonet attached, he ran me back to the barracks. In a few minutes all of the men were out looking at the cities burning.

On July 10, we planted soybeans in among the sweet potatoes and put small limbs over the sweet potato slips that had just been planted. This would protect the tender plants from the hot sun. Our food ration of rice was increased slightly when we were working and even then everyone in camp lost weight. July 12, ten packs of Kinchi cigarettes were issued to each prisoner. This was the first issue in this camp; we also received one safety razor blade per person. It had to last us one month. We would sharpen the blades on the palms of our hands. Our beards were like fuzz from the lack of vitamins or protein. On the fourteenth, someone stole the Japanese carpenter's lunch and they could not find out who did it. The next day was Sunday, so the punishment for stealing the lunch was that every able-bodied man had to work on the road repair.

Monday the Japanese rewarded the hardest workers by giving them one and one-half cucumbers. I did not get any cucumbers. After about two days of heavy rains, we started clearing more land. Sometimes we would find small snakes when we were clearing some brush. They would bring the snakes to me to identify and see if they were poisonous or not. I would dress the snake for half of it and we would cook it over a brush fire. We also found some land crabs that had a small clump of white meat on their abdomens about the size of the end of my thumb. We would pull this off and cook it. We were careful to stack the brush so that when we set it afire it was not a hazard.

We had a Lieutenant Mollette from the 31st Infantry in camp. He was very sick and weak. We started taking all of the snake meat to him after we cooked it. We thought the protein would help him even though there was never very much meat on a small snake.

On July 19, there was another heavy bombing at Fukui at about quarter-past eleven in the morning. Our next ration of rice was polished rice and scorched barley. This was the aftermath of the burning of the food warehouse at Fukui. This was the first all-white rice we had received since leaving Yodogawa on August 1, 1943. We thought this was a good sign that the raids were hurting their food supply. We began to get wild rhubarb in our soup with cabbage. We were also issued two spoonsfuls of rice bran, which had some vitamins in it. On July 23, a Japanese general, who was in charge of the Osaka area prison camps, inspected our camp. The commandant showed him all the land we had cleared and planted to potatoes and soybeans.

26. *Close to a Breakout*

Our rice ration had dwindled gradually, until on July 25 the prisoners started to refuse to go to work. Everyone was losing weight and growing weaker by the day. The commandant promised more potatoes and *meshi* in our soup at noon. We received an increase in rice and vegetables for supper. The next Sunday we weighed again, but they would not let us see what we weighed. They made us stand on the scales backward. The man in line next to the one on the scales could see what the man on the scales weighed, so the word was passed down to remember what the man in front of you weighed. I weighed ninety-six pounds this time, a loss of two pounds since I had arrived in this camp. They thought they could keep us from knowing that we were losing weight and prevent us from complaining to the commandant too much.

July 29 we had two air-raid alarms, one early in the morning and one late, around ten o'clock that night. August 2 there was a large air raid. The drone of planes lasted from ten o'clock to midnight. It seemed that the bombers were unmolested. There was no anti-aircraft fire or fighter planes. We seemed to have complete control of the skies. August 3 there was no work, because we had no food, and we were on the verge of breaking out to find something to eat. August 4, Lieutenant Mollette, of the 31st Infantry, died of tuberculosis. He was the last man to die before we were liberated. He was cremated in a baby crematory.

August 5, Second Lieutenants Travis Smith and Dillard escaped during the night. Lieutenant Bill Lewis had charge of the section they were in. The lieutenants put pillows in their beds so it would look as if someone were sleeping there when the guards made their check. They just flashed their lights over the area and assumed everyone was there. The next morning at roll call, they were missing. The guards took Lieutenant Lewis to the commandant's office and they tried to make him say that he knew they were going to escape. They drew a circle on the outside wall of the commandant's office, just high enough to make Lieutenant Lewis have to stand on his tiptoes to put his nose in the center of the circle. It was a very hot day and this was on the south side of the building. Each time he would get tired and let down from the tiptoe position, the guards would hit him and make him get his nose back in the circle. He still would not acknowledge knowing anything about their plans to escape.

August 6, Lieutenants Smith and Dillard were caught about three o'clock in the afternoon. The day before, two grade school children had seen them cross the road in front of them as the children were on their way to school. The children could tell that they were white so they reported them. Both officers were brought back to camp and tied under the wood shed. An investigation was made by the district adjutant and it was decided that they should stand trial by the Japanese army. They were brought by our barracks on their way to be put in a car. Their hands were tied behind them and their faces were swollen; both had black eyes. They had been beaten. The Japs paraded them in front of us to keep us from trying to escape. We were told that they were taken to Osaka and put in jail.

August 7 the enlisted men were issued cigarettes. We received very little food and did not go to work. The days following we had to work. The night of August 14 there were no air raids. All was quiet. we usually heard sirens and the drone of planes sometimes during the night.

August 15, I was in charge of a thirty-man work detail. When the guards came after us, they said we were to clean out the latrines. I told them it was against the international law for prisoners to clean out *benjos* (latrines). They said this was the commandant's order. I told the detail to sit down until I found out what we were to do. (The guards were speaking Japanese and we did not have an interpreter in this camp.) I said, to the guards, "Tell the commandant that we are not going to clean out the *benjos*." The guard went into the commandant's office, which was about one hundred feet from where we were, and told him what I had said. The commandant had me brought into his office and he was sitting behind his desk. He said, "Captain Coleman, you must take this detail and clean out the *benjos*."

I told him, "It is against the international law for you to make us clean out the *benjos*."

He replied, "Your people are using illegal weapons of warfare and we can treat you any way we want to; we only comply with international law where we see fit."

I said, "Two wrongs do not make a right."

He had a newspaper in his hand, with one-half of the front page a picture. He said, "Look at this; just one bomb did this." He held up one finger when he said this. The picture showed a lot of charred buildings that had been blown down and burned. There were civilian dead lying all around the buildings. The commandant's voice was trembling as he talked to me. I could not tell if he was mad or scared, probably a little of both. I could not read the Japanese language, so I could not tell what the large headlines were reporting. It was such good news to me that I could hardly keep my face straight. It was encouraging to know that we had a bomb so devastating.

The commandant did not say what kind of bomb it was. He was so shocked he did not know whether to be hard or easy on us. He finally called out the guards with the bayonets. They came running out to our work detail that was still sitting on the ground. The guards, about twelve in all, began jabbing the prisoners lightly with the bayonets. A lot of our men had not tried to learn the Japanese language because they hated them so much. The men said, "What happened, you sure have made them mad." I told them, "They want us to clean out the latrines and it is against the international law." The latrine excretion was to be carried off in ten-gallon wooden buckets. Each person was to carry two buckets on a yoyo pole across his shoulders. I suggested to them to go get the wooden buckets and to try to hit them on the rocks as they came down where the guards were. The buckets were so dry they would fall to staves rather easily. They did as I had suggested and the buckets did begin to fall apart. The guards were shouting at them to be more careful. The men guessed at what the guards were shouting about. The guards put the buckets back together and put them to soak in the creek that ran through our compound. The buckets would swell and would not leak after they were soaked. The Japanese never wasted any of this fluid. It was used as a fertilizer. We had to wait about an hour for the buckets to swell enough to be used.

The guard said, "OK, let's go." I said, "It's noon now and we will need to go to lunch." He looked at his watch and said, "OK, take them to lunch." Every day at noon we changed details. When we got back to the barracks, a lieutenant colonel was supposed to take this same group of men out for the afternoon. I told him that the guards would want him to clean out the *benjos* that afternoon and for them to be sure and not do it. If he did, they would keep making us do it. He said, "I sure won't do it." I did not tell him the trouble we had encountered that morning.

That night when he came back in with the detail, he was tired and dragging in his tracks. He had this juice sprinkled around on him. He said, "That was the maddest bunch of guards that I have ever gone out on a work detail with, and we had to clean the latrines because they were waiting for us with fixed bayonets."

27. End of War Seems Nearer

The next morning not anyone went out to work. The commandant had gone to Osaka, leaving the first sergeant in charge. There were no air-raid sirens or sounds of bombers going over that night. The night of August 15, after seeing the newspaper picture in the commandant's office, we paid a truck driver 250 yen to bring us a paper. This driver delivered rice to our camp almost every night about midnight. When he came the next night, we asked him about the paper and he told us it was under the seat in the cab of the truck. Navy Lieutenant Commander Bill Wilson, who could read Japanese, read the paper and then burned it so the Japs would not catch him with it. They watched him very closely because they knew he could read Japanese. He told us the paper told of a bomb that had been exploded at Hiroshima and how devastating it was.* That hundreds and hundreds of people had been killed and many more hundreds badly burned. He said it did not name the kind of bomb it was.

Our rice rations were increased, with some barley mixed with it. Some of the barley was scorched. It probably was in the warehouse at Fukui that had been burned down. Since our rice ration had been increased and we did not have to work, we felt for sure something was happening in our favor.

The paper that Commander Wilson read just reported the second bomb explosion. Evidently the first one was thought to be an accident and was not reported. They did not want to panic their people. The newspaper also reported that the Japanese parliament was in closed session about a very grave subject.

The next few days the prisoners just sat around playing bridge or cribbage. My bunk mate, Captain Mike Ushakoff, continued to teach the Russian language class. Some others were teaching Spanish and shorthand. Late on the afternoon of August 20, which was my birthday, the Japs faked an air raid. Usually when we had an air raid within forty miles, a large bell would ring in the community of Roku Roshi, but we could also hear air-raid sirens at Fukui. This time only

---

* On July 16, 1945, President Harry Truman ordered General Carl Spaatz to drop one atomic bomb on one of four cities in Japan. The city was to be determined according to weather conditions anytime after August 3, 1945. On August 5, the bomb was dropped on Hiroshima from a B-29. The second bomb was dropped August 9 on Nagasaki.

the bell in Roku Roshi rang. The first sergeant came out of the office building and ran toward our barracks, shouting, *"Denki nai,"* which meant "Lights out." Those on the outside of our barracks just laughed at him. He came within one hundred feet of our barracks and no one made any attempt to turn out any lights. We kept laughing and jeering him. He finally turned around and went back to the office. The next morning we had all new guards, except the first sergeant. The commandant still had not returned.

The next morning the first sergeant sent a guard to bring me to his office. I thought maybe we were going to have to start to work again. When I went into his office he said, "Who told you the war is over?"

I said, "No one has told me that the war is over."

He said, "The prisoners are acting very disobedient and will have to be punished unless they show more respect." I knew he was referring to the way we had laughed at him when he faked the air raid.

I said, "What happened to the air raid? We never did see any planes or hear any motors."

He said, "They were forced back off the mainland." I acted so ignorant, he said, "You can go back to the barracks." We continued to listen for our bombers to come over, but they never came again after August 14. Everyone thought the war was over or that there had been some arrangements made to exchange prisoners. We did not know anything about how many Japanese prisoners the American forces had captured. When we were taken prisoner in 1942, the Japanese belief was that they would not surrender under any conditions. I believe that by this time they had changed their minds.

On the twenty-second of August, the commandant returned from Osaka. He put on his first-class uniform and came to our barracks. Usually he had the first sergeant come ahead of him and call us to attention by yelling *"Skilski."* We would each bow at a forty-five–degree angle and hold this position until the commandant saw that everyone was bowing; then he would salute and say, *"Wakare,"* which meant "at ease" or "dismissed." This time the commandant had an interpreter with him and he did not call us to attention. No one bowed or saluted. He went straight to our senior officers' room. The commandant saluted our officers first, and then he read a statement he had prepared. It was something like this:

For the last few days we have been holding a peace conference in Manila and have reached an agreement. You will be notified by me as soon as the orders come through for you to be moved to the ship. I will have trucks here to take you, your baggage, and the sick men to the railroad station. It was not my fault that your sick men had to walk from the station at Fukui to this camp. I had no authority at that time. [He was referring to the man on crutches and the sick men who had to walk all the way from Fukui to this camp on that dark, cold, and rainy night.] You may open the doors that have been nailed closed and reduce the anchor watch from four men to two. We will keep guards on because we are responsible for your safety until you are turned over to your troops. I arranged for some meat to be delivered here tomorrow and will try to get more food. Your rations will not be decreased again.

The commandant saluted and did an about face to leave. Colonel Unrhue, our senior officer, said, "Wait just a minute; will our troops come for us or will we be taken to them?" (His answer would tell us whether or not the surrender was unconditional.)

The commandant said, "Your troops will come for you." With this answer Colonel Unrhue knew it meant that the American troops would occupy Japan and it was an unconditional surrender.

Colonel Unrhue said, "You will have all your arms and ammunition stacked out here in the front yard near the flag pole in thirty minutes for us to take over."

The commandant said, "But we are responsible for your protection until you are returned to your troops."

The colonel said, "The civilians are friendly to us and, if we have the arms, we can take care of ourselves." The Jap said, "But, sir, my side arm is a part of my uniform and I cannot be separated from it." (He was speaking of his samurai sword.)

The colonel said, "You use that weapon on the battlefield; therefore, we consider it a weapon of war, and you will surrender it, too."

The commandant said, "Would it be asking too much of the colonel to go to Osaka and ask my superior officer if I should turn in my side arms?"

The colonel said, "It might not be too much to ask, but I am telling you now, you will surrender your side arms."

The commandant said, "Yes, sir," saluted, and went back to his office. Colonel Unrhue came out of his office and a large number of prisoners were waiting to find out what had happened in their meeting. The colonel immediately said, "The war is over, the Japanese have capitulated." This was at 3:57 P.M. on August 22, 1945. We learned later that the Japanese had surrendered on August 14, 1945.

There was laughter, shouting, and crying. There were too many different remarks made to remember all of them, but some said, "We've made it, thank God." "We've weathered this terrible nightmare." Lieutenant Colonel Satterwhite came to me and said, "Stub, you saved my life last winter and I owe my life to you." Others said, "Thank God, we could not have lasted much longer under these conditions." "It is all over and we have the best nation in the world."

Colonel Unrhue issued orders for us to arrange for a surrender ceremony to take place in forty-five minutes. I was told to organize a platoon of officers and to get the front doors opened that had been nailed closed all of this time. The ceremonies were to take place in front of the flag pole that was flying a Japanese flag as big as a bed sheet. Everyone was so happy and talking incessantly. It was hard to get their attention. I had to get enough officers for a platoon, and when the officers finally understood that we were going to have a formation, they all wanted to be in it. I had enough for two platoons. When we went out to take up our positions, the Japanese had already stacked their arms and ammunition in a military formation. My platoon did not get to take the guns, as there was another platoon assigned to do that.

When I told the platoon to fall in and gave them "right dress," they snapped to the orders as if they had been training every day. I was surprised to see the colonel and the color guard unfurl a small silk American flag. It had been folded and pressed for a long time by some prisoner. The colonel called us to attention; the Japanese commandant came with his sword across his arm and surrendered it to Colonel Unrhue. The commandant was crying. The color guard lowered the Japanese flag and hoisted our small American flag up on that sixty-foot pole. Everyone in the ranks and those out of the ranks held a salute from the time the color guard put the flag on the rope until it was hoisted to the top of the flag pole and secured to the base. When the colonel ordered us to dismiss our troops, I did an about face and looked at this platoon. Every eye was on that tiny American flag, with tears streaming down their faces. When I dismissed them, the celebration was really on again. The reality that we were free men was hard to believe, but we were confident.

The Japanese paid us the back pay that they had been holding in what they referred to as a savings account. This consisted of the pay for a captain in the Japanese army, which was 220 yen. For each officer they had given us 60 yen per month. Of this 60 yen we had to pay back 30 yen to the Japs for our rations, and if we bought a pair of socks or a G-string, we would have to pay for them. My savings in the three years and five months that I was a prisoner amounted to 1,800 yen. Then we found out that, since the Japs lost the war, the yen wasn't worth anything. At first we could buy some articles, but the prices were enormous.

After paying us our savings, they issued us some cigarettes and a jigger of saki. This was my first taste of saki and I did not like it. I gave my part to Captain Cameron Starnes. We had tin cans with handles on them for our water or tea. This is what we used to pour the saki in, and those who could drink it had half a can of saki. It lasted them most of the night.

After supper we gathered for a service of prayer and thanksgiving led by our Chaplain Moe. Later we sang songs. Someone had managed to get an accordion. We sang our national anthem and other patriotic songs, then some love songs, as we were all thinking of our wives and sweethearts and going home. Some sang solos and Captain Starnes found a cornet that he blew all night. He had been a band instructor at Fort Worth, Texas, before the war. A lot of men stayed up all night talking and singing. Most close friends talked about their wives, mothers, fathers, brothers, sisters, and children.

August 23 we had a good dinner. It consisted of bread and one pound of meat for each twenty men; Captain Mike Ushakoff and I made the last batch of tea that we had saved for just this occasion. That night we took our own muster. We counted off in English and made our report in English. This was the first time since we were taken prisoners that we were able to do this.

28. *Contact Made with Outside World*

Colonel Unrhue asked five of us officers to go down into Roku Roshi and get a radio, so we could contact the outside world and find out what we should do. The five of us went to Roku Roshi about ten o'clock the next morning, which was August 24. We did not see but one radio aerial that indicated there was a radio in the house. We went to this house and there were two pairs of skivvies just outside the door. We knocked on the door several times and no one came to the door, so we opened the door and went in. There was a radio over in one corner of the room. Japanese have partitions in a room that are movable screens. When we were taking the radio from its electrical connections, a woman peeped her head around the screen and said, in Japanese, "Sir, that is the mayor's radio and I do not know what he will say if you take it away." We told her, in our best Japanese, that we were going to take it to our prison camp, and that it would be left there, unharmed, when we left. When we started out the door with the radio, another woman, who we thought was the mayor's wife, said, "That is the mayor's radio and he will not like it if you take it away." We also told her they would find it in our prison compound when we left.

We brought it back to camp and someone tried to hook it up so we could find out what we were to do. About sundown that evening, the mayor from Roku Roshi, who owned the radio, came to our camp. He brought about everything this village could afford in the way of food. He had about three hundred pounds of cucumbers, which we ate like bananas; four hundred pounds of grapes; some watermelons that were small but delicious. The mayor made us a chamber-of-commerce talk, except that it was in reverse, for he was praising our country, not his. He said, "You should be proud that you live in a nation so blessed by God with all the raw materials in abundance so you can whip any nation on earth." Our military might had made a believer out of him.

That night after the mayor had left and things began to quiet down, General MacArthur came on the radio broadcasting where and when they would drop food for each prison camp. He said, "We will drop food for the Roku Roshi camp on August 28, at eleven o'clock in the morning. You must print a large PW in white on the roof of your barracks." Even though the twenty-eighth was several days away, the next morning we painted a large PW on the roof of our barracks on the west and east sides.

We talked about what they would drop from the air, just as if it were going to be Christmas morning, when it arrived. Would they drop us clothes? Just Type C rations? Anything would suit us as we had learned not to be particular.

On August 25, our rations had increased from 1,200 calories to 3,100 calories a day. We had mango beans for breakfast, a large serving of potatoes, and onions. We had grapes and pears that were just turning, but could be eaten. They issued us one suit of Japanese uniforms. The people of the community gave us cookies made from rice and barley flour, with sweetened mashed beans rolled in the center. They were very tasty.

There were thirty or forty of us who organized a walk through the Roku Roshi community. This was a picturesque mountain village. They had some kind of mining tunnels dug into the side of the mountain. These were used for bomb shelters. There were several small streams of water, with a water wheel on every stream. There were some small plots of irrigated rice. The water wheels furnished the power to grind rice and barley flour. There was a crematory on top of the mountain. This was called a baby crematory for it was just two feet wide and four feet long.

29. *Intelligence Report*

Now that the war was over we knew we would be asked for reports concerning the treatment in each of the prison camps in which we had been held. Since there were twenty-five officers that had come from Yodogawa Bunshaw camp at Osaka, we decided that we would consolidate a report to be given to our military intelligence when we returned to the States. On August 27, 1945, we made the following record to be submitted to our intelligence department:

Captain John S. Coleman, Jr.

ROKU ROSHI PRISONER OF WAR CAMP

FUKUI PROVINCE, JAPAN

AUGUST 27, 1945

Subjects: Report of deaths of Americans held prisoners of war and statement of general conditions in Yodogawa Sub-Camp, Osaka District, Osaka, Japan, from November 26, 1942, to July 31, 1943.

To: Commanding General, U.S. Army of Occupation in Japan.

1. Location of Camp.

(a) This camp was located in a suburb northwest of Osaka on the bank of the Yodogawa River. It was a factory, the Yodogawa Seiko, which produced sheet steel, steel barrels, small steel casings, and diesel motors for canal barges.

(b) Four hundred prisoners from the Philippine Islands were moved into this camp, November 26, 1942. Of these, forty-six (46) were officers and three hundred and fifty-four (354) were enlisted men, of the Navy, Army, and Marine Corps.

(c) The camp was under the jurisdiction of the Osaka Prisoner of War Bureau.

2. Food.

(a) Under the Japanese army, which had direct control of the camp at the beginning, the rations issued were as follows: Approximately 600 grams of cereal consisting of rice and barley per man per day, variable vegetables issued, usually between 120 to 200 grams per man per day. In addition, beans, salt, sugar, soy sauce, etc. were issued; however, frequently individual members of the Japanese staff appropriated varying amounts of this issue for themselves. This was particularly true of such items as beans, sugar, salt, etc.

(b) After March 10, 1943, supply administration was turned over to the Yodogawa Seiko. At this time nominal rations were reduced to 570 grams of rice per man per day. The vegetable ration was appreciably decreased. The beans were eliminated entirely, and smaller amounts of sugar, salt, etc. were issued.

(c) Very infrequent issues were made of protein foods, such as meat or fish.

(d) The diet was very unbalanced and very deficient in vitamins, proteins, calorific content; quantity and quality were very poor.

3. Clothing.

(a) During the month of December there was no clothing issued and prisoners had to rely, for warmth, on the few remnants of tropical clothing they had been able to bring from the Philippines.

(b) At the end of December, prisoners were issued castoff overcoats of poor quality and a suit of very thin material in addition. The latter wore out very rapidly and were not replaced.

(c) On February 2, after most of the cold weather had passed, each prisoner received a suit consisting of heavy trousers and a blouse, some long underwear, and socks. All of these items were second-hand castoffs and in poor condition. At this time all personal clothing, except our suit of underwear, as well as other articles, was confiscated by the camp authorities.

(d) At no time did the prisoners have enough clothing to provide a change.

(e) Service shoes, with which the prisoners were equipped upon arrival, were confiscated early in the winter and replaced with rubber-soled canvas shoes. On April 14, 1943, new American service shoes were issued to all men. Shortly afterward these were collected and put in storage and their use was not permitted.

4. Housing.

(a) Until December 10, 1942, prisoners were housed in a partitioned-off corner of the factory buildings. Each man was limited to a space two and one-half feet wide and six feet long. There was no possibility of protection from the smoke and soot generated in the factory just on the other side of the partition. One steel drum served as the sole heat source for the barracks.

(b) The camp was moved on December 10, 1942, into a newly constructed loft in the upper part of another factory building. All prisoners were housed in the same room and the space per individual was not increased. Heating again was provided by one stove which was allowed to burn only at specified times during the day. No attempt was made to make either of the buildings weather tight.

(c) The most severe cases of illness were isolated from the barracks by a short partition, which prevented visual communication only.

(d) Prisoners slept on boards covered with straw mats and had five poor-quality, thin cotton blankets.

5. Medical Facilities.

(a) In our original group of four hundred, there were no doctors or medical corps personnel. After strong representation by prisoners, one doctor and three corpsmen were transferred in from another camp.

(b) Medical supplies and equipment were at no time sufficient.

Medicines were limited to ointments or powders of little or no value, and were under strict supervision of the Japanese medical corps privates. Issues were often delayed until even their questionable value was useless. The only tools in camp were a small field kit which was the personal property of the American doctor. After the arrival of Red Cross supplies in April, 1943, medicines were more abundant, but never available for use at the discretion of our doctor. Bandaging materials were always short and had to be used over and over.

(c) The main aim of the Japanese at all times was to show on their records a maximum number of men at work. As a result the decisions of our doctor were constantly ignored or overruled and men were sent to work who were hardly able to walk. Often disease and ailments that would not normally be fatal or even serious, if properly treated, were aggravated to such an extent that the patient died.

(d) Most common ailments were the results of malnutrition and dietary deficiencies: beriberi, edema, dysentery, pellagra, etc. In addition, flu, pneumonia, and malaria were common. Due to malnutrition, resistance was low and contracting an illness was of grave concern. In cases of the beriberi patients, these became gangrenous and the amputation of all or a part of the foot became necessary.

(e) Living conditions for the patients were even more trying than for the well ones. They were packed into bays with scarcely enough room and it was impossible to segregate infectious cases from the others. The Japanese did not supply us with sufficient sick-bay workers to maintain more than the most rudimentary sanitary precautions. Patients were liable at any time and in any kind of weather to be forced outside for exercise, regardless of their physical condition.

(f) Visits were made at intervals by the Japanese medical officer, but his examinations were mostly perfunctory and constructive action was rarely taken.

(g) A list of deaths and causes during this period is given in the attached Appendix A.

6. Working Conditions.

(a) All men were forced to work in all parts of the factory, doing the hardest kind of physical labor, such as carrying too heavy a load, serving at the blast furnace, working in rolling mills in extreme heat, etc.

(b) Work was allotted to men regardless of their physical condition and despite the protest of the prison doctor. This was in all kinds of weather. Not only were sick men required to work, but they were forced to keep the pace set by the Japanese workers.

(c) Officers were forced to work as laborers, under duress. This took the form of physical punishment as well as mental hazing.

(d) No attempt was made to protect the men against occupational hazards. As a result, injuries occurred daily. Most noticeable were the cases of those men who worked in the sand-blasting department. Goggles and masks were not provided and the casualties in this department were particularly heavy. Many cases of lung trouble were contracted here.

7. Punishments.

(a) The smallest infraction of rules was punished by severe physical violence. These were often meted out to the group as a whole as well as to individuals directly concerned. As an example: On March the eleventh, 1943, it came to the attention of the Japs that some service shoes had been sold to a factory workman for food. They could not find the prisoner involved, so they forced the whole camp, sick and well alike, to strip naked and kneel on the cinder-surfaced compound yard for two hours. This was particularly hard for those whose feet and legs were swelled and painful from beriberi. The day was cold and blustery. This resulted in several of the men being sent to bed seriously ill. When the culprit was found he was severely beaten with fists, belt buckles, and leather shoe heels. His nose was broken and he had many lacerations about his face. After this treatment, he was tied with his hands behind his back; the rope was then passed over the roof beam and tightened so that he was forced to stand on tiptoe to avoid excruciating pain in his arms. He was left in this position all night. Many other such examples could be cited.

(b) The Japanese staff took great pleasure in inflicting pain and humiliation on prisoners. They went out of their way to create provocation.

8. Red Cross.

(a) Red Cross food parcels were issued on December 17, 1942, on the basis of one parcel for every three men. Lieutenant Yamada personally supervised its fair and equal distribution.

(b) Other Red Cross food supplies, both bulk and parcels, were broken up and issued to individuals as prizes for "good work." Sick men and those that had incurred the displeasure of the camp authorities received almost nothing, while others received several articles. Much of the food, especially sugar, candy, cocoa milk, and cereal were retained and used by the guards. The American senior officer was forced to sign a receipt for these supplies, before they were issued. All of this was done under the personal supervision of Gunsō (Sergeant) Hirose, the camp commander.

(c) At no time in our stay in this camp were the prisoners visited by or allowed contact with the representatives of the International Red Cross.

(d) Three letters were received in the camp during the period.

9. General.

(a) Every effort was made to create animosity between the prisoner officers and the enlisted men.

(b) Officers were continually subjected to humiliation in front of their own men.

(c) All prisoners, regardless of rank, were forced to render salutes to the lowest-ranking Japanese personnel.

(d) Officers were not furnished separate quarters.

(e) Despite constant and strong representation by the prisoners, the Japanese authorities, both military and civilian, remained indifferent to the welfare of the camp. They even went so far as to issue a written order that these representations cease.

(f) The daily ration of those too sick to work was reduced to one-half the daily ration of the working personnel.

10. Designation of Responsibilities.

(a) It is the opinion of the undersigned that the direct responsibility for the high death rate and the conditions mentioned in this report rests on the shoulders of the Osaka District authorities and the administrative personnel of the Yodogawa Sub-Camp, a list of whom follows:

DISTRICT: Lieutenant Colonel Murata, Commanding Captain Nosu, Medical Officer

SUB-CAMP: Second Lieutenant Yamada, Camp Commander from November 26, 1942, to March 10, 1943

Sergeant Hirose, Camp Commander from March 10, 1943, to June 16, 1943

Sergeant Tanaka, Camp Commander from June 16, 1943, to the end of the period.

Corporals:

Akamatsu

Nakagima

Sto

Maishita

Interpreters:

Asui

Suwa

Shitagawa

SIGNED:

Russell B. Johnson
First Lieutenant, Infantry,
0-381012

John S. Coleman, Jr.
Captain, Air Corps,
0-243526

Thomas R. Harrison
First Lieutenant, E. A.,
0-446400

Cameron S. Starnes
Captain, Infantry,
0-291283

The foregoing report has been examined and approved by all of the twenty-five officers who were removed from Yodogawa Seiko, July 31, 1943, to Zentsuji Prisoner-of-War Camp, Shikoku, Japan.

We also recorded a list of eighty-seven men who died at this camp, giving the name, rank, date of birth, and what the Japs said was the cause of death. When we left this camp, July 31, 1943, there were thirty men who were confined to sick bays, too sick to work.

30. *Food from Heaven*

When August twenty-eighth came, everyone was up early anticipating the dropping of food. When we looked out and scanned for the possibility of good weather, it was dark and cloudy. A slow rain was falling. We thought, this is early and surely by eleven o'clock it will clear and the planes can locate our camp. We walked the floor and listened to the rain, hoping that it would stop. It did slow down by ten o'clock, but it continued to be dark and cloudy. When eleven o'clock came and conditions were not any better, we could have cried. We heard the drone of the motors of the planes as they flew directly over us, but there was no break in the clouds anywhere. We were very disappointed, but knew that no one could help the conditions of the weather, except God. We wondered when they would try again to drop us some food. We did not know how far they were having to fly to get to our camp. Were they coming from Okinawa or had they secured a base in Japan?

That night we all huddled around the radio hoping to get a report. For a long time all we could hear was the Japanese language and they talked too fast for us to get much out of their conversation. Finally General MacArthur came on the air and said it was too cloudy to drop food at Roku Roshi that day, but it would be dropped at eleven o'clock the morning of September 2, weather permitting. This was four more long days to wait. We were just marking time until we received more American food or they gave us orders to come to Osaka or Yokohama. The only information we had received about getting us moved out was what the commandant had told us, that our troops would come for us. One time it was reported via radio that all POWs were to stay in camp until someone came for them.

We had cleared the brush and stumps from about four acres of land and had planted it in sweet potatoes and some soybeans, since we came to Roku Roshi. I walked around the garden plot for the last time. We were leaving them with a very good garden. The vines were dark and healthy. We had had plenty of rain since the plants were set out.

The morning of September 2 finally arrived; again we got up early to check the weather. It was cloudy again and foggy, but not raining. We thought it best for no one to stay in the building for fear a parachute would rip open and come down through the roof. Anyway, everyone wanted to be outside to see what happened. It stayed cloudy and dark until about ten-thirty; then we could begin to see a few breaks in the cloudcover.

About eleven o'clock a long slit opened up in the clouds and a big B-29, which few of us had seen, came through this opening. The pilot tipped his wings to let us know he had seen our camp and then went out of sight into the clouds. In a few minutes another B-29 came through the opening and dropped many parachutes of all colors. As soon as one group of parachutes got near the ground, another B-29 came through the opening, another B-29 bay was opened, and more came floating down. This was the most beautiful display of colors I had ever seen. Each individual article had its own colored parachute. The canned foods were dropped in two fifty-five gallon drums welded together. Sometimes a parachute would rip open and the barrels would slam into the ground like a bomb. Cans and packages would scatter everywhere. We had to keep on the alert and run to keep from being hit by one of these packages.

One bale of clothes burst open soon after the parachute opened up and air would get in the shirts and trousers. They would flutter and slowly drift downward giving the appearance of a scarecrow. After each plane had passed over twice, emptying the rear bay first, then the front bay, everything cleared up. I think there were three B-29's making six drops. There was no wind to scatter the parachutes and they all landed in a ten-acre area, except some clothes that floated a little farther away, but all were retrieved.

As soon as all of the packages and parachutes had landed, and there was no further danger of a barrel coming down on our heads, each of us went to a barrel of canned goods first. The ones that had burst open were the first surrounded. Not one bit of food was wasted. We had exhausted ourselves to keep from getting hit. We sat down by the barrels with all of the canned food pouring out and this reminded me of the pictures I had seen of the horn of plenty, with lots of money pouring out, but this was a much more attractive sight to us than anything else in the world. We first looked for any cans that had been broken open enough to leak so that we could use them immediately and the food would not be ruined or wasted.

The first can I found was a can of fruit cocktail. It was dented just enough for some juice to leak out, so I opened it and ate it. Then I saw a can of peaches that had burst open, and a lieutenant and I ate the sliced peaches from this can. There were some Type C rations marked dinner, supper, and breakfast on the wrappings. I ate three days' ration of these. Each package had four cigarettes in it. Next I started on some chocolate bars and ate five of them. They were a type of emergency ration. By this time I felt full, but I still had a hungry feeling in my stomach. Each of us took an armload of food to the kitchen until all that had been dropped was picked up.

We assembled in one place all of the clothes that had been dropped. There was not enough clothing for each prisoner. We drew for the clothing and we got either a shirt or a pair of trousers. I drew a size-17 shirt and I normally wore a size 15. Since no one wore a size-17 shirt, I could not trade it for a smaller one.

By twelve o'clock I was very sick. I had eaten too much. I went to the rest room and vomited; then I began to squirt at both ends. I was so sick I could hardly sit up, but I had to take care of nature's actions. After about twenty minutes of heaving, I was able to go back to my bunk. In about two hours after running to the latrine and coming back to my bunk to rest, my stomach settled down. I was not the only one who was sick. Sometimes I would have to wait my turn to get into the latrine.

They brought our dinner to us about half-past twelve, but I had to send most of mine back to the kitchen. I could not stand the thought of eating. I remember waking up during the night and there were small campfires out in the prison compound, with three or four men squatted around, trying to cook something they thought they would especially like. I heard a conversation where they were mixing green beans, potatoes, and some kind of meat. Then they fixed another dish of Type C rations warmed up. Every kind of combination that a person could think of, but none of this was appetizing to me. That night my hands and feet swelled and had fever in them. In a few days the outer skin peeled off my hands and a ridge grew on my finger and toe nails. I had seen this happen to foundered horses. My finger nails grew twice as fast as my toe nails. In two days I began to eat lightly. Everyone had all the food he could eat until we left camp.

31. *The Day of Liberation*

On the eighth of September just before noon, a group of eight soldiers and two nurses arrived at our camp. They were to take us back to Yokohama. This was our liberation force. The commandant had enough trucks brought up to take us to Fukui to the railroad station. We left Roku Roshi the morning of the ninth of September. When we arrived in Fukui, it was raining. Most of the city of Fukui had been burned to the ground. This city had close to one million in population and now it lay in ruins. The depot had been burned down, but they had built a small building about thirty by one hundred feet in size. They had tents set up to keep us out of the rain. There was one five-story office building still being used. One of the burned-out buildings that had part of the top left was filled with urns, the ashes of dead people. Each room was stacked full of these square white boxes. They were about one and one-half feet square.

We had to wait three hours for our train. While we were waiting, we walked around the ruins of this large city during the intermittent showers. Five of us went into the five-story office building. We could hear people running upstairs, but we could not see anyone. When we would come to an office we would open the door and look in. The Japanese had heard us coming or had seen us. Realizing that we were ex-POWs, they just left their offices and kept going higher and higher in the building. Apparently they were afraid that we were there to cause trouble, but we had not planned to do this at all. Of course, it would not have taken much to start trouble with us after three years and five months of Japanese oppression. The lights would be on in the offices and there were papers on the desks and we could tell they had left in a hurry.

When we had been in Fukui about one hour, the Japanese Red Cross set up several tents and we were invited in for tea. This was a pleasant surprise. They served us hot tea, some little biscuits or crackers about one-half inch square, and one tangerine. The ladies who served it were friendly and pleasant. The atmosphere was very congenial and no one got out of line. This was my first knowledge that the Japanese permitted their Red Cross to function. During the war they didn't allow any gathering to take place without strict supervision, for fear of getting antigovernment actions started.

Some passenger trains came through Fukui and stopped for a few minutes each time. The coaches were loaded with soldiers of all kinds. They were hanging on the outside and completely filled the inside. It looked like they had just told the soldiers to go home if they could get there. The Japanese officers continued to carry their samurai swords, but they were not carried on their belts. The police who were on duty at Fukui had no guns of any kind, just light swords.

We left Fukui on the passenger train just before dark. Since we had no watches, we had become used to guessing at the time just from the position of the sun. No one slept much that night on the train; however, there was heat and it was comfortable. Our freedom became more and more a reality. We were headed for home, to our families and loved ones. We wondered about our relatives. My mother was old when I left the States in 1941, but was in good health. My brother, Wood, was a lieutenant colonel and was in Italy the last time I heard. Another brother, Jesse, was a lieutenant in the Air Corps, but had not been sent overseas the last time I heard from my wife, which was in 1944. My heart ached because of the worry I knew my mother must have suffered over the safety of her three boys, but most especially for the worry I had caused her.

Sam Kinch and Charles Boatner from the *Fort Worth Star Telegram* were with those who came to liberate us. They were with the army unit. Sam Kinch interviewed me since I was the president of the Texas POW organization. There were 52 Texans in this camp. I had not had a chance to send a telegram to my wife to let her know I was still alive after this ordeal, so I asked Sam Kinch if he would send a telegram to my wife. I knew he would have access to this mode of communication at Yokohama. He said he would be glad to do this for me. It just so happened that we were thinking of two different kinds of telegrams. My wife did receive a *Fort Worth Star Telegram*, which was the name of the newspaper Sam Kinch represented, and it did have my name circled in red. I had thought she would receive a telegram by wire, instead of a newspaper. I did appreciate his willingness to do this for me and she probably received the newspaper as quickly as a wire.

32. *San Francisco Here We Come*

We arrived in Yokohama about nine o'clock the morning of September 10. When we got off the train a battalion of the best-looking soldiers that I had ever seen were there. They were bronze in color, from taking Atabrine to prevent malaria; they were all dressed neatly and all straight and healthy. These men were holding a "present arms" with small field rifles. General MacArthur and General Eichelburger were holding a hand salute, with tears running down their cheeks. Several nurses were at each coach landing. They would ask us if we wanted a cigarette or gum and they would ask us how we were feeling. The one I talked to put her hand on my shoulder, looked at me with tears in her eyes, and finally said, "I will help you around the corner to a hospital boat," but I told her, "I have never felt better in my life." She smiled and said, "Each of you is just wonderful." The band was playing "San Francisco Here I Come."

I was wearing an old pair of patched-up shorts, with the new khaki shirt, size 17, that I drew at Roku Roshi. This shirt fit me like a Mother Hubbard dress. The tail of the shirt came below my blue denim shorts, which were the regulation trousers in the Philippines. I had cut the legs off to patch the seat. At the time, I wasn't thinking of seeing all those beautiful nurses. They had a way of making you feel like they really cared about your health and general well being.

We were escorted a few hundred feet to the dining hall. When we entered we couldn't believe our eyes! There were tables and chairs. The tables had cloths on them and, "gee whiz," there were even waiters, waiting to serve us! Soon General MacArthur entered the room, we were called to attention, then at ease. The general made a short talk and told us how glad he was to see us free men again. Then he said, "Order anything you want and I have also ordered the galleys on the ships taking you home to stay open day and night. Order anything they have and eat as much as you want, day or night."

Golly! This was a great breakfast, with the smell of hot cakes, bacon, and coffee. All the men that I noticed ordered hot cakes and bacon with coffee. The general also told us, when we had finished our breakfast, to come into the room next door and get some clothes and shoes. When I went to the supply room, General MacArthur was helping fit the men with clothes. He was smiling and seemed so happy for us. I was having a problem finding a six and one-half in shoes and was sitting on a folding canvas cot. While I was trying on a size seven and one-half G.I. shoe, the general sat down beside me and asked my name, what branch of the service I was in, and my rank. When I told him I was an administrative officer in the Air Corps, he said, "That was the biggest mistake I made at the beginning of the war. I did not believe any airplane could sink a battleship. Of course, the sinking of the *Prince of Wales* and the Pearl Harbor incident made a big believer out of me."*

I did not tell General MacArthur that my commanding officer had recommended me three times for a major's commission before we surrendered. The table of organization required the rank of major to command an Air Corps squadron. When General MacArthur was sent to Australia and General Wainwright took his place, my commission was approved about April 3, 1942, but things were happening so fast and the fighting so fierce on the front, that I had never had the opportunity to take the oath of office for this commission. Therefore, I didn't receive the commission until September 10, 1945, but it was dated September 2, 1945. Because of all of this, I lost three and one-half years' salary as a major.

We had been in Yokohama about two hours when we heard that a lot of ex-POWs had been flown to the United States. Most of the group that I had been with were in the Air Corps of the Army. Now they found they were going to have to return to the States by ship, while other branches of the service were going to fly home. I heard lots of fussing among them about having to return the slow way. Some inquired into the possibility of flying home, but were told that there would not be any more air transportation because the heavy transport planes had torn up the air strip runways so badly that it would not be safe to take off with a load. Naturally all of these men wanted to get home as soon as possible. Most had been away from the States four years.

I was fitted with two field uniforms and a pair of over-size field shoes. We were taken to a ship by landing barges. The ship was anchored in Yokohama Bay, out about one-half mile. The ship was the combat transport *Goodhue*. Here we were assigned to cabins for our voyage to Manila. We stayed anchored all night and part of the next morning, while they took on more troops. We pulled anchor and started for Manila about ten o'clock the morning of September 12.

---

* On December 10, 1941, the British battleship *Prince of Wales* was sunk by the Japanese air force. This was at that time the largest battleship in the world and was commanded by Admiral Tom Phillips. The cruiser *Repulse* and the destroyer *Electra* were also sunk. This left the west side of the Philippines unguarded.

It was reported by the weather bureau that a typhoon would hit the Okinawa territory the next day. We were to vary to the east of Okinawa, which would have been a nearer route to the Philippine Islands. Most of the trip was very hot and sultry, and lasted six days. Some of the marines on the ship, who had not been POWs, brought me a green marine uniform. My other clothes had been so soiled by perspiration. I appreciated their thoughtfulness. One of the marines said he was going to come back to Japan and serve in the occupational forces. He asked me how many dollars I would take for 100 yen. I did not know what a yen was worth, so when he offered me fifteen dollars for 100 yen, I was glad to trade. I had not seen American money in several years.

The second night on the boat I woke up about ten o'clock and felt a little hungry. Thinking of the many months I had really been hungry and remembering what General MacArthur had said about the galley being open all night, I decided to go get something to eat. When I got to the galley it was lit up brightly and several ex-POWs were eating. I saw a basket filled with fruit: apples, bananas, oranges, pineapple, and other kinds of fruit. I took an apple because I had missed apples most. It tasted like I had remembered them, when I had wished for one in prison. This was the only time I went to the galley at night. While I was there, a mess sergeant asked, "Is there anything I can cook for you?" I thanked him and felt well satisfied with the apple.

33. *Manila Again*

When we came to Manila Bay the morning of September 18, there were sunken ships as far as the eye could see. They were large ships, some with bows extending out of the water as much as thirty feet and some had settled flat in shallow water, with smoke stacks extending out of the water. Our ship weaved around these sunken ships slowly. There must have been at least one hundred sunken ships you could see at one time. This bay looked like a cemetery for ships. We anchored at Pier Five and there were army trucks there to take us to the 29th Replacement Depot.

I saw an amphibious boat come out of the water and up on the shore to the street, and there was an airplane that looked like it was flying slow. I later found out that it was called a helicopter. The ship we came back to Manila on was equipped with radar. This was all new equipment to us. On the way to the replacement depot, we passed tall, long ricks of food and supplies of different kinds. This was to be used if we had to invade Japan proper. These supplies were to help the Okinawa invading forces, too. When we arrived at the replacement depot it was a tent city. They were unloading some work details of Japanese prisoners. This was the first time I had seen a large number of Japanese prisoners.

We were assigned tents and given some supplies. We were issued a number-one uniform, a steel helmet liner to use as a wash basin, a khaki web belt with a canteen and a first-aid kit, two Australian woolen blankets, a duffle bag, and a mess kit. We were told to go to the infirmary for a physical checkup. This was also in a large tent. They looked us over and gave us some kind of shots. Since I did not have any feeling in my forearm these shots did not bother me. The nurses seemed to think we were getting an awful lot of shots at one time. When I started out of the infirmary, one of the nurses asked me in a very low voice, as if it were a secret, if I wanted a toddy after having all of those needles jabbing and probing me. I said, "Yes." She gave me a jigger of whiskey. Before I got out of the tent entrance I noticed she was giving all of the men a toddy and was not showing any partiality to me.

We went to the finance department to get a partial payment of our salaries. It had been three years and ten months since I had been paid. I drew seven hundred dollars thinking this would last me until I returned to the States. I went to the post exchange and bought a pocket knife. This two-bladed knife cost me twenty-seven cents and I had to sign for it. I had not owned a knife since I threw mine in Manila Bay on April 11, 1942, just before going in to surrender. I went to the communications center to send a telegram to my wife. Here I received my first correspondence from home since I had been liberated. The telegram read: "For Captain John S. Coleman, Jr., 0243526, the children and I are eagerly awaiting news of your liberation. Sunday, September 2 is our seventeenth wedding anniversary. Remember I love you truly. Mrs. John S. Coleman, Jr."

I also sent a telegram telling my family that I had been liberated

September 8 and would be back in the States in October. This tele-gram was never received by my wife. It was sent from a Red Cross tent where they were taking written messages. If you were an ex-POW, the first twenty-five words were sent free, but I wrote more than the allotted number of words. The extra cost was one dollar and twenty-five cents. I put a one dollar bill along with a quarter on top of my message and left it on the table. The clerks were very busy and probably a mix-up of who was paying for what caused the message not to be sent. I did not learn that the telegram was never received until I arrived at home.

When I got back to my tent, my bunk was made up and every-thing had been put in order by an orderly. I lay down to rest for a little while. It had started to rain. I tried to think of someone I had known in Manila before the war. I remembered a Mr. Boone, who was a Spanish American War veteran who had come to Manila with Admiral Dewey and had stayed. When World War II started, he was having heart trouble and I did not expect to find him. He was the brother-in-law of a friend of mine in Hartley County, Texas, whose name was O. H. Finch. Mr. Boone's daughter, Alice, was more likely to have survived the war, so I tried to locate her through the federal post office. They would look up the names and if they lived in Manila they would tell you very soon. I found out later that I had asked for Alice Finch instead of Alice Boone. This was a mental mix-up on my part.

I slept on an army cot that night and I could hear it raining very hard all night. The next morning a group of Japanese prisoners were policing the grounds near my tent. I spoke to them in Japanese. When they found out that I could speak Japanese and that I had been a prisoner of war in Japan, they crowded around me asking questions about their homeland. I told them that most of the large cities were destroyed, but they did not believe me. I told them that Osaka and Fukui had been burned to the ground. They were shocked. The American guard would come and run them away so they would get their work done. They would filter back one by one to ask more questions and the guard would scatter them again. By the second morning they had begun to believe me. Although I could not speak fluent Japanese and they could not understand English too well, they seemed to understand most of what I told them. I told them that their people were dying from malnutrition due to starvation.

They all looked as if they were in perfect physical condition. I told them that many of our prisoners had died of starvation in Japan. I also told them that they would soon be released to go back to their homeland as free men. This brought a smile to their faces and I could understand why. Even though we had been enemies, the longing to go home was a mutual feeling.

September twentieth I received orders that I would board the transport ship *Admiral Hughes* on September twenty-first to go to San Francisco. The post canteen was the meeting place of all branches of the service. All were soon to go home. The ex-POWs were treated like royalty everywhere we went. They would not let us pay for drinks, candy, popcorn, eats of any kind, or whatever we wanted. The kitchens were always open. There were hundreds of soldiers and officers who had served long enough overseas to have enough points to qualify them to go home. One lieutenant in my group had received a telegram from his parents telling him that his wife had remarried. She had not heard anything from him in the three years and five months that he had been a prisoner. There was one master sergeant who received the same news and, of course, they were very sad. We all sympathized with them.

September 21 those who were leaving on the *Admiral Hughes* were up at daylight and ready to leave. The thought of going home was still hard to believe. We had been gone over four years and many times over those four years it looked as if it would be impossible to live. There were many times it would have been much easier to die than to try to live. During this time the greatest war that had ever beset our nation had been fought. The process of getting home seemed to move very slowly. I had packed everything that I owned that I could carry in my duffle bag and it was about half full and very heavy for my weak body to carry. I had to leave on my cot, two wool blankets, the helmet liner, a pair of booties, a mess kit, and a first-aid kit. My duffle bag was still too heavy and I wondered how I would ever get it up the gangplank of the ship.

It was raining when the trucks pulled up to the replacement depot. Everyone was on time and ready to leave. We passed the old

Manila Hotel and could see where artillery shells and machine gun bullets had penetrated the outside walls of this once-beautiful building. It was said that the Japanese had to be fought out of this hotel and were chased to the top story before they were killed or surrendered. The Americans had declared Manila an open city when we left in January 1942, thinking it would keep it from being destroyed, but the Japanese did not try to prevent its destruction when it was retaken by our troops in 1945. We stopped at the old walled city near the ship docks; and the walls that had been twenty feet wide, with a moat around them, had been torn down by artillery shells and bombs. This had to be done to dislodge the Japanese from the old fort. We walked up on the old walls from the outside, and where they had once been twenty feet wide they now lay in ruins.

When we arrived at Pier Five where the *Admiral Hughes* was docked, I dragged my duffle bag out of the truck and started down the pier to the gangplank. Just then an enlisted man came up and asked if he could carry my duffle bag up the gangplank for me. After we got to the top of the gangplank he said, "Where is your cabin?" I was so glad to have him carry my duffle bag up the gangplank that I didn't expect him to take it to my cabin. After we found my cabin and he set the bag down, I tried to give him a five dollar bill, but he said, "I would not think of taking pay for helping you." I did not want to embarrass him by insisting. I thanked him and told him that this was the nicest thing that had happened to me in a long time. When he left, I sat down on the bunk to rest for a little while. I thought of all those things that I had left on my cot at the replacement depot that I could have put in my duffle bag had I known I was going to find someone nice enough to carry it aboard for me. Soon the other three came in who were assigned to this four-bed cabin. There was so much visiting going on that only when we went to bed could you tell who bunked where as far as the cabins were concerned. The war was over and at last we were going home. The bad memories of past battles were beginning to take a back seat to the anticipated reunions with our families.

As the *Admiral Hughes* threaded its way through the sunken ships in Manila Bay, we passed land marks that were familiar. Mt. Natib in the distance, where my unit first met the Japanese Imperial Army coming down to the entrance of Bataan; the town of Balanga, which the Japanese held for so long a time and near where we spent our first night and were interrogated on the death march. Then Orion, near where our front lines were for two months and where my unit made several counterattacks.

Pilar, between Balanga and Orion in no man's land, where we did some trading on the black market from Manila until the Japanese intercepted their boats and sank all of them. Pilar was also where the syrup mill was that we got black strap molasses from until the Japanese put kerosene in it. We also fought some skirmishes with the Japanese patrols trying to get the millstone to be used for grinding rice flour.

The village of Limay was where our first hospital was located. Later it was moved farther back on the peninsula. Then there was the Little Baguio, sitting high on a hill, surrounded by a beautiful virgin forest. The little village of Lamao, where I had given first aid to a woman and child who had been in a bombing raid two weeks before Bataan fell.

The ship glided past Cabcaben, the nearest boat dock from the Bataan Peninsula to Corregidor. It was also from here that most troops departed when Corregidor was invaded. This is where Captain Dorman and I were ordered to take a boat from on April 9, 1942, to go to Corregidor, a trip we were unable to make. Captain Dorman and I crossed the Japanese lines on the Real River to enter our front lines on the same morning before the surrender. The ship passed the Gibraltar of the East, Corregidor, that defended the Manila Bay.

Then we passed Mariveles, where the Air Corps from Nichols Field landed on Christmas Day, 1941. Now we were out of the mouth of Manila Bay and those historical scenes would, for most of us, fade into history and never be seen again for hundreds of ex-POWs. My son, Spencer, and I did visit here again in 1967. Some scars of the war were still visible.

The Philippines was a beautiful country and there were many wonderful people living there. It was a tragedy that the invading armies of Japan overcame them.

We were about one day's journey from the east side of Mindanao when the ship's captain sighted what he thought to be a floating mine. One of the crew shot at it with a .50-caliber machine gun at a distance of about one-quarter of a mile. It was hit but did not explode.

When we were north of the Hawaiian Islands the captain of the ship received a radiogram that altered our course and destination from San Francisco to Seattle. This was done because we had a number of British and Canadian troops on board and they were to disembark at Victoria, Canada. I was glad that I had not wired my wife to meet me in San Francisco. When we arrived at Victoria, we, as well as the British and Canadian military personnel, received a big welcome. When we were anchored at the pier the Canadian people threw fine, large apples up to us on the deck. Their bands were playing and everyone was in a very merry mood.

Several officers of the United States military intelligence came aboard at Vancouver to ride to Seattle. They questioned us about atrocities that may have been committed by the Japanese and inquired if any of our personnel had committed any acts of treason that we knew about. The investigations were also to find out if there had been any illegal breach of the Geneva Conference agreement. I had the report ready that the twenty-five officers had made and certified on the camp at Yodogawa Bunshaw. This was a seventeen-page report written in longhand. I told the investigating officers that if they would take the original report, they would need to make me twelve copies for my future use. They made me fifteen copies and I did use them at other stations.

Just after I finished making my report to the investigating officers, we were on our way to Seattle. An entertainment boat pulled along side our ship. It was just after sundown. It had all of its bright lights on and was really well lit. All of the army personnel, which consisted of about four thousand men, ran over to the side of the ship to get a better view of the entertainment boat. An urgent announcement came over the ship's communication system, "Now hear this, an urgent announcement to all passengers. Please move back to the center of the ship immediately. You are about to capsize the ship. Give us a few minutes to pump water into the ballasts." Eventually the crowd complied with the request, but these were the first American girls that most of us had seen in four years. They were beautiful women.

It was almost dark when we pulled into the harbor at Seattle. Here we really received a welcome befitting a king. Factory whistles blew, battleships anchored there sounded their whistles, and all the fire sirens in Seattle blew for fifteen minutes. This was October 8, 1945. When we docked at the pier another announcement came over the ship's intercom, "Now hear this, no ex-POW will disembark tonight. You will be taken through the hospital in the morning."

When we tied up to the pier and the gangplank came down, all except the ex-POWs began disembarking. There were 2,610 liberated POWs and the other men who were to get off at Seattle. All the men getting off the ship were carrying duffle bags over their shoulders. All were happy that they had served their country through this terrible war but were now coming home.

Most of the ex-POWs were standing along the rail on the top deck of the ship. We were happy for the hundreds of people and soldiers who were meeting their families there. You could tell those that were meeting their sons, husbands, fathers, and brothers. These soldiers were men to be proud of. Major Mike Ushakoff, a close friend of mine, was standing beside me. I knew Seattle was his home. It was not publicized that there would be any ex-POWs on the transport *Admiral Hughes*. I did not expect Major Ushakoff's folks to be at the pier, but looking down at the large crowd that was waiting, I asked Mike what his wife looked like. Mike was too blind to identify anyone ten feet away. He said, "She is a short, blond-haired woman." I looked the crowd over again and noticed two women together who seemed to be looking for someone. One of them did fit Mike's description of his wife. I shouted down to them, "Mrs. Ushakoff." She raised her hand. I said, "Come on up the gangplank. Mike is here." She and the other woman hurried up the gangplank, but were stopped by the guard. I explained to him that her husband was here and was blind. That she had not seen him in four years. The guard stepped aside and let the two women on board the ship. The other woman was the wife of Chaplain Leslie Zimmerman, an ex-POW. They all had a wonderful reunion and visited on board the ship until about two o'clock that morning.

Early the next morning we began to disembark and were taken to the Madagen General Hospital at Fort Lewis, Washington. We were assigned beds and then began filing through the doctors' offices. We were checked for all kinds of Asiatic diseases and given chest X-rays. Many of these men responded positively to the tuberculosis test. I continued to have the hurting in my right side, but otherwise I felt in good shape. I tried to get them to release me and let me fly home, but they said that I would have to stay there nine days and then go by hospital coach to Brooke General Hospital in San Antonio, Texas.

The tenth of October was my wife's birthday so I decided to call her right after midnight and surprise her by saying, "Happy Birthday to you." I tossed around on my hospital bed and could not sleep, but I had asked the nurse to wake me at midnight if I did happen to drop off to sleep. By half-past ten, I just could not wait any longer to call Ethel. All of this time I had thought that she had received the telegram I had sent from Manila. I tried for one and one-half hours to get my phone call through to Wellington, Texas. Finally an answer came, but when she answered the phone, I forgot all about wishing her a happy birthday. She had not received the telegram and this call came as quite a shock to her. I told her that I would be staying at Madagen General Hospital in Fort Lewis for nine days and would come through Childress, near my home, on a certain date. I would let her know as soon as our travel orders were confirmed. She told me about receiving the *Fort Worth Star Telegram* newspaper with my name circled in red as having been liberated on September 8. My daughter, Lennie Lou, talked to me too. All of this was so exciting to me, I really did have a time going to sleep.

The next day Major Mike Ushakoff had arranged for us to go to a football game between Oregon State University and Washington State University. That night we went to a big dinner party. We were mixing back into civilization gradually. I was still having problems sleeping in a bed. It felt like sleeping on a cloud after sleeping on the ground or a hard floor for three years and eight months.

The hospital administration had arranged to keep a kitchen open all night, just for the ex-POWs. They would cook a short order or almost anything one could want. Many of the men used these facilities during the night and between meals during the day.

Two days before leaving Madagen General Hospital, a nurse came to me and said she would be in charge of our hospital coach on the trip to San Antonio, Texas. She was a second lieutenant and had been reared in Massachusetts. She was eager to visit Texas. She told me that they would have pajamas for all of us and would take our clothes; that we were not to leave the coach until we arrived at

Brooke General Hospital in San Antonio, Texas. I told her that en route to San Antonio we would be passing through my home area and I might want to get off a few minutes at different places to see some of my friends or family. She said, "I have orders that no one is to leave the coach at any time."

We finally boarded the hospital train about two o'clock one afternoon. This train consisted of fifteen hospital coaches with the destination Denver, Colorado. Here three coaches were to be switched to the Fort Worth and Denver Railway. The others were to continue east and would be sent to other destinations. We arrived in Denver, Colorado, about one o'clock the next afternoon. We had a three-hour layover before continuing to San Antonio, Texas. While we were waiting to leave Denver, the nurse in charge of our coach had to go to the depot to send a wire. The depot was about one-quarter of a mile from where our coach was stopped. While she was gone two of our men got their clothes out of the nurse's room, where they had been stored when they took them after issuing us pajamas. They went downtown far enough to get a beer and to have a telegram typed for her. When they came back they changed back into their pajamas and left the telegram on her desk. The telegram read, "We will meet you in sunny San Antonio." When she returned and found the telegram, she came crying to me. She said, "Major, two of our men have left the coach without permission and left this telegram saying they will meet me in sunny San Antonio." Then she showed me the telegram. She said, "You are the ranking officer in this coach and you should not have let them go."

I said, "Lieutenant, you did not give me any authority to do anything. You took my uniform and put us all in pajamas. I have no more authority than anyone else in this coach." This made the tears fall faster. I tried to console her by telling her, "Those are Texas boys and if they said they would meet you in San Antonio, they will be there."

She said, "But I had orders not to let anyone leave this coach. From now on you are second in charge."

I said, "To reimburse me for being second in charge, you will let me have my clothes so I can stand on the platform and greet some of my family and friends in Dalhart, Channing, Amarillo, and Childress, will you not?"

She said, "Maybe." I suggested to her that we count the men in the coach. "Could be they are all here." When we counted them and they were all there, she dried her tears and laughed about the joke that had been played on her. She was a very sincere and dedicated officer and wanted to carry out her orders to the letter.

When the lieutenant had gone to the depot to send the wire, she made arrangements for six USO girls to come to the coach and entertain us. We had gotten all of the confusion cleared up before the girls arrived and this was a pleasant surprise for us. The girls sang and danced for us. They sang new songs that we had never heard. They had to put on their show in the aisles between our beds, but they performed well and then visited with us for about an hour. It surely did make the three-hour layover pass a lot faster.

When we left Denver, I was given my uniform so I could go to the coach platform and visit at different stops when we arrived in the state of Texas. On the way to Dalhart, I got to talk to the conductor of the train. He had been reared in Shamrock, Texas, near my home. I knew many of the same people he knew. I told him that I had been overseas four years. He told me that he would try to give me a little extra time at Dalhart, Channing, and Childress so I could visit with friends and family. When we arrived in Dalhart, about thirty people were waiting for me, all of them old friends. We stayed here about fifteen minutes. When we rolled into Channing, the county judge, his wife, some of the county commissioners, and a host of friends were there to meet me. This is where I had been working as county agricultural agent until I was called into the service. When we arrived in Amarillo, my brother Jesse and his wife, Margaret, and other friends met me. My brother was a first lieutenant stationed at the Amarillo Air Corps Base. He told me one of our older brothers was in Europe. He was a lieutenant colonel in the United States Army.

I talked to the conductor again between Amarillo and Childress. He said the train would take on water at Childress and that was the end of his run. He would have to go north again from there, but he would get someone to take me from the water tower to the depot so I would have more time to visit with my folks. He would also hold the train an extra ten minutes in Childress. In all I would have about twenty minutes to visit with my family. All of this was greatly appreciated.

When the train arrived at the water tower in Childress, there were several cars parked around, but no one to drive them. A hand car came along headed west and the depot was east of us. The conductor stopped the hand car and had it turn around and take me to the depot. The hand car was on the track next to the depot platform. My family and a lot of friends were on the platform looking down the track to where the train was taking on water and they did not notice the hand car. I stepped onto the platform right in front of them before they knew I was anywhere around.

I was greeted by my wife, daughter, and son along with my mother. Another brother, Frank, and his wife, Willie, were also there, as were many friends. My son and daughter had changed so much in my four years' absence that I would not have recognized them if I had met them on the street. We had twenty happy minutes of visiting. The Fort Worth and Denver conductor was waiting for me to get back on the hospital coach and I thanked him for being so considerate and giving me this extra time.

Ethel, my wife, had not been able to get a ticket on the train, as tickets were sold out several days ahead. She said she would drive to San Antonio and meet me the next evening at Brooke General Hospital. It was over a four-hundred-mile trip, but I was hoping to get a thirty-day pass and come home.

When I entered the hospital coach and got into my pajamas again, several of the men said, "Say, let's get going to San Antonio. Are you a railroad commissioner or some big shot with the railroad?" I told them that there would be no more delays on my part and San Antonio would be the next stop.

When we entered Brooke General Hospital on October 23, the receiving doctor asked me, "How are you feeling?"

I said, "I've never felt better in my life."

"How is the hurting in your side?" he asked.

I told him, "It is better."

He felt my side and I told him I wanted to go home on a thirty-day furlough.

He said, "Who is your family doctor?"

I told him, "Dr. E. W. Jones."

He said, "I will send a letter to him and he will be in charge of you for thirty days." I went into another office and asked the clerk to cut orders for me for a thirty-day furlough, beginning today. She said, "You cannot leave for two days. It takes that long for your furlough to go through." I asked her to let me speak to her commanding officer. I talked to the colonel in command of this part of the hospital.

He said, "Ordinarily one would have to wait two days, but in this case I will mail your orders to you in Wellington, Texas."

Soon my wife arrived and we were on our way home. There were many times I had doubted if I would ever get to come home again. As we drove toward home, my mind began to flash back to some of these times. Days on the death march when death seemed so near; the many times I had been so hungry, so sick, or so exhausted that death would have been a blessing; the night of April 8, 1942, was the worst night of my life as we tried to keep just ahead of the Japanese, not really knowing where we were going or what would be our fate. Then there were the inhumane punishments we had had to endure, and worse yet were the humiliations we were forced to suffer that made us feel more like animals than human beings. Watching men die from disease and starvation and being unable to help them was especially hard for me. I wondered if I would ever be able to forget some of the horrible, grotesque scenes that I had witnessed. I thank God that there are some pleasant things to remember too, like the day the B-29's broke through the clouds bringing us food and clothing, but more than that was the realization that we had not been forgotten as so many times it seemed we had. The most beautiful sight of all was the day we saw the tiny American flag hoisted high over the prison camp Roku Roshi and grown men filled with so much emotion they were unashamed to cry. From deep down inside came the overwhelming sense of humility as I breathed a prayer of thanksgiving to God for His watchful care. Yes, I had been an eyewitness.

Epilogue

On my return to the United States, I was assigned to an army hospital for one year and five months. During this time I was granted two thirty-day leaves and my family and I were given a two weeks' paid vacation in Corpus Christi, Texas.

I was retired from the United States Air Corps at Brooke General Hospital in San Antonio, Texas, on March 11, 1947. When the doctors were discussing my retirement, I heard one of them say that in my physical condition I might live five years. Hearing this made me determined to take care of myself. My wife was very instrumental in seeing that I got the right amount of rest and proper food and that I did not overwork. She took all of the responsibility possible off me.

After I returned home I began little by little to take my place in the life of my community. I secured a job as co-ordinator of veterans' schools in Collingsworth County. This job lasted until 1957. At the same time I was managing our farm and ranch interests in the county. I served six years as mayor of the city of Wellington, Texas; president of the Collingsworth County Chamber of Commerce; commander of the American Legion, home post; president of the Wellington Kiwanis Club and later lieutenant governor of the Kiwanis Clubs, Division Eighteen, Texas and Oklahoma District; president of Region II of the Texas Municipal League; secretary of the Panhandle Regional Planning Committee; and secretary of the Wellington Housing Authority.

I have had the privilege of seeing my children married and establishing homes of their own. I have five grandchildren, three of whom graduated in the Bicentennial classes of 1976. One granddaughter will be entering Texas A&M University and my twin grandsons will be entering West Texas State University.

These almost thirty years have been good years and, although I shall never forget the years spent in prison camps, time has a way of healing. I was glad to be able to serve my country, still the best in the world, and if called upon I would gladly serve again.

Index

Abney, Captain, 76, 85

Abucay line, 22, 24

Admiral Hughes (transport ship), 193, 194, 197

Air Corps Regiment, 15, 20, 21, 27, 105, 189; health of, 86–87; infantry training of, 19, 20; lack of food for, 44; before surrender, 41, 57–58; at surrender, 69; weapons of, 60; withdraws, 46. *See also* individual units by name

Akamatsu, Corporal, 182

Albuquerque, N.M., 89

Amarillo, Tex., 199

Amarillo Air Corps Base, 200

American flag, 105, 174, 202

American Legion, 203

Anderson, Sergeant, 124

Army Engineer Corps, 3

Asui (interpreter), 182

Australia, 13

Australians, 70, 129; as prisoners, 108, 141; officers of, 155, 157; troops of, 44

Balanga, P.I., 30, 69, 194–195

Bataan, 14, 20, 21, 39, 70; American objective in, 66; bakery at, 63; defense plan for, 15; fall of, 95–96

Bataan Death March: condition of troops on, 69–70, 72; condition of wounded after, 93; deaths on, 76, 77; food on, 82, 83; Hosetana apologizes for, 144; international law during, 71, 72, 74; maltreatment on, by guards, 71–72, 74, 75–76, 81; starvation during, 72, 75, 76, 80

Bird, Chief, 116

Boston, First Sergeant, 24

Blue Moon Dance Hall, 83

Blumel, Gen. Clifford, 71–72

Boatner, Charles, 187

Boone (Spanish American War veteran), 192

Boone, Alice, 192

Brady, Col. Jasper, 50, 57–58

Brennison, Master Sergeant: and wife and son, 19

British, 70: officers of, 155; overcoats of, 135; as prisoners, 108, 128, 129; troops of, 44, 196

Brooke General Hospital, 198, 199, 201, 203

Buck, Frank, 17

Burns, Lieutenant, 63

Cabcaben, P.I., 37, 38, 40, 58, 59

Cabcaben Air Field, P.I., 20

Cadmus, Captain, 135

Camp Bowie, Tex., 8, 26

Camp Cabanatuan, P.I., 128; baths at, 102; black market at, 104; blood-brothers at, 99, 101; civilian prisoners at, 103; clothes at, 104; death penalty at, 94, 96; food at, 97, 102; description of, 90, 91; disease at, 102, 103; doctor for, 104; escape from, 99; latrines at, 103; punishment at, 94, 99–100; sick bay at, 92–93, 104; suicide at, 104; water for, 93–94

Camp O'Donnell, P.I., 69; black market at, 104; burial at, 87; commandant of, 84, 164; conditions at, 86, 90; death penalty at, 84, 85, 88; death rate at, 89–90; disease at, 86, 90; starvation at, 87–88; statistics of, 84, 85, 90; water for, 84, 85, 88

Cane, Col. Emeral, 3

Canadian, Tex., 124

Canadians, 129, 196

Capas, P.I., 83

Caroline Islands, 127 n

Cavite, P.I., 12